A TRADER'S FIRST BOOK ON COMMODITIES

EVERYTHING YOU NEED TO KNOW
ABOUT FUTURES AND OPTIONS TRADING
BEFORE PLACING A TRADE

T0204739

A TRADER'S FIRST BOOK ON COMMODITIES
EVERYTHING YOU NEED TO KNOW ABOUT FUTURES AND OPTIONS TRADING
BEFORE PLACING A TRADE
Carley Garner

T H I R D   E D I T I O N

ISBN: 9781948018005
Library of Congress Control Number: 2017956607

This book was previously published by: Pearson Education, Inc.

Published by DeCarley Trading, LLC
an Imprint of Wyatt-MacKenzie

www.DeCarleyTrading.com

DeCarley Trading, LLC

A TRADER'S FIRST BOOK ON COMMODITIES

EVERYTHING YOU NEED TO KNOW
ABOUT FUTURES AND OPTIONS TRADING
BEFORE PLACING A TRADE

CARLEY GARNER

COMMODITY MARKET ANALYST & BROKER AT DECARLEYTRADING.COM

DeCarley Trading, LLC

RISK DISCLOSURE

There is a substantial risk of loss in trading futures and options. Past performance is not indicative of future results.

The information and data contained in this text was obtained from sources considered reliable. Their accuracy or completeness is not guaranteed. Information provided in this book is not to be deemed as an offer or solicitation with respect to the sale or purchase of any securities or commodities. Any decision to purchase or sell as a result of the opinions expressed in this text will be the full responsibility of the person authorizing such transaction.

Seasonal tendencies are a composite of some of the more consistent commodity futures seasonals that have occurred over the past 15 or more years. There are usually underlying, fundamental circumstances that occur annually that tend to cause the futures markets to react in a similar directional manner during a certain calendar year. While seasonal trends may potentially impact supply and demand in certain commodities, seasonal aspects of supply and demand have been factored into futures & options market pricing. Even if a seasonal tendency occurs in the future, it may not result in a profitable transaction as fees and the timing of the entry and liquidation may impact on the results.

No representation is being made that any commodity trading account has in the past, or will in the future, achieve profits using these recommendations. No representation is being made that price patterns will recur in the future. There is an unlimited amount of risk in option selling or open-ended option spreads.

ACKNOWLEDGMENTS

This book is dedicated to loyal DeCarley Trading brokerage clients, my colleagues, and Jim Cramer. The markets are treacherous and unforgiving at times but I'm fortunate to be surrounded by supportive, intelligent, and encouraging people.

ABOUT THE AUTHOR

Senior Commodity Market Strategist and Broker, Stocks & Commodities Magazine Columnist, TheStreet.com Contributor, and Author

Carley Garner is an experienced futures and options broker with DeCarley Trading, a division of Zaner Group, in Las Vegas, Nevada. She is also the author of *Higher Probability Commodity Trading*; *A Trader's First Book on Commodities*; *Currency Trading in the Forex and Futures Markets*; and *Commodity Options*. Her e-newsletters, *The DeCarley Perspective,* and *The Financial Futures Report,* have garnered a loyal following; she is also proactive in providing free trading education.

Carley is a magna cum laude graduate of the University of Nevada Las Vegas, from which she earned dual bachelor's degrees in finance and accounting. Carley jumped into the options and futures industry with both feet in early 2004 and has become one of the most recognized names in the business. Her commodity market analysis is often referenced on Jim Cramer's *Mad Money* on CNBC and she is a regular contributor to TheStreet.com and its Real Money Pro service.

Carley has also been featured in the likes of *Technical Analysis of Stocks & Commodities*, *Futures*, *Active Trader*, *Option Trader* magazines, and many more. She has been quoted by *Investor's Business Daily* and *The Wall Street Journal* and has also been known to participate in radio interviews. She can be found on the speaking circuit. Visit Carley at www.DeCarleyTrading.com.

Keep in touch on social media:

 @carleygarner

 DeCarleyTradingCommodityBroker

 decarleytrading

PRAISE FOR A TRADER'S FIRST BOOK ON COMMODITIES BY CARLEY GARNER:

"As an industry insider and active trader, Carley provides excellent perspective in trading commodities. She simplifies the process and explains in detail how to gain access to the markets and how to avoid the common mistakes for novice traders. This is a must-read and one that has shelf life as an important resource in commodities trading."—**Stephanie Link, TIAA Investments Equity Portfolio Manager, an affiliate of Nuveen**

"This book provides the type of information every trader needs to know and the type of information too many traders had to learn the hard and expensive way. Carley offers practical need-to-know, real-world trading tips that are lacking in many books on futures. It will help not only the novice trader but seasoned veterans as well. This book will serve as a must-have reference in every trader's library." —**Phil Flynn, Futures Account Executive at Price Futures Group, and a Fox Business Network contributor.**

"This easy-to-read introduction to futures trading provides a comprehensive overview while being honest about the risks. If you are as hard working as Carley is, it will surely whet your appetite to read more about the incredible business of trading commodities!" —**Linda Raschke, LBRGroup/FuturePath**

"This book has the perfect name, the perfect message, and the necessary information for any beginning trader. Take this book home!" —**Glen Larson, President, Genesis Financial Technologies, Inc.**

"As a 35-year veteran of the CME/CBOT trading floor, I can tell you...those who think they can begin trading commodities without knowing the less talked about topics that Carley discusses in *A Trader's First Book on Commodities* are sadly mistaken. Anyone who trades their own account, or would like to, should read this book."—**Danny Riley, Mr.TopStep.com**

"I own and operate one of the longest running independent brokerage firms in the industry. Take it from me, there is a lot more to futures trading than studying charts and reading the news; this book delivers what most commodity books are missing. Carley goes a long way toward shortening the learning curve for anybody that is serious at getting involved in the futures and options markets. *A Trader's First book on Commodities* is a must-have for newbies or experienced traders looking for a fresh perspective."—**Matt Zaner, Zaner Group LLC**

"Carley does a masterful job connecting the rich history of commodity trading with the modern day trading markets. It's not easy trading any market, but this book gives any trader a chance to advance their knowledge. While times have changed, the art of trading commodities has not; this piece is a must-have for a trader getting started."—**Bob Lang, Founder, ExplosiveOptions.net and Contributor at TheStreet.com**

TABLE OF CONTENTS

Risk Disclosure 2

Acknowledgments 3

About the Author..4

Praise for A Trader's First Book on Commodities by Carley Garner: 5

Intro: To Know Where We Are Going, You Must Know Where We Have Been 16

Why has the Boom and Bust of Commodities Become so Dramatic? 16

Easy Market Access...17

European Debt Crisis 18

Quantitative Easing..19

Fear of a US Financial System Collapse...19

The New Investment Fad...20

Fracking: the Battle Between US Shale Oil Producers and OPEC 21

The Speculator's Role in Volatility 22

Meanwhile, in the Equity Markets 23

Commodity Volatility Leads to Fortunes Made and Lost...24

Commodity Brokers Boom and Bust Too...26

Brokerage Firm Business Models Breakdown 27

Hard Times and Desperate Measures..28

Customer Segregated Funds Violations..28

Collateral Damage 29

How to Protect Yourself from the Unlikely Event of a Brokerage Firm Failure 30

Follow the FCM Financial Data Report 30

Spread Funds Among Multiple Brokers 31

What Regulators Are Doing to Protect Clients 31

Conclusion 31

Chapter 1: A Crash Course in Commodities...33

The Chicago Board of Trade..33

The Chicago Mercantile Exchange..34

The New York Mercantile Exchange 34

The CME Group...35

Intercontinental Exchange..35

Evolution of the Forward Contract into a Futures Contract 36

The Forward Contract...36

The Futures Contract 37

Cash Market Versus Futures Market 38

    Cost to Carry 38

    Arbitrage 39

Contract Expiration 40

    First Notice Day 40

    Futures Expiration 41

The Mechanics of Futures Contracts 41

    The Long and Short of It 41

    Buy or Sell in Any Order 42

    Offsetting and Rolling Over Trades 42

    Bid/Ask Spread 45

    Round Turns and Transaction Costs 46

    Price Speculation 47

Futures Spreads 47

A Brief Introduction to Commodity Options 49

    What Is an Option? 49

    Option Spreads 50

    Understanding Option Pricing and Tendencies 52

    What Are Weekly Options 54

    The Bottom Line on Options 54

Chapter 2: Hedging Versus Speculating 55

    Hedging Commodities 55

    Why Hedge? 55

    Nothing in Life is Free 56

    Hedging Versus Speculating 56

    Using Futures to Hedge Price Risk 56

    Long Hedge Versus Short Hedge 58

    Commodity Speculators 59

    Leverage in Hedging and Speculating 60

Chapter 3: The Slow Death of Open Outcry and the Growth of Electronic Trading ...61

    Don't Judge a Book by Its Cover 62

    The Pit 62

    Electronically Traded Markets 63

Confusing Contract Symbols 64

The Good and Bad of Electronic Trading 64

    Market Liquidity 65

    Quicker and More Efficient Execution 65

    Stricter Intraday Margin 65

    No Sleep for the Weary 66

    Option Spreads Don't Translate to the "Screens" 66

    More Market Access & Info 67

    Weekly Options 67

    Better Charting 68

    Order Flow, Chatter, and Sentiment 68

Where Are the Floor Traders Now? 68

Chapter 4: Account Access, Trading Platforms, and Exchange Data Fees 70

Commodity Market Access Can Be Costly, But It Doesn't Have to Be 70

Subscribing to Commodity Quotes 71

    CME Data Fees 71

    ICE Price data fees 73

Charting 74

Free Trading Platforms and Market Access 75

Paid Trading Platforms 75

    Per-Side Transaction Costs Versus a Flat Monthly Fee 76

Option Trading Platforms and Brokers 77

    Not All Brokers Allow Clients to Sell Options 77

    Accessing the Greeks, IV, and Option Calculators 78

Platform Risk Parameters and Order Approval 79

    Don't Panic over Rejected Orders 81

Choosing a Trading Platform 82

Mobile Applications 84

    Popular Mobile Futures Platforms 84

Order Desk ("The Desk") 85

Is It Worth Paying Platform Fees? 86

Chapter 5: Choosing a Brokerage Firm 88

What Is an FCM? 88

What Is an IB? 89

What Is a Broker/Dealer? 91

Fill Quality 92

Behind the Scenes of Transaction Costs 93

Discount Brokerage or Full-Service Specialization? 94

What You Should Know About Commission Structure: Blanket or Variable Rates? 95

    Clients Are Risky 95

    Commission Should Be Based on Client Risk and Not a Predetermined Flat Rate 96

Real-time Account Stats, Trading Platforms, and Mobile Device Access 97

Margin Policy 98

    Day Trading Margin 98

    Short Option Trading Margin 99

Beyond Your Broker 99

    Customer Service and Back-Office Operations 100

    Technical Support 100

Conclusion 101

Chapter 6: Finding a Broker that Fits and Choosing a Service Level 102

Understand your Broker's Business 103

    The 80/20 Rule 104

    What It Takes to Be a Commodity Broker 104

Get to Know Your Futures Broker 104

    Use Available Resources 105

    Work Ethic 106

    Work Experience 106

    Trading Background 106

    Trade Execution 107

    Help in Choosing a Trading Platform 107

    Market Research 108

    Consider the Future 108

Full-Service Broker or Self-Directed Online Trading? 108

    Sometimes Less Actually Is More 109

    Full Service Doesn't Have to Be Expensive 109

    Is Your Broker Working for You or for Your Commission? 110

Why Using a Broker's Assistance Might Be a Good idea 110

    Avoid Overtrading and Panic Liquidation 111

Shifting Risk of Order Placement 111

Margin Calls 112

Companionship 112

Conclusion 112

Chapter 7: Order Types and How to Use Them 114

Order Types 114

Market Order 114

Limit Order 115

Stop Order (a.k.a. Stop Loss) 117

Trailing Stop 118

Stop/limit order 119

One Cancels the Other (OCO) or Brackets 120

One Sends the Other (OSO) 121

Market If Touched (MIT) 122

Fill or Kill (FOK) 122

Immediate or Cancel (IOC) 123

Market on Open (MOO) 123

Market on Close (MOC) 124

Cancel (Straight "Can") 124

Cancel/Replace (Modified Order) 125

Good Till Canceled (GTC) 125

Multiple Entry, Multiple Exit (MEME) 126

Placing Stop Orders on Options 126

A Disclaimer to Stop Loss and Market Orders in an Electronic Trading World 127

Placing a Trade with Your Broker 129

Calling Your Broker or a Trade Desk 130

Placing a Trade Online 131

Chapter 8: Making Cents of Commodity Quotes 132

Rule #1: Use Multipliers, Not Contract Sizes 133

Rule #2: Stay Positive 133

Corn, Soybeans, Wheat, and Even Oats 134

Understanding Grain Market Fractions 134

Calculating Profit, Loss, and Risk in Grain Futures and Options 135

Not All Grains Are Created Equal 137

Soybean Meal Futures 137

Soybean Oil Futures 138

The Meats 139

Live Cattle and Lean Hogs 140

Foods and Fiber (The Softs) 142

Cocoa 142

Coffee 143

Orange Juice 143

Sugar 143

Cotton 145

Lumber 145

Precious Metals Futures 146

Gold 146

E-Mini and E-Micro Gold 147

Platinum and Palladium 148

The Other Metal Futures 148

Silver Futures 149

Copper Futures 149

The Energies 150

Crude Oil Futures 151

Natural Gas Futures 151

Chapter 9: Figuring in Stock Index Futures 153

The Boring but Necessary Basics 153

E-Mini Dow Jones Industrial Average Futures 155

E-Mini NASDAQ 100 Futures 156

S&P 500 Futures 157

The Original S&P 500 158

E-Mini S&P 500 159

Arbitrage 160

Russell 2000 Futures 161

Chapter 10: Calculating Interest Rate Futures 162

A Complex "Complex" 162

Fixed Income Securities 163

Discount Securities 163

Inverse Relationship Between Price and Yield 164

What Does a Treasury Futures Contract Represent? 165

Treasury Futures 166

T-Bond Futures 166

T-Bond Options 168

10-Year Note 170

Five-Year Note 170

Two-Year Note 171

Short-Dated Discount Bond Futures 171

Eurodollar Futures 172

Fed Fund Futures 174

Chapter 11: Counting Pennies with Currency Futures 176

Euro, Franc, and Yen 176

Aussie and Canadian Dollars 178

British Pound 178

Conclusion on Figuring Profit, Loss, and Risk in Futures and Options 179

Chapter 12: Coping with Margin Calls 180

What Is Margin? 180

Initial Margin 180

Maintenance Margin 181

Day Trading Margin Versus Overnight Margin 181

What Are Margin Calls? 182

How to Handle a Margin Call 183

The Margin Call Countdown 184

Day One 185

Day Two 185

Day Three 185

Accepting Margin Calls 186

Chapter 13: The Only Magic in Trading—Emotional Stability 187

The Three Emotions in Trading: Fear, Greed, Frustration 188

Fear 188

Greed 190

Frustration 191

Vengeful Trading Is Counterproductive 193

Capital Preservation, a.k.a. Risk Management 193

Chapter 14: Trading Is a Business—Have a Plan 195

The Trading Game Plan 195

Automated Trading Systems 196

Constructing a Business Plan in Trading 199

Price Speculation (Ideally, Prediction) 200

Timing Is Everything 200

Choosing a Trading Vehicle 201

Risk Management 202

Option Selling Provides Favorable Odds But Doesn't Guarantee Success 203

The 10% Rule 205

Don't Be Ashamed of One-Lot Orders 205

Managing Risk with Stops 206

It Is Your Money 207

Chapter 15: Why you Should Speculate in Futures and Options 209

Speculating in Futures Versus Speculating in Stocks 209

Leverage and Margin 210

Liquidity and Efficient Execution 211

Buy or Sell in Any Order 211

Low Account Minimums 212

No Interest Charges or Borrowing Fees 212

Level Playing Field 213

Favorable Tax Treatment 213

Excitement 213

Commodities Won't Be Delisted and Reflect True Position 214

You *Can* Trade Futures and options in an IRA 214

Risk Capital Only 215

Conclusion 215

Chapter 16: Futures Slang and Terminology 217

Bull Versus Bear 217

Bull and Bear Slang 217

Spread 218

BID/ASK SPREAD 218

Option Spread 219

Futures Spread 219

Contract Month Slang 219

Red Months 219

Fill 219

    Split Fill 220

    Partial Fill 220

Blowout 220

Blowup 221

Keypunch Error 221

Busted, Moved, or Canceled Trade 221

Fat Finger Error 222

Net Liq 222

Equity 223

Customer Segregated Funds Account 224

Beans 224

Commodity Currency 224

    The Aussie and the Loonie 225

Pound, Pound Sterling, Sterling, the Cable 225

Dead Cat Bounce 225

Bottom Fishing 225

Chasing the Market 225

Limit Moves 226

    Limit Up 226

    Limit Down 226

The Tape 226

Trading Solution, Environment, and Front-End 227

Proprietary Trading 227

    Prop Desk 227

Running Stops 227

Short Squeeze 228

Babysitting 228

Scalp 228

Slippage 229

Working Order 229

Unable 229

Handle 230

Overbought/Oversold 230

Debit Balance/Account Debit 230

Round Turns 231

Index 232

INTRO: TO KNOW WHERE WE ARE GOING, YOU MUST KNOW WHERE WE HAVE BEEN

Witnessing the grain complex shatter all-time-high price records and continue to climb in the now-infamous 2007–2008 commodity rally was nothing less than breathtaking. However, by late 2008, the party had ended. Many retail traders and fund managers watched in horror as the grains and energy markets made their way relentlessly lower in sympathy to the notorious financial crisis. The selling pressure and losses in the commodity markets during this time were so profound that hedge fund managers experienced unprecedented numbers of

> "There is no tool to change human nature … people are prone to recurring bouts of optimism and pessimism that manifest themselves from time to time in the buildup or cessation of speculative excesses." — Alan Greenspan

redemption requests; the associated liquidation added fuel to the already raging fire. Investors in all corners of the market, with the exception of US Treasuries and gold, were in full risk-off mode. Ironically, the same asset class that investors swarmed to for "diversification" from stocks in the early 2000s played a role in the demise of equities during the 2008–2009 bear market; margin calls in commodity accounts were met via stock liquidation and vice versa.

We now know that this boom-and-bust cycle was destined to be repeated, although in slightly less dramatic fashion. Commodity markets such as the grains, energies, and meats soared between 2010 and 2015, but fast forward to 2016 and the complex was in a crisis of its own. Perhaps a feast-or-famine trade is a new reality: high margins, high risk, high reward, and even higher adrenaline rushes.

WHY HAS THE BOOM AND BUST OF COMMODITIES BECOME SO DRAMATIC?

Several theories attempt to explain the historical volatility in the commodity markets throughout the previous decade. Valid contributors are likely ethanol demand and the government programs promoting it, the European debt crisis, sheer market exuberance, sidelined cash looking for a home, government stimulus such as quantitative easing, the emergence of US shale oil accompanying the attempted resurgence of OPEC and, most of all, advances in technology offering easy market access for the average retail trader. One thing is certain: The commodity euphoria causes the agricultural, energy, and metals markets to overshoot equilibrium prices in both directions on a seemingly regular basis. This provides both opportunity and risk to traders.

In the midst of the excitement, the lure of a swift commodity rally clouds the judgment of many. Looking back at boom-and-bust cycles, which are now relatively common, it is rather obvious that expecting market fundamentals to maintain boisterously lofty prices is simply unrealistic. However, in the heat of the moment, nobody knows how high is "too high," and speculation runs rampant. Countertrend traders who enter the market "early" with bearish strategies likely pay dearly for their aggression. Yet when the tides finally turn, they do so in a vicious fashion, enabling well-timed bears to reap substantial rewards. After all, the stunning fall from grace is typically even steeper than the preceding rally. On the other hand, trend traders aren't always flush with profits even in a swiftly moving one-direction market. For instance, those riding the wave late in the cycle might be entering the trend just as it is ending. Or, they might have sustained massive losses in choppy markets before the big commodity move occurred. We discuss the idea of trend trading and countertrend trading in my book *Higher Probability Commodity Trading.*

In a speech delivered at the American Enterprise Institute in the late 1990s, then–Federal Reserve Board Chairman Alan Greenspan warned that the equity market might be overvalued through the use of "irrational exuberance." In my opinion, this is a good explanation of the illogical rallies and bear market sell-offs in the commodity markets. In an environment in which anyone with a computer (and a mouse) can buy or sell commodities with a single click, logic sometimes has little control over the outcome. Nevertheless, such cycles of excess and price contraction open the door for speculators to achieve abnormal profits, assuming that they are willing to manage and accept the corresponding risks.

Naturally, speculators aren't buying or selling commodities on a whim. They are holding on to some fundamental story that justifies the initial price move, but the bandwagon mentality often takes reality into fantasy. Here are a few of the primary factors driving the wave of commodity market volatility that began in 2007 and has continued to thrive for over a decade.

EASY MARKET ACCESS

Investors trading commodities in the 1990s knew that the only way to place a trade in the commodity markets was to pick up a phone and call a broker. Because brokerage firms relied on paper tickets and statements, they weren't necessarily able to keep close tabs on client trading accounts throughout the trading day. This posed large risks to traders and the firm. Accordingly, commodity trading was typically reserved for well-capitalized and sophisticated investors. That simply isn't true anymore. Anybody with at least a thousand dollars and an operable computer can buy or sell commodities online without ever picking up the phone.

> At first it is easy to confuse a bull market with trading genius, but it can't last.

Individually, such traders have little influence on the market, but collectively, this new breed of futures speculators can have a significant impact on price movements. If you don't believe me, look at the roller-coaster ride gold futures took following the S&P's credit downgrade of US debt in 2011 (Figure 1). I speculate that much of the late-comer buying was done by inexperienced, yet convinced, retail traders who were unaware of the risks of having convenient online access to buy or sell commodities without being properly educated. Once the last of these buyers had taken action, the market immediately reversed their impact on pricing as they were forced to liquidate at what were likely large losses. We saw something similar in gold following the November 2016 US Presidential election. The price of gold plummeted on a Donald Trump victory due to the perception that the new administration's policies would be pro-growth leading to higher interest rates (which is antagonistic to gold prices). However, after a gross overreaction by what my colleague, Jim Cramer, refers to as "pajama traders" (those clicking their mouse to trade futures from their basement computers), gold prices reverted to a more reasonable price level.

In the fall of 2011, a US credit downgrade triggered a massive but fundamentally unsustainable gold rally as inexperienced retail traders jumped on the bandwagon. The market quickly gave back all of its gains.

Trump victory selling in gold was swift and relentless, but it was also erased rather quickly as "pajama traders" were forced to cover their short positions.

Figure 1: It has been argued that the one-month rally in 2011 that spanned $1,500 per ounce to $1,910 was largely fueled by small retail traders and herd mentality. Once the last buyer was in, the market quickly retreated to eliminate most of the gains, which equated to about $40,000 per contract. There was a similar bandwagon trade on the short side of gold following the 2016 US Presidential election. (Chart courtesy of QST)

EUROPEAN DEBT CRISIS

The US credit crunch of 2008/2009 eventually sent Europe into a tailspin. For years, the domestic financial and commodity markets were hijacked by the possibility of a similar credit market collapse overseas, despite improvements in the homeland. Obviously, a healthy economy leads to healthy demand for commodities, but certainly, other fundamental factors are at play. Nevertheless, at the turn of the decade, there were years in which traders focused European headlines and put individual commodity market fundamentals on the back burner. Their concern was the failure of the highly leveraged members of the European Union such as Greece would trigger a contagion throughout the region, which could destabilize financially sound countries such as Germany. The thinking at the time was the EU was only as healthy as its weakest link, and that wasn't a pretty picture.

Prior to the 2008 US debt crisis and similar chaos to follow in Europe, financial market speculation only moderately influenced commodity prices. Yet in a post–credit crunch world, when the financial markets became enthralled with European headline risk, the commodity markets went along for the ride. As a result, commodities, currencies, and the US stock market often become highly correlated; in short, they all traded as if they were one asset going up and down together in lockstep.

When all three asset classes begin moving in the same direction, it can be nearly impossible to stop the bleeding. This is because excessive moves simultaneously occurring in all three arenas trigger margin calls galore and enhance investor panic. Imagine being an investor under the belief that their well-diversified portfolio would reduce their risk of drawdown only to find out there was no escaping the fallout. In such an environment, liquidation becomes a seemingly never-ending endeavor.

QUANTITATIVE EASING

In late 2008, the Federal Reserve announced that it would be undertaking a little-known practice known as quantitative easing. In summer 2012, the Fed declared it would continue to implement the quantitative easing program indefinitely.

Quantitative easing is now a household phrase, but it is most commonly referred to as QE. QE is a rather complex scheme in which the US government essentially buys the Treasury bonds it issues. In layman's terms, the federal government is selling bonds to itself. The net result is a cash injection into the economy, or simply money printing.

The increase in money supply stemming from the Fed's QE campaign tends to put upward pressure on asset prices of all types, including commodities. This is because, all else being equal, more money is chasing the same number of goods; therefore, prices are driven higher. Another way to look at it is, the larger the money supply, the weaker the US dollar. A discounted dollar tends to put upward pressure on asset prices because it results in more purchasing power for foreign buyers and, thus, higher demand.

Accordingly, much of the boom-and-bust pattern we've seen in commodities likely is exaggerated by artificial price inflation via QE and the subsequent correction from unrealistic levels.

FEAR OF A US FINANCIAL SYSTEM COLLAPSE

Fearful savers have been known to store wealth in nonfiat currencies, namely gold and silver. The theory is that if the financial system as we know it fails, the "gold bugs" will manage to maintain their prosperity by exchanging precious metals holdings for goods and services. For example, in the summer of 2012, an older man in Nevada died in a modest Carson City home with about $200 in his bank account. As the home was being cleaned and prepared for resale, approximately $7 million in gold bullion was found hidden in secret compartments in the walls and in boxes in the garage. The metals hoard was said to be in response to the man's lack of faith in the current fiat money financial system.

Despite years of stability in the US economy, such practices were still going on in 2017 (at the time of this writing). In my opinion, this type of thinking has had a profound impact on overzealous rallies in precious metals in 2011 but has also contributed to deep and dark corrections as those with cooler heads prevail. I suspect this feast and famine volatility in the precious metals might continue for quite some time. Figure 2 depicts just how far fear of a failing domestic currency can drive precious metals prices beyond reason in both directions. To put this figure into perspective, the move from $18.00 per ounce in silver futures to $50.00 represents a profit or loss of $160,000 per contract! The near-immediate reversion to $34.00 from $50.00, which erases the last leg of the rally, equates to about $80,000.

$50.00 per ounce

By 2011, the financial crisis was over but silver traders were convinced the turmoil had only just begun. Consequently, speculators of all sizes forced the price of silver to astronomical levels that might not be seen again in our lifetimes.

$18.00 per ounce

Years of switchback trading occurred as investors attempted to predict whether the next economic phase would be expansion or contraction. Each of these moves represents about $60,000 in profit or loss per contract.

Figure 2: Fear of another US financial system collapse in 2011 triggered a historical rally in silver prices that simply couldn't be sustained by fundamentals. It took years for the market to work out the panic. In recent years, silver has found comfort in the $14.00 to $18.00 per ounce price range. Unless we get a repeat of the 2008 calamity, we might not see $50.00 silver again. (Chart courtesy of QST)

THE NEW INVESTMENT FAD

Swirling newscasts, financial newspaper editorials, never-ending infomercials, and social media buzz regarding the emerging opportunities in the commodity markets have successfully lured an enormous number of investors looking for opportunities other than traditional stocks and bonds. The craze began in the early 2000s but has extended well into the current environment.

For all intents and purposes, the US equity markets made little or no progress from the year 2000 through 2013, causing many investors to lose faith in the system. Ironically, this mindset also caused many of them to miss out on the historical equity market rally that began in March 2009 and was still in full swing by mid-2017. Nevertheless, frustrated by the stock market and with Treasury bond yields at record lows compliments of QE efforts by central bankers, savers found themselves intrigued by the commodity story. Accordingly, the general investing public has made it a habit of allotting substantial amounts of capital to trading and investment arenas that were previously much more difficult to access, such as the commodity markets. Included in this new allocation concept enjoying relatively consistent money flow since the trading tech boom of the early 2000s are self-directed or full-service commodity accounts, commodity hedge funds, commodity equity products such as exchange traded funds (ETFs), and Commodity Trading Advisors (CTAs).

"If the models are telling you to sell, sell, sell, but only buyers are out there, don't be a jerk. Buy!"—William Silber (NYU)

The simplicity of participating in the futures and options markets has greatly benefited the commodity industry but it also likely plays a part in the relentless boom-and-bust cycles. Unfortunately, in many cases, money is flowing into commodities from investors who have little experience in the futures markets and limited knowledge of the high levels of risk involved in participating. As you can imagine, this leads to volatility in the trading accounts of market participants as well as their family life.

Not only do I believe too many speculative investors are relatively undereducated about the futures markets, but I also argue that numerous money managers might be as well. For instance, many of them fail to recognize a few things, such as the fact that the commodity markets aren't as deep as equity markets and are thus highly influenced by bandwagon trading. Naturally, this occurs in the equity markets as well—just look at social media shares such as Twitter and Snapchat—but in the futures market, it takes arguably fewer dollars chasing assets to see a price reaction. In some of the smaller commodity markets, such as rough rice or even cotton futures, it is possible for prices to make substantial moves on the buying or selling of a moderate number of contracts. In other words, it isn't difficult for deep-pocketed speculators to temporarily alter the price of some commodities. With droves of cash making its way to commodities, it doesn't take long for things to get out of hand. This is why it is important to limit your trading activity to futures contracts with ample liquidity. Leave the exotic commodity markets to the "other guy."

In addition, commodity prices normally trade in envelopes instead of ongoing inclines, as stocks tend to do. Yet commodity market newcomers sometimes behave as if this isn't the case, causing prices to increase sharply beyond what are feasibly sustainable levels. These simple concepts seem obvious, but fear of missing out on a rally, and the greed that prevents profit taking, sometimes overshadows the red flags and concerns of commodity veterans who "know" that the hysteria that accompanies a bull market in commodities can't last. Similarly, green traders often fail to recognize the simple fact that commodity prices can't go to zero. When a commodity gets cheap, it can turn on a dime without any obvious change in supply and demand fundamentals. In fact, commodity prices generally lead published fundamental data; this is because the data itself is outdated by the time it is distributed to the public.

Of course, the assumption of undereducated market participants is my personal perception, and it is in stark contrast to the opinions of some other analysts. In fact, well-respected and well-known market commentators believe that the original 2007 commodity boom was purely the result of tight supply and high demand and subsequent collapses in price were merely the unwindings of those fundamentals. Although I agree 100% that concrete fundamentals are often the initial cause of boom cycles and are eventually the cause of a bust, I am not convinced that fundamentals alone blazed the trail for the unprecedented volatility we've witnessed over the last decade.

Unfortunately, markets and their participants are complex, and this often makes pinpointing the driving force behind any price move impossible. At first, it is easy to confuse a bull market with trading genius, but it can't last.

FRACKING: THE BATTLE BETWEEN US SHALE OIL PRODUCERS AND OPEC

A more recent culprit to commodity market volatility is the realization that the practice of fracking has brought US energy products to the forefront of the industry. The process of injecting liquid at high pressure into subterranean rocks forces open existing cracks to extract oil and natural gas was a game changer. Suddenly, US frackers were flooding the market with natural gas (so much so that many were burning off excess inventory because it was cheaper than transporting it to sell). In the end, the price of natural gas fell from a high of over $13.00 MMBtu (one million British Thermal Units) in 2008 to under $2.00 by 2012 and has generally traded below $5.00 since.

This energy market revolution also dramatically increased the supply of crude oil as US frackers relentlessly drilled wells and ramped up production. As a result, the price collusion of OPEC nations no longer works as a means to control oil the long-term price of oil. Instead, OPEC production cuts aimed at boosting sluggish oil prices have merely created short-term market volatility but hasn't been the magic bullet it has been historically been (Figure 3). Fracking and other factors have helped oil prices retreat from $110 per barrel in 2012 to as low as $27 in early 2016. Talk about volatility!

Figure 3: Crude oil futures are susceptible to changes in OPEC policy, but the cartel is less powerful than it once was. Nevertheless, the war between OPEC and US shale oil producers is heating up and causing sharp volatility. (Chart courtesy of QST)

THE SPECULATOR'S ROLE IN VOLATILITY

Much debate centers on the speculator's role in commodity valuation. On more than one occasion in the mid- to late 2000s, commodity market regulators testified before Congress and participated in interrogation hearings regarding the speculator's role in excessive market pricing. The popular view in Washington seems to be that most of the blame falls on traders when it comes to high commodity prices. Ironically, the government's own QE program arguably played a bigger role in elevated food and energy prices than speculators ever could. Nonetheless, for those of us with the luxury of being within the industry and understanding the nature of the marketplace, it is nothing short of scary to see our elected leaders making such uninformed assumptions and, eventually, decisions about what are intended to be free markets. The truth is, there is plenty of blame to go around, but there probably isn't a better alternative than capitalistic price discovery as barbaric as it might seem to some.

The futures markets were formed to facilitate the transfer of risk from producers and users to unrelated third parties hoping to profit from price changes; I cover this in detail in Chapter 1, "A Crash Course in Commodities." Nevertheless, the commodity markets are built on speculation; without it, there would be no market.

Some evidence seems to suggest that speculation causes artificially inflated prices, at least temporarily. After all, commodities boomed when anxious investors poured money into the alternative asset class in search of higher returns. Not only that, what was once an investment arena utilized only by the uber-rich and risk-hungry investors now sees money inflows from average retail investors and even pension funds. However, the door swings both ways; during waves of liquidation, as investors redeem funds from their commodity holdings, the market sometimes behaves as if someone is pulling the floor out from underneath it. Consequently, commodity prices often fall much further and faster than they might have without speculative excess. In such a scenario, the economy enjoys commodities at highly discounted prices. Naturally, you will never hear complaints that speculators are driving gas prices too low!

In my opinion, speculators don't cause bubbles or even pop them, but unfamiliar, inexperienced, or greedy speculators might share some of the blame for their magnitude. Without support from basic supply-and-demand fundamentals, a market cannot sustain pricing in the end. Thus, if and when speculation does move prices beyond

> For every winner, there is a loser. Nonetheless, the winners get all the attention.

what the equilibrium price might be, it eventually has to correct itself. The problem is that there is no telling how far and how long prices can remain distorted. Unfortunately, many traders are introduced to this the hard way.

It is critical to realize that, from a trading standpoint, it doesn't necessarily matter whether the market is driven by fundamentals, technicals, speculators, hedgers, or central bank efforts. What does matter is that prices move, and you want to be on the right side of it—or at least get out of its way. Markets are unforgiving; regardless of how strongly you feel that prices should behave in a particular way, they are sometimes driven by irrational speculation for much longer than you can financially and psychologically afford to be involved.

Excessive commodity market volatility and price extremes create unparalleled opportunities for futures, and options on futures, traders. With that in mind, it is imperative that traders approach the markets with the simple premise that anything is possible, and positions should be taken and risks managed with this in mind.

MEANWHILE, IN THE EQUITY MARKETS

Despite continued volatility in the commodity markets, the equity markets have experienced an implosion of volatility beginning in 2009 on the heels of the financial crisis and was still playing out in mid-2017 as this edition was going to print. The CBOE's volatility index, known simply as the VIX, was hovering at an all-time low and the S&P 500 was on pace to have the tamest year since 1960. It was as if all of the volatility had been sucked out of the stock market.

Obviously, most investors enjoyed the low-stress and never-ending stock market rally spanning over several years, but the reality is, overly calm markets aren't healthy. They are fun while they last, at least for buy-and-hold investors, but they are also more prone to dramatic corrections such as the 2010 *flash crash* or the August 2015 *mini-flash crash*.

There are several theories on why volatility in the stock market collapsed to historical lows by 2017; the most prominent explanation is algorithmic trading, or simply algo trading. Algorithmic trading is the automated signaling and execution of futures and stocks via computers and coded programs. These trading systems often buy and sell instruments minutes, or even seconds, apart.

All along, algorithmic trading advocates argued that the added liquidity in the marketplace would work toward lowering overall volatility and now it seems as though that theory holds some water. Nevertheless, many believe that the active market liquidity resulting from algorithmic trading is a two-sided coin. In low volatility environments, it smooths out price changes even more, but if things heat up, algorithmic trading will likely add to volatility, not detract from it.

In 2008, it was determined that computer trading exacerbated losses in the equity markets and the same was said of the 2010 flash crash, which started in the E-mini S&P 500 futures markets. It is easy to forget these things when everything is going well, but equity traders will be reminded of the downside algo trading brings to the financial markets the next time the stock market goes into correction mode (if it ever does).

On a side note, I've noticed that algo traders seem to be mass contributors to *commodity* market volatility. In my opinion, around the clock trading in commodities such as gold, crude oil, and the grains offers algo traders an opportunity to utilize sizable quantity orders to push markets around during what are expected to be illiquid times of the day. I specifically recall a sharp gold rally in 2011 in which most of the gains were forged in the overnight market because there simply wasn't anybody to sell and the *machines* were executing a constant stream of buy orders.

COMMODITY VOLATILITY LEADS TO FORTUNES MADE AND LOST

By nature, when we think of large price moves in leveraged markets, we assume that there are riches to be made. However, this isn't necessarily the case; traders must be on the right side of the trade to make money, and that is easier said than done. Even worse than missing a big price move is being caught on the wrong side of it. The media's (and politicians') arguments against "greedy" speculators seem to imply that a majority of traders make money and that it is somehow easy to do so. This couldn't be further from the truth; if it were, wouldn't they be doing it too? Profitable trading is possible for those who are dedicated and capable of controlling their emotions, but it is far from being a surefire way for the "rich to get richer," as many assume.

Because of its profound impact on the economy and our daily lives, crude oil futures are often at the center of the debate. Believe me, not all speculators in the energy complex make money. Crude oil is one of the most challenging markets to trade successfully, regardless of whether you are a futures or options trader. The margin requirements are extremely high at times, and so are the volatility and risk. Figure 4 portrays the magnitude of risk and reward energy traders might face.

Surprisingly, based on my experience and conversations with those within the futures and options industry, the 2007 commodity rally was paralyzing for many veteran traders but a likely gold mine for investors who simply didn't know that wheat shouldn't trade in double digits, nor crude oil in mid-$150s. For investors who had been trading grains and energies for many years, it was not only unimaginable but in some cases, career-ending.

The 2008 decline in crude oil from $150.00 to $32.00 per barrel respresents a profit or loss of $118,000 per contract.

$150.00

$115.00

$110.00

The collapse from $110.00 to $27.00 would have made or lost a trader $83,000 per contract.

$32.00

The OPEC production cut rally from $32.00 to $115.00 equates to a profit or loss of $83,000 per contract.

$27.00

Figure 4: Crude oil traders have the potential for large gains, but the risk is of equal magnitude. Not many could have predicted that crude oil would rally to $150.00 per barrel, only to collapse to nearly $32.00. Such a move represents nearly $120,000 per contract. (Chart courtesy of QST)

Traders who spent the bulk of their adulthood speculating on grain and energy prices as they moved from high to low within their historical price envelopes quickly discovered that the markets no longer had boundaries. For example, before 2007, wheat was a commodity that was most comfortable trading between $2.00 and $4.00 per bushel, with a few brief stints in the $6.00 range. Looking at a long-term wheat chart, it is easy to see how a trader could unexpectedly get caught on the wrong side of a move that eventually got close to doubling the previous all-time high of the commodity. Those who did find themselves in such positions were in a state of denial and had a difficult time liquidating positions with large losses. As a result, the situation became worse as losses mounted, as did margin calls (see Figure 5).

You might have heard about the rogue (unauthorized and reckless) wheat trader whose actions during the historic wheat rally resulted in a large loss at a major financial institution. Without permission from his brokerage firm, MF Global, the trader greatly exceeded his trading limits due to a loophole in the trading platforms. The culprit was a commodity broker located in Memphis, Tennessee, who reportedly put his account—and, ultimately, MF Global—in the hole more than $141 million. This is believed to be the largest unauthorized loss in the history of the agricultural markets. Ironically, MF Global survived the debacle despite its stock immediately losing nearly a third of its value but claimed bankruptcy a few years later due to large losses in trades authorized by its own CEO, Jon Corzine. We'll discuss this next.

Figure 5: Few could have predicted the magnitude of the 2007–2008 wheat rally that made a mockery of its previous all-time high. (Chart courtesy of QST)

Prior to the unauthorized wheat trade, the MF Global broker triggering the debacle had been a responsible and regulator-registered participant of the futures industry for more than 15 years; perhaps, in this case, his experience worked against him, in that he was overly bearish in a market that simply wasn't "playing by the rules."

Conversely, in early 2016 the opposite landscape was in play. Crude oil, natural gas, and many other commodities plunged to ridiculously low prices. In some instances, the commodity futures contracts were trading below the cost of production! For instance, crude oil was under $30 per barrel and natural gas fell well under $2.00 mmBtu. It was obvious prices couldn't stay depressed forever, but at the time TV pundits and flashy analysts were calling for $15.00 crude oil and $1.00 natural gas; the negative sentiment and massive losses in commodity trading accounts forced many commodity bulls to the sidelines at the worst time. The energy markets eventually recovered but left quite a bit of carnage in their wake.

Keep in mind that in the pre–commodity boom world, the margin to hold a wheat futures position overnight was less than $1,000 and crude oil was under $2,000. During the commodity heyday, each of these margin requirements were well into the several-thousand-dollar range. Therein lies much of the problem: As commodities become more volatile, they also become more expensive for traders to hold. In such an environment, traders are forced to fold their hands due to a lack of margin or, worse, funding. The liquidation of underfunded traders adds momentum to the direction of the trend causing prices to quickly become unreasonable. Unfortunately, temporarily irrational prices wreak real havoc on trading accounts. What *could have* or *should have* been being irrelevant.

COMMODITY BROKERS BOOM AND BUST TOO

In the late 2000s, the commodity markets made history, but in the early 2010s, it was commodity brokerage firms that were grabbing headlines. More specifically, the epic failure of two prominent players, MF Global and

PFGBEST, showcased epic stories of insolvency plagued by a lack of integrity. As Warren Buffett said, "Only when the tide goes out do you discover who has been swimming naked."

BROKERAGE FIRM BUSINESS MODELS BREAKDOWN

For decades, futures brokerage firms had operated within a business model in which revenues were generated by the trading commission in addition to interest earned on the deposits made by clients to meet margin requirements. Simply put, if a client wires $10,000 to a futures broker to fund a trading account, the brokerage firm is free to invest that money in regulatory-approved interest-bearing securities such as Treasuries, bank deposits, and CDs while utilizing the assets to post margin requirements with the exchange on behalf of the client. Historically, the interest generated from such investments accounted for a rather significant percentage of a brokerage firm's income. Yet federal programs forcing interest rates to near-zero levels eliminated the capability of firms to benefit from client deposits; accordingly, profitability was hindered and exclusive to the generation of commissions and fees. Not surprisingly, brokers invented fees such as inactivity and margin call charges.

Before the Federal Reserve's never-ending quest for near-zero interest rates, futures brokerage firms enjoyed returns on client deposits between 3% and 5%. Accordingly, as technology improved trading execution, many firms traveled the path of discounting commissions to attract client funds and, in turn, relied on earning somewhere near 4% interest on client deposits. They knew that carrying large profit margins on the commission wasn't necessary if they could earn "the float," which is the industry term for interest earned on client money. However, this business plan didn't consider the possibility of unfathomably low-interest rates for prolonged periods of time and eventually proved to be a highly flawed manner of conducting a futures brokerage business.

Unfortunately, the practice of discounting commission to attract new clients is a slippery slope that eventually resulted in cannibalism of the industry. Firms went from competing on service to competing on price; ultimately, profit margins shrank to levels at which brokers simply couldn't operate profitably in a low-interest-rate environment.

In addition to low interest rates and lower commissions, the financial collapse of 2008 tightened the purse strings of many speculators. This dealt another blow to the commodity brokerage industry, causing many brokerage firms to fold their hands.

I entered the commodity industry in early 2004; during that time, I've witnessed the number of registered Futures Commission Merchants (also known as futures brokers) fall from about 90 firms to fewer than 50 in 2012. It has since increased to roughly 63, but of those only about half will accept retail trading accounts of smaller traders. Instead, the majority of them are only interested in institutional business trading large accounts and high volume. Simply put, there is likely less than half the number of retail accessible commodity brokerages in operation now relative to when I stepped into the business. Regretfully, I worked as a broker for one failed firm and operated as an Introducing Broker for another. Chapter 5, "Choosing a Brokerage Firm," covers the definition of an Introducing Broker and a Futures Commission Merchant.

Through no fault of my own, or any of the other hard-working employees and brokers of these collapsed firms, I faced significant challenges in regrouping my life and business in the wake of the industry downsize. Ensuring the most efficient transition to new brokerage arrangements possible for my firm and, more important, my clients was a difficult task. Part of the process involved establishing new relationships with the risk-management departments of our new trade-clearing arrangements to make sure each of our clients had the opportunities and leeway they needed to better their odds of success. In addition, we faced the burden of matching our clients with new trading platforms appropriate to their strategies, ensuring favorable margining and fee structures, and much more.

On the bright side, the commodity industry is known as the "last bastion of capitalism"; therefore, survival of the fittest is always in play. As difficult as it is for a broker and its clients to migrate to a new brokerage firm in the wake of the collapse of another, I can attest that the odds are in favor of an overall improvement in service and quality simply because only the strongest and most efficient survive.

HARD TIMES AND DESPERATE MEASURES

The difficult futures brokerage environment following the financial collapse of 2008 led some brokers to turn to highly questionable and illegal practices to stay afloat. Specifically, at least two firms violated long-standing, and previously concrete, safeguards of client funds by using customer margin deposits for business operations or, worse, personal embezzlement.

In fall 2011, MF Global, a mammoth commodity brokerage house, went down in dramatic fashion while misappropriating client funds to finance a "trade gone bad" on its proprietary desk in a fast and furious demise. Less than a year later, it was learned that the owner of PFGBEST, one of the 10 largest privately held commodity brokerage firms, had been secretly pilfering funds from client accounts to finance operations, pay regulatory fines, and fund a comfortable lifestyle for himself.

As outlined in an episode of *American Greed* on CNBC in which I was featured as a victim, the top executive at PFGBEST was reporting false customer segregated funds figures to the overseeing bodies and using falsified bank statements to deter regulators from detecting the fraud. In a letter written before an attempted suicide, he pleaded, "I had no access to additional capital and I was forced into a difficult decision: Should I go out of business or cheat? I guess my ego was too big to admit failure. So I cheated, I falsified the very core of the financial documents of PFGBEST, the Bank Statements."

Prior to this dramatic confession and the sudden unraveling of PFGBEST, the brokerage firm was considered to be well-respected and among the most compliant in the commodity industry. Regrettably, for these reasons, I chose to use PFGBEST as the exclusive brokerage firm to clear my clients' trades. My clients and I paid a hefty price for doing business with PFGBEST. As a small consolation prize, the mastermind of the fraud, Russell Wasendorf, is living out the remaining years of his life in a Federal prison.

CUSTOMER SEGREGATED FUNDS VIOLATIONS

Before October 2011—more specifically, before the collapse of MF Global—few outside the futures industry were aware of the term *customer segregated funds*. In July 2012, the failure of PFGBEST to uphold the sanctity of *customer segregated funds* catapulted the phrase into daily usage in national media outlets, and maybe even the homes of many Americans.

Customer segregated funds are exactly what the name implies; they are monetary deposits made by clients that are segregated from the assets of the brokerage firm. Expressly, when a client wires funds to a brokerage account in his name, the money is sent to a bank account in the name of the brokerage firm but titled "Customer Segregated Funds." For example, if your account was housed at Gain Capital, the title of the account holding your trading margin might be **Gain Capital Group LLC - Customer Segregated Funds Account**. All funds held within this account are to be client monies and are not to be commingled with firm money.

The requirement that brokerage firms hold client funds in segregated accounts is a safeguard against brokerage firm bankruptcies. In theory, if the FCM (Futures Commission Merchant, a fancy word for brokerage firm) suffers financial trouble and files for bankruptcy, any client funds on deposit will be unaffected. In fact, in such a case, it is common practice for the funds and open positions to simply be transferred to an alternative brokerage firm, leaving the insolvent FCM to deal with its issues and its former clients unscathed. Before MF Global and PFGBEST, commodity brokerage bankruptcies, mergers, and acquisitions an inconvenience to traders, but no client had ever lost a dime in the process; that changed in 2011.

The failure of MF Global and PFGBEST to avoid the commingling of the firm and client money crudely reminded us that segregated funds rules are only as good as their followers—and enforcers. Both FCMs displayed a flagrant disregard to compliance stipulations intended to protect the very customers who had enabled their long-standing success as brokerage firms. Deplorably, in both cases, industry regulators weren't able to detect the violations until after it was too late. Client funds had already been misappropriated and either spent or lost.

At this time this edition was going to print, MF Global clients had recouped nearly all of the money they had on deposit through liquidation of firm assets and other sources, but the process took over a year. PFGBEST clients hadn't fared so well; it took nearly four months after the firm's failure in July 2012 for the bankruptcy trustee to release 30% of the funds in what was a chaotic transfer of client assets to another brokerage firm, Vision Financial, who also later went out of business. At the time of this writing, PFG clients had recovered nearly 70% of their trading accounts in a total of five separate distributions spread out over five years. Even if the funds are eventually fully restored, the burden of having money unwillingly tied up and the emotional turmoil caused by the fiasco is substantial.

COLLATERAL DAMAGE

Brokerage clients were the obvious losers of the MF Global and PFGBEST breakdowns. However, other casualties have often been overlooked, including the firm's employees, its brokers, third-party vendors (platforms, trading systems, and money managers), floor traders, market makers, and more. When MF Global and, later, PFGBEST went under, not only did they nearly take their clients with them, but the situation devastated the lives of many hard-working industry participants. The trading pits in Chicago saw an immediate and dramatic decline in participation. In fact, many believe that these brokerage firm failures dramatically sped up the inevitable death of the trading pits. By the end of 2016, the open outcry pits were nearly dead. This cut out the need for floor brokers in the industry and shrunk the employment base substantially. In short, the commodity industry downsized almost overnight.

Painfully, my trading firm, DeCarley Trading, worked exclusively with PFGBEST until its demise in July 2012. I'll never forget July 9 of that year: A single email near the close of trading devastated all of our hard work and dreams. Without any knowledge of troubles brewing at the firm, nor any reason to have suspected wrongdoing, we were notified that PFGBEST's assets and client funds had been frozen pending an FBI investigation into the fraud of its president, Russell Wasendorf.

The commodity brokerage business is extremely demanding; few brokers achieve financial success and those who do succeed spend years building their business to get there. DeCarley Trading opened its door four years before the failure of PFGBEST and worked tirelessly around the clock to build clients' trust. Sadly, it was taken from us in the blink of an eye, without any culpability of our own. Fortunately, we were able to quickly recover by creating an even better trading environment for our brokerage clients; over time and through dedication, DeCarley Trading was able to emerge from the rubble as a "bigger and better" firm.

However, we were not alone in our hardship. Approximately 120 firms were engaging in a similar exclusive trade-clearing relationship with PFGBEST. More than half of such firms had thrown in the towel and closed shop on news of the debacle. After all, their ability to generate commission revenue stopped immediately and PFGBEST owed its brokers about a month and a half in commission at the time of failure, leaving little capital to work with. The thought of building a business from scratch in a nearly impossible environment for commodity brokers was a gut-wrenching task many weren't willing to attempt.

Each of us doing business with PFGBEST chose the firm with careful consideration and due diligence; nonetheless, each of us also learned that even doing your homework and confirming with the data reported by regulators isn't always enough. With that said, the industry and its regulatory bodies have gained insight and implemented practices that should successfully prevent a repeat of the PFGBEST and MF Global heartache. If you are interested in learning more, CNBC replays the *American Greed* episode featuring PFGBEST titled "The Falcon and the Conman" with regularity. As previously mentioned, I was interviewed and highlighted in the episode as a victim of the fraud.

HOW TO PROTECT YOURSELF FROM THE UNLIKELY EVENT OF A BROKERAGE FIRM FAILURE

The wounds left by MF Global and PFGBEST on the commodity industry were deep, but there have been positive developments in their aftermath such as improvements in the way regulators audit futures brokerage houses and maybe even the potential for deposit insurance at some point in the future. Similarly, although the odds of a repeat of this type of failure appear to be slim, futures traders should take the lessons learned from these events to safeguard themselves from potential hardships; as the saying goes, "It is better to be safe than sorry."

FOLLOW THE FCM FINANCIAL DATA REPORT

The Commodity Futures Trading Commission (CFTC) requires that FCMs regularly report the status of their customer segregated funds account to regulators; as a reminder, an FCM is simply a type of brokerage firm that will be discussed in detail throughout this book. With the data collected, the CFTC publishes a monthly report on the financial data of each FCM. Reports leading up to the PFGBEST debacle were a painful reminder that data portrayed on the CFTC's reports might not always be verified properly. However, this situation has largely changed. Government regulators now have electronic access to the customer segregated funds accounts of each commodity brokerage firm, enabling reliable and accurate real-time verification of funds.

The report includes information such as the total value of customer segregated deposits, whether the amount the brokerage firm has in the customer segregated funds account is enough to be compliant, and any excess or deficiency in the account. You might be wondering why an FCM would have more in its customer segregated funds account than its customers actually have on deposit. Cash inflows and outflows are constantly taking place as clients deposit and withdraw funds, buy and sell options and futures contracts, and pay brokerage fees. Plainly, the math isn't quite as easy as one might think; instead of being a black-and-white figure, there is quite a bit of gray.

Nonetheless, this data gives market participants the ability to see relatively timely data on how their broker is complying with the regulations in place that require brokerage firms to segregate customer funds from their own to protect client funds.

SPREAD FUNDS AMONG MULTIPLE BROKERS

Clients trading substantial sums of money might consider using more than one brokerage firm to clear trades with the exchange. Traders choosing to work with an *Independent Introducing Broker* (defined in Chapter 5) enjoy the luxury of having one individual broker service their trading accounts at multiple brokerage firms. This cuts down on the additional hassles of maintaining multiple trading accounts while providing clients the advantage of diversifying the risk of a brokerage firm failure in which client segregated funds have been tampered with. Accordingly, my experience in the PFGBEST debacle leads me to conclude such an arrangement is necessary for probable success as a commodity broker. Not surprisingly, I am now operating under an *Independent Introducing Brokerage* arrangement and therefore offer my clients access to several brokerage houses while still dealing exclusively with DeCarley Trading as their point of contact.

Again, the odds of another incident similar to those with MF Global or PFGBEST occurring are lean but having peace of mind is important. After all, if the unthinkable happens again, it won't occur at more than one firm at the same time.

WHAT REGULATORS ARE DOING TO PROTECT CLIENTS

As painful as back-to-back system failures were for clients, employees, and brokers of both MF Global and PFGBEST, some long-term good has come of it. For instance, as mentioned, in the aftermath of these events, the National Futures Association (NFA) has been provided electronic access to the bank accounts of FCMs, enabling frequent verification of customer segregated funds balances. On a handful of occasions, there has been a proposed insurance fund discussed within the CFTC that would provide deposit insurance to commodity traders on up to $250,000 of the account balance. This insurance fund would be similar to the banking system's FDIC deposit insurance and would eliminate the risk of unforeseen events such as bank insolvency or a brokerage failure to comply with segregation rules. Unfortunately, excessive costs involved in such deposit insurance for futures traders is more of a desire than a reality, but I predict it will eventually be implemented in some form as the commodity industry thrives to compete with leveraged ETFs for speculative dollars.

CONCLUSION

Despite the 2010–2012 hiccup in its track record, violation of customer segregated funds regulations is a rare and infrequent event. In fact, even without new regulatory safety nets already put in place to avoid another calamity of this sort, it likely would not happen again anytime soon. Nevertheless, those of us whose livelihood depends on a properly functioning marketplace in which we can all be confident welcome positive changes in oversight with open arms. I sleep well at night confident that my clients' funds and, therefore, my business are in safe hands.

Throughout this text, you find what I believe to be a realistic and candid view of the commodity markets. My intention isn't to deter you from trading commodities. After all, I am a broker who makes a living from the commission, and I would love nothing more than to attract traders into what I believe to be some of the most exciting markets available to speculators. However, as a broker, it is also my job to make sure that you are aware of the potential hardships and, accordingly, that you will properly prepare yourself before putting your hard-earned money at risk.

If you walk away from this book with something, I hope it is the realization that anything is possible in the commodity markets. Never say "never"—if you do, you will eventually be proved wrong. In addition, trading the markets is an art, not a science. Unfortunately, there are no black–and-white answers, nor are there fool-proof strategies—but that does not mean there aren't opportunities.

I am often asked what is the best technical tool or indicator to use when speculating in a market. My answer is always the same: No "best tool" exists, nor is there a best way to use the tool. The paramount approach to any trading tool, whether technical, seasonal, or fundamental, is to use it—or, better yet, a combination of a few tools—to form an educated opinion in your expectations of market price. With their findings, traders should approach the market with a degree of humbleness and realistic expectations.

Remember, as a trader, you compete against the market—specifically, each participant in that particular market. Therefore, assuming that you can always beat the markets is assuming that you are somehow smarter and better informed than all other participants. Not only is this arrogant, but it also might be financial suicide. Instead, you should approach every trade with modesty and the understanding that you could be wrong. Having such an attitude might prevent you from sustaining large losses as the result of stubbornness.

With that in mind, in its simplest form, trading is a zero-sum game. Aside from commissions paid to the brokerage firm and fees paid to the exchange, for every dollar lost in the market, someone else has gained a dollar. Becoming a consistently profitable trader isn't easy, but it isn't synonymous with chasing the proverbial end of the rainbow either. With the proper background, hard work, and the experience that comes with inevitable tough lessons, long-term success *is* possible. I hope this book is the first step in your journey toward victory in the challenging, yet potentially rewarding, commodity markets.

CHAPTER 1: A CRASH COURSE IN COMMODITIES

Given the urban nature of the city of Chicago, we often forget that it is located in the agricultural heart of the Midwest. In the mid-1840s, the Windy City emerged as the agricultural market center for neighboring states. Chicago was the meeting place for farmers looking for buyers of their crops and grain mills looking to purchase the product for their operations. However, despite the central location, timing and logistic issues created inefficient means of conducting business and thus inflated commodity prices.

At the time, grain elevators were sparse, so lack of storage made it critical that a farmer sell his crop upon harvest at the annual meeting in Chicago. Even those who did have a method of storing the grain faced frozen rivers and roadways that made traveling to Chicago nearly impossible during the winter months. Likewise, the springtime trails were often too muddy for wagon travel. Thus, during and immediately after harvest, grain supply was in such abundance that it was common for unsold grain to be dumped into Lake Michigan, for lack of means to transport and store unsold portions.

> Commodity prices have always been a function of supply and demand, but before the futures markets, excess and shortages wreaked havoc on consumers and producers.

As you can imagine, as the year wore on, the grain supply dwindled, creating shortages. This annual cycle of extreme oversupply and subsequent undersupply created inefficient price discovery and led to hardships for both producers and consumers. The feast-or-famine cycle created circumstances in which farmers were forced to sell their goods at a large discount when supplies were high, but consumers were required to pay a large premium during times of tight supplies. Luckily, a few of the grain traders put their heads and resources together to develop a solution: an organized exchange known as the Chicago Board of Trade (CBOT)—or, more accurately, what is now the CBOT division of the CME Group.

The Chicago Board of Trade was created by a handful of savvy grain traders to establish a central location for buyers and sellers to conduct business. The new formalized location and operation enticed wealthy investors to build storage silos to smooth the supply of grain throughout the year and, in turn, aid in price.

After spending the last decade and a half as one of the largest futures trading organizations in the world and a direct competitor to the Chicago Mercantile Exchange (CME), the CBOT and the CME merged July 12, 2007, to form the CME Group, creating the largest derivatives market ever.

THE CHICAGO BOARD OF TRADE

The CBOT division of the CME Group is the home of the trading of agricultural products such as corn, soybeans, and wheat. However, prior to its inclusion of the CME Group the CBOT exchange added several products over the years, to include Treasury bonds and notes and the Dow Jones Industrial Index. Since 1930, 141 West Jackson Boulevard in

> Established in 1848, the CBOT is the world's oldest futures and options exchange. Native Chicagoans describe the organization as "old money."

downtown Chicago has been known as the Chicago Board of Trade Building. It is now designated as a National Historic Landmark.

The success of the CBOT fueled investment dollars into exchanges that could facilitate the process of trading products other than grain. One of the offshoots of this new investment interest was the Chicago Mercantile Exchange. The CME was formed in 1874 under the operating name Chicago Produce Exchange; it also carried the title Chicago Butter and Egg Board before finally gaining its current name. The contract that put this exchange on the map was frozen pork belly futures, or simply "bellies," as many insiders say. Hollywood and media portrayals of the futures industry often focus on the pork belly market. How could anyone forget the infamous scene in the movie *Trading Places* in which Billy Ray Valentine plots his speculation of belly futures? Ironically, the CME Group delisted pork belly futures in July 2011 due to a "prolonged lack of trading volume."

THE CHICAGO MERCANTILE EXCHANGE

Local Chicagoans refer to the CME as "The Merc."

The CME, now a division of the CME Group, is responsible for trading in a vast variety of contracts, including cattle, hogs, stock index futures, currency futures, and short-term interest rates. The exchange also offers alternative trading vehicles such as weather and real estate derivatives. In fact, they are constantly adding futures and options products to be traded, in my opinion at their own peril. The goal should be to lure more commodity traders and market volume, not grow the product list beyond reasonable liquidity. Nonetheless, at the time of this writing, and likely for some time to come, the CME has the largest open interest in options and futures contracts of any futures exchange in the world.

THE NEW YORK MERCANTILE EXCHANGE

Although the futures and options industry was born in Chicago, New York was quick to get in on the action. In the early 1880s, a crop of Manhattan dairy merchants created the Butter and Cheese Exchange of New York, which was later modified to the Butter, Cheese, and Egg Exchange and then, finally, the New York Mercantile Exchange (NYMEX).

In March 2008, NYMEX accepted a cash and stock offer from the CME Group that brought the New York futures exchange into the fold, along with the CBOT and the CME. On August 18, 2008, NYMEX seat-holders and shareholders accepted the proposal and the rest is history. The NYMEX division of the CME Group was fully integrated with the CME and CBOT divisions of the exchange despite being located hundreds of miles away from downtown Chicago. However, the NYMEX is currently a 100% electronically traded exchange. The last of the open outcry trading pits in New York were closed on December 30, 2016.

According to New Yorkers, there is only one "Merc," and it isn't in Chicago. However, the CME Group has been slowly winding down NYC operations in recent years and closed the last trading pit in December 2016. All New York Merc products are traded exclusively via electronic trade matching.

The NYMEX division of the CME Group currently houses futures trading in the energy complex. Examples of NYMEX-listed futures contracts are crude oil, gasoline, and natural gas. A 1994 merger with the nearby Commodity Exchange (COMEX) allowed the NYMEX to acquire the trading of precious metals futures such as gold and silver under what is referred to as its COMEX division. As you've probably assumed, the COMEX now operates as a division of the CME Group.

THE CME GROUP

The CME Group consists of the four aforementioned divisions: the CBOT, CME, NYMEX, and COMEX, which previously stood as independent exchanges. Accordingly, the CME is officially the world's largest derivatives exchange. As previously mentioned, on July 12, 2007, the merger of the CBOT and the CME created the CME Group, but NYMEX (along with its COMEX arm) was acquired in 2008 to create a powerful and innovative entity.

Trade on the CME Group represents a majority of futures trading in the United States, but its largest competitor is the Intercontinental Exchange known simply as ICE.

The CME Group currently serves the speculative and risk management needs of customers worldwide. Among the four divisions, the CME Group offers derivative products across nearly all imaginable asset classes.

Upon merging, the CBOT and the CME consolidated all floor-trading operations into a single location: the historic CBOT building on 141 West Jackson Boulevard in downtown Chicago. The actual move took place over three weekends, and no details were spared. The new combined trading floor spanned 60,000 square feet. However, since the move but not because of it, the trading floor has slowly dwindled to a whisper. Instead of thousands of traders waving their hands to buy and sell future and options, there are dozens of traders fighting over a handful of orders hitting the pits. Most predict that by the year 2020 the practice of open outcry will be completely eliminated.

INTERCONTINENTAL EXCHANGE

Intercontinental Exchange (ICE) is the newest player in US futures trading. ICE was established May 2000; by 2001, it had acquired a European energy futures exchange, but it didn't dig its claws deep into the heart of the US futures industry until its acquisition of the New York Board of Trade (NYBOT) in 2007, along with the responsibility to facilitate trading in the softs complex. The term *soft* generally describes a commodity that is grown rather than mined; examples of contracts categorized as soft and traded on ICE in the United States include sugar, cocoa, coffee, and cotton. Their claim to fame is the Brent crude oil futures traded in Europe. More recent additions to the US Intercontinental Exchange (ICE) are financial products including the US Dollar Index and other currency products. However, liquidity in products other than the softs and Brent crude oil has been sluggish.

In stark contrast to the original models of the CBOT, the CME, NYMEX, and COMEX, ICE exclusively facilitates over-the-counter energy and commodity futures contracts. This simply means that there is no centralized location for open outcry trading; all trading takes place in cyberspace via electronic trade matching. We discuss the two types of execution in greater detail in Chapter 3, "The Slow Death of Open Outcry and the Growth of Electronic Trading." As discussed, the CME Group is slowly following suit but ICE was the first to set the precedent. Ironically, despite ICE's stance as a trail blazer for electronic trading, they are particularly bad at offering simple conveniences for traders such as good until canceled orders on options and allowing traders to modify existing orders as opposed to canceling an order and replacing a new ticket. In many aspects, the CME Group has surpassed ICE in its electronic trading technology. In addition, ICE charges traders $110 (plus NYC sales tax) for access to live price data. Not surprisingly, most retail traders opt not to subscribe. Instead, they choose to participate in CME Group products or endure the inconvenience of trading ICE products with delayed price data.

EVOLUTION OF THE FORWARD CONTRACT INTO A FUTURES CONTRACT

The futures markets and the instruments traded there, as we know them today, have evolved from what began as private negotiations to buy and sell commodities between producers and users. The agreements that resulted from these negotiations are known as forward contracts. Fortunately, efficient-minded entrepreneurs discovered that standardized agreements can facilitate transactions in a much quicker manner than a privately negotiated forward contract. Thus, the futures contract was born. Next, we take a look at the advent of the forward contract and how the concept eventually bred the futures contract.

THE FORWARD CONTRACT

The ingenuity of agricultural trade didn't end with the creation of organized and centralized grain trade in the 1800s. Although this certainly worked toward price stabilization by leveling shortages and surpluses throughout the growing and harvest cycles, other factors worked against price efficiency. As a means of mitigating price risks, farmers and merchants began dealing in forward contracts.

A forward contract is a private negotiation developed to establish the price of a commodity to be delivered at a specific date in the future. For example, a farmer who has planted corn and expects it to be harvested and ready to sell in October might locate a party interested in purchasing the product in October. At that time, both parties might choose to enter an agreement for the transaction to take place at a specific date, price, and location. Such an agreement locks in the price for both the buyer and the seller of the commodity and, therefore, eliminates the risk of price fluctuation that both sides of the contract face without the benefit of a forward contract.

Along with a centralized grain trade, the forward contract was another big step toward price stability, but there was a problem. Forward contracts reduce price risk only if both parties to the arrangement live up to their end of the agreement. In other words, there is no protection against default. As you can imagine, a farmer who locks in a price to sell his crop in the spring through a forward contract and later discovers that he can sell the product for considerably more in the open market might choose to default on the forward contract.

It is easy to see the lack of motivation for parties to a forward contract to uphold their end of the bargain. Even the most honest man would be tempted to default if it means a better life for his family.

To resolve the issue of merchants and farmers defaulting on forward contracts, the exchanges began requiring that each party of the transaction submit a good-faith deposit, or margin, with an unrelated third party. In the case of failure to comply with the contract, the party suffering the loss would receive the funds deposited in good faith to cover the inconvenience and at least part of the financial loss.

THE FUTURES CONTRACT

Exchange-traded forward contracts were extremely helpful in reducing the price risk that farmers and merchants normally were exposed to. In addition, with the advent of exchange-traded forward contracts along with good-faith deposits, much of the default risk was eliminated. However, because forward contracts were negotiations between two individuals, it was a challenge to bring together buyers and sellers who shared the same needs in terms of quantity, timing, and so on. Also, forward contracts were subject to difficulties arising from uncontrollable circumstances such as drought. For example, a farmer obligated to deliver a certain amount of corn via a forward contract might not comply due to poor growing conditions, thus leaving the counterparty to the transaction in a dire predicament.

> In its simplest form, a futures contract is a standardized forward contract.

The exchanges' answer to problems arising from forward contracts was the standardized futures contract. In its simplest form, a futures contract is a forward contract that is standardized in terms of size, deliverable grade of the commodity, delivery date, and delivery location. The fact that each contract is identical to the next made the trading of futures much more convenient than attempting to negotiate a forward contract with an individual. The concept of standardization has allowed the futures markets to flourish into what they have become today.

According to the CME, the formal definition of a futures contract is as follows:

> *A legally binding, standardized agreement to buy or sell a standardized commodity, specifying quantity and quality at a set price on a future date.*

In other words, the seller of a futures contract agrees to deliver the stated commodity on the stated delivery date. The buyer of a futures contract agrees to take delivery of the stated commodity at the stated delivery date. The only variable of a futures transaction is the price at which it is done, and buyers and sellers determine this in the marketplace.

Although the futures contracts bought or sold represent an obligation to take or make delivery, according to the CME Group, approximately 97% of futures contracts never result in physical delivery of the underlying commodity. Instead, traders simply offset their holding prior to the expiration date. We discuss this in more detail later in the chapter.

In the evolution into the futures contract and away from the forward contract, exchanges also eliminated default risk associated with buying or selling futures contracts by guaranteeing the other side of the transaction. Thus, unlike a forward contract, or early versions of the futures contract, in which both parties are left to depend on the other to live up to their end of the contract, a futures contract is backed by the exchange. This exchange guarantee covers the entire value of the position, instead of being limited to the margin posted by participants.

Thanks to the standardization of each contract, the subsequent ease of buying or selling contracts, and a lack of default risk, futures trading has attracted price speculation. Participation is no longer limited to those who own or would like to own the underlying commodity. Instead, unrelated third parties can easily involve themselves in the markets in hopes of accurately predicting—and, therefore, profiting from—price fluctuations.

CASH MARKET VERSUS FUTURES MARKET

Currently, commodities are traded in two separate yet related markets: the cash market and the futures market. The cash market refers to the buying and selling of physical commodities. In a cash market transaction, the price and exchange of product occur in the present. In contrast, the futures market deals with the buying or selling of future obligations to make or take delivery instead of the actual commodity.

> A cash market transaction occurs in the present, but a futures market transaction is an agreement for an exchange of the underlying asset in the future.

COST TO CARRY

Prices in the cash and futures market differ as a direct result of the disparity in the timing of delivery of the underlying product. After all, if a commodity is going to be delivered at some point in the future, it must be stored and insured in the meantime. The costs associated with holding the physical grain until the stated delivery date are referred to as the costs to carry.

Naturally, in normal market conditions, the cash price is cheaper than the futures price because of the expenses related to carrying the commodity until delivery. Likewise, the near-month futures price is generally cheaper than a distantly expiring futures contract. The progressive pricing is often referred to as a normal carrying charge market (see Figure 6). You might also hear this scenario described by the term *contango*.

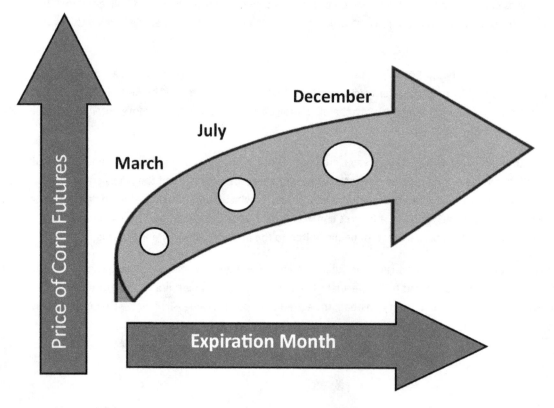

Figure 6: Normal carry charge market or contango.

Normal carrying charge markets are possible only during times of ample supply, or inventory. If there is a shortage of the commodity in the near term, prices in the cash market will increase to reflect market supply-and-demand fundamentals. The supply shortage can reduce the contango or, if severe enough, can actually reverse the contango if the spot price, and possibly the price of the nearby futures contract, exceeds the futures price in distant contracts, as shown in Figure 7.

It is important to understand that the contango shouldn't exceed the actual cost to carry the commodity. If it did, producers and consumers would have the opportunity for a "risk-free" profit through arbitrage.

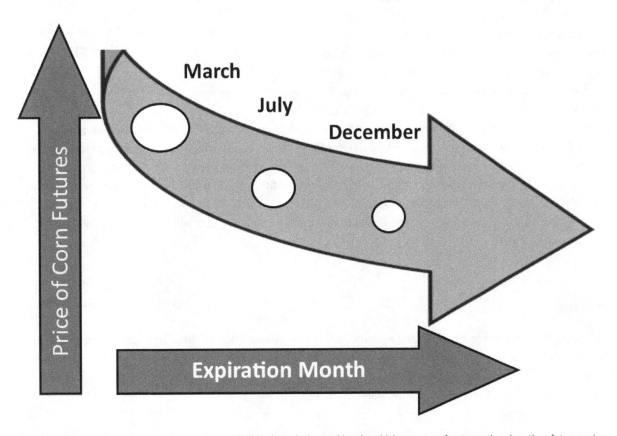

Figure 7: The opposite of contango is sometimes called backwardation and involves higher spot, or front month, prices than futures prices.

ARBITRAGE

Arbitrage is the glue that holds the commodity markets together. Without arbitrage, there would be no incentive for prices in the futures market to correlate with prices in the cash market—and as I discuss in Chapter 2, "Hedging Versus Speculating," arbitrage enables efficient market pricing for hedgers and speculators. Specifically, if speculators notice that the price difference between the cash and futures prices of a

> "If you can take advantage of a situation in some way, it's your duty as an American to do it." —C. Montgomery Burns (from *The Simpsons*)

commodity exceeds the cost to carry, they will buy the undervalued (cash market commodity) and sell the overvalued (futures contract written on underlying commodity). This is done until the spread between the prices in the two markets equals the cost to carry.

The true definition of arbitrage is a risk-free profit. Sounds great, doesn't it? Unfortunately, true arbitrage opportunities are uncommon, and those that do occur are opportunities for only the insanely quick. Chances are, you and I do not possess the speed, skill, and resources necessary to properly identify and react to most arbitrage opportunities in the marketplace.

For further clarification, an example of an arbitrage opportunity, unrelated to cash market pricing but relevant to the discussion, is a scenario in which the E-mini S&P is trading at 2380.50 and the full-size version of the contract is trading at 2380.70. In theory, if you noticed this discrepancy in a timely fashion, it would be possible to buy five mini contracts and sell one big S&P. The mini contract is exactly one-fifth the size of

> Arbitrage is a "risk-free" profit, but for most of us, it might as well be a mirage. Markets are quick to eliminate such opportunities.

the original and is fungible; this means that trading five E-mini futures contracts is identical to trading one big contract. Consequently, a trader who can execute each side of the trade at the noted prices can request that the positions offset each other to lock in a profit of 20 cents, or $50 before transactions costs. It doesn't sound like much, but if it truly is an arbitrage opportunity, a $50 risk-free profit isn't such a bad deal. On a side note, the days of the full-sized S&P 500 futures contract is likely numbered. I predict that by the fourth edition of this book is released its memory will be completely wiped from the text, but for now, it exists and creates trades with some arbitrage opportunities.

CONTRACT EXPIRATION

By definition, futures contracts are expiring agreements for buyers and sellers of those contracts to exchange the underlying physical commodity. Most market participants choose to avoid dealing with the underlying assets by offsetting their obligation at some point before the futures contract expires or, in some cases, prior to first notice day. I cover the process of offsetting positions later in the chapter.

FIRST NOTICE DAY

First notice day occurs before the corresponding futures contract expires. The official definition of first notice day is the day on which the buyer of a futures contract can be called upon by the exchange to take delivery of the underlying commodity. On this day, the exchange estimates the number of traders who are expected to make delivery of the commodity (those short futures contracts) and distributes delivery notices to those long futures on a first-in basis. Simply put, traders who hold long positions into the first notice day run the risk of being delivered upon but might not actually be delivered upon, depending on the amount of time the position has been open. For instance, a trader who has been long a futures contract for several weeks will receive a delivery notice before a trader who has established a position the day before first notice day. Note that the danger of receiving a delivery notice applies to those long the market only. Short traders don't have to worry about delivery until expiration day—yet they should be out of the market well before expiration because the market volume and liquidity dry up immediately preceding and beyond the first notice day.

After a delivery notice is distributed, a trader isn't forced to accept it, so panicking is unnecessary. Instead, he can instruct his brokerage firm to "retender" the notice, which equates to selling the obligation in an open market to an interested party. Although the trader avoids being forced to find a home for 5,000 bushels of corn, or whatever the commodity might be, he faces substantial processing fees. All speculators should diligently avoid being part of the delivery process.

Not all futures contracts have a first notice day; some stipulate a cash settlement process instead of delivery of the underlying product. Cash settlement works just as it sounds and is explained next.

FUTURES EXPIRATION

Expiration is the time and day that a particular delivery month of a futures contract ceases trading and the final settlement price is determined. The actual delivery process begins at the expiration of the futures contract for markets that involve a physical commodity exchange. Conversely, a select number of futures contracts are cash settled. If this is the case, investors who hold positions into expiration agree to allow the exchange to determine a final valuation for the futures contract at hand and adjust the value of individual trading accounts accordingly. In my opinion, it is generally a bad idea to hold positions into expiration in cash-settled markets because it leaves the fate of profit and losses in the hands of a relatively arbitrary exchange-derived contract value. I've seen cash settled contracts base the trader payout on a price considerably different than the last price the futures contract traded. Nobody should be interested in trading that type of Russian roulette in the commodity markets. Likewise, unless you are willing to make, or take, delivery of the underlying commodity, you shouldn't have an open position in a deliverable commodity contract into expiration.

THE MECHANICS OF FUTURES CONTRACTS

So far, we have learned that futures contracts are standardized and are guaranteed by the exchange. However, there is a lot more to be learned, and you must fully understand the basics before you can expect to be a successful futures trader.

THE LONG AND SHORT OF IT

Commodity trading is a world full of insider lingo; it is almost as if the industry created a language of its own. If you want to be a participant, you must become familiar with commonly used terms and phrases. Doing so avoids miscommunication between yourself, your broker, and any other party you might be communicating with.

I cover several commonly used phrases and terms in a later chapter; however, the two most critical terms to be aware of are *long* and *short*. In essence, the term *long* is synonymous with *buy*, and the term *short* is synonymous with *sell*. This is the case

> In futures market slang, *long* and *short* describe a speculative position.

whether the instrument in question is a futures contract or an option. Specifically, if a trader buys a futures or options contract, he is *going long*. If a trader sells a futures or options contract, he is *going short*.

It is important to realize that you will sometimes hear industry insiders say that they are *long the market* with options, futures spreads, and such. Although in the strict context of the phrase *long* implies that something has been purchased, in loosely used lingo, being *long a market* might simply mean having a bullish stance. This can mean long futures, long call options, short put options, bullish option or futures spreads, or any other speculative play that profits from an increase in the price of the underlying asset. Consequently, you might hear a trader mention that she is *short the market*; this might mean that she is short futures, short call options, long puts, or engaged in a bearish option or futures spread. Despite the alternative uses, however, beginning traders should first be comfortable using *long* and *short* in the context.

BUY OR SELL IN ANY ORDER

One of the most difficult concepts for beginning commodity traders to grasp is the fact that a futures contract can be bought and sold in any order. The common thinking is that you can't possibly sell something before you own it, and even if you could, some interest likely would be charged for borrowing the asset that you intend to sell. Although that might be true in stock trading, that logic doesn't apply to the futures markets. Let's take a look at why this is the case.

> Futures traders don't have to own or borrow assets before they can sell.

Unlike stocks, futures contracts are not assets; they are liabilities. The purchase of a futures contract does not represent ownership of the underlying commodity; instead, it represents an obligation to take delivery of the underlying commodity at a specified date. Likewise, the seller of a futures contract isn't selling an asset; he is simply agreeing to make delivery of the stated asset on the appropriate date.

> Trading futures and options is as simple as buying low and selling high—but simple doesn't mean it is easy.

Because there is no ownership or exchange of the asset at the time the futures trade is made, it isn't necessary to own the underlying commodity or even be prepared to take ownership. Thus, buying or selling in any order isn't an issue for futures traders.

OFFSETTING AND ROLLING OVER TRADES

As mentioned, most investors who participate in the futures markets are simply attempting to profit from variations in price movement and are not interested in taking or making delivery of the underlying commodity. Again, to avoid the delivery process, it is necessary to offset holdings prior to expiration—or, more specifically, the first notice day.

> When a trade is offset, the trader is said to be flat the market. This means that all positions are closed and there is no exposure to price risk, aside from a potential missed trade.

The notion of offsetting is simple: To offset a trade, it is necessary to execute a position opposite the one that you originally entered the market with. To illustrate, if you bought a December corn futures, you would need to sell a December corn futures to get out of the position. When you are out of the market, you are said to be flat. This means that you do not have any open trades and are no longer exposed to price risk or margin. Of course, being flat the market doesn't necessarily mean that the risk of emotional turmoil is eliminated. Unfortunately, many beginning traders have incorrectly looked at missed opportunities as monetary losses. We look at the psychological impact of such emotions in Chapter 13, "The Only Magic in Trading—Emotional Stability."

Figure 8: Futures traders can buy and sell in any order but must take the opposite action to exit. This trader is going long an August soybean futures contract and will later have to sell it to offset the position. (Chart courtesy of QST)

The concept of offsetting can be best explained by an example. In mid-2017, soybean futures were trading at multi-year lows but had shown signs of holding long-term support. A trader who believed that prices would appreciate might purchase a futures contract in hopes of a rally. At that point, the trader has an open long position with the exchange and continues to have an open position until it is offset. As mentioned, the only way to offset an open position is to execute a transaction opposite the one used to enter the market. Looking at Figure 8, you can see that the trader purchased an August soybean futures contract at $9.50. In Chapter 8, "Making Cents of Commodity Quotes," I explain the details in quoting and calculating grain futures.

To get out of the market, the trader must sell an August soybean futures contract, hopefully at a higher price. Naturally, if a trader can buy low and sell high, regardless of the order, he will be profitable (see Figure 9). As simple as this premise is, execution can be challenging. In fact, a majority of speculators walk away from the game with less money than they started with merely because they couldn't find a way to consistently buy low and sell high.

To exit a long position the trader would need to sell a futures contract to get even with the exchange. He hopes to do this at a much higher price than the original purchase.

S 1 ZSQ17 @ $10.45

Figure 9: When a trader no longer has an open position, he is said to be "flat" the market. This trader is hoping to sell his contract, and his obligation with the exchange, near $9.50. (Chart courtesy of QST)

The same concept would be true for someone who sold an August soybean futures contract to enter the position rather than buying one. Aside from holding the futures into expiration and actually making delivery of the underlying asset, the only way to get out of a short August futures trade would be to buy an August futures contract to offset the position.

The term *rolling*, or *rolling over*, is commonly used to describe the practice of offsetting a trade in a contract that is facing expiration and entering a similar position in a contract with a distant expiration date. *Rolling over* is simply offsetting one position and getting into another. Many beginning traders make the mistake of assuming that *rolling* into a new contract somehow avoids exiting the original position and simply changes the contract month. Perhaps it is wishful thinking for those who would prefer not to lock in a loss on an open position; unfortunately, doing so is a necessary evil if the goal is to move into an alternative contract month.

To illustrate, a trader who is long a June T-note futures contract with the first notice day quickly approaching might choose to roll into the September contract to avoid delivery while still maintaining a bullish speculative position in the market. In this case, rolling would include selling the June contract and buying September.

BID/ASK SPREAD

The notion of a *bid/ask spread* can be confusing. This is especially true given the differing perspectives of written literature available for beginning traders. Some articles and books seem to insist on explaining the *bid/ask spread* from both a market maker's point of view and a retail trader's

> Nothing is free. Paying spreads are a part of trading costs. Don't get mad; get savvy.

perspective. However, in my opinion, providing details of both sides of the story simply creates more confusion than is necessary to get a good grasp of what a *bid/ask spread* is and how to cope with it as a trader.

The easiest way to understand the spread between the *bid* and the *ask* is to come to peace with the fact that there are essentially two market prices at any given time. There is a price at which you can buy the contract (the *ask*) and a price at which you can sell it (the *bid*). As a retail trader, you will always be paying the higher price and selling the lower price. It takes money to make money, and if you want to participate in a market, you must pay the *bid/ask spread*. For instance, a corn trader might buy corn at $3.75 and sell corn at $3.75 1/2. The difference of half a cent is the *bid/ask spread*, and it translates into a component of the transaction cost associated with executing a trade in this market.

Keep in mind that the *bid/ask spread* is how market makers are compensated for executing your trade and providing liquidity to the markets. In the not too distant past, market makers were mostly floor brokers or those standing in the trading pits executing orders that flowed through the market. Just as you pay a commission to the retail broker who took your order or provides you trading access via an electronic platform, the market maker must be paid in the form of the *bid/ask spread*. Think about it: If as a retail trader you are always paying the *ask* and selling the *bid*, you are a net loser even if the price of the futures contract remains unchanged. In options markets, the beneficiary of the difference between the *bid* and the *ask* is the market maker making fluidity of trade possible. In liquid futures markets, market makers are generally not needed. Thus, the conglomerate of market participants absorbs the bid/ask spread.

The spread between the *bid* and the *ask* is not something that investors should resent—in liquid markets, anyway. After all, the market maker must be compensated for accepting the risk involved with taking the other side of your trade. In general, he wants to offset his position and risk as soon as possible; his intention is to "make a market" and profit from the difference in the *bid/ask spread*, not to speculate on price movement. In highly liquid markets, there are often no market makers but there is still a natural bid/ask spread of about a tick. More specifically, options traders will almost always be executing orders in which a market maker is on the other side of the transaction earning the spread. However, futures traders are often having their trades matched with other retail traders rather than a designated market maker. This is because there is ample liquidity for the market to function and discover prices without the aid of a liquidity provider.

As a trader, it is important to be aware of the *bid/ask spread* and the implications that its size will have on your trading results. A couple prominent factors that affect the size of the spread are market liquidity and volatility. As market liquidity decreases, the size of the *bid/ask spread* widens, and thus the costs associated with participating in such a market increases. This makes sense. If the market maker is anticipating a lack of volume and the corresponding difficulty offsetting his trade, he will require more compensation for taking the other side of your trade.

Likewise, if volatility is high, the market maker faces more price risk during the time in which he takes the other side of your trade and can subsequently offset the position. Thus, he requires higher compensation for his efforts, which creates a relatively wide *bid/ask spread*.

One of the biggest mistakes I have witnessed beginning traders make is to ignore the repercussions of large *bid/ask spreads*. Most futures contracts are fluidly traded enough for this to be a non-issue. However, in the options trading arena, this is a big concern. It is extremely important that you understand that bid/ask spreads are a part of doing business and know how to adjust your trading strategy accordingly.

Bid/ask spreads hinder a trader's ability to make money; the wider the spreads, the more difficult it is to be profitable. In fact, certain markets have *bid/ask spreads* so wide that I believe investors have no incentive to trade them. This avoidance stems from the idea that excessively wide spreads create a scenario in which the trader must not only be right in the direction of the market but must also be extremely right to overcome the hefty transaction cost. Imagine trading copper options that often have *bid/ask spreads* in excess of 1 cent in premium, or $250. Immediately after initiating the trade, it is a loser in the amount of $250, regardless of movement in the futures price. As you can see, this can make trading even more challenging.

ROUND TURNS AND TRANSACTION COSTS

Unlike the world of stocks, in which transaction costs are often quoted on a per-side basis and in the form of a ticket charge, commodity trades are typically charged on a round-turn basis. However, as the nature of the industry shifts from broker-assisted trading to discount online, futures brokers are beginning to quote commissions per side in an effort to make the transaction costs seem cheaper than they actually are. Further, broker-dealers (stock brokers who offer futures and options on futures on the side) also frequently quote commission on a per-side basis. Nevertheless, commodity commission is traditionally measured on a round-turn basis. A single round turn consists of the purchase and sale of the same futures or options contract. Simply put, it is getting in and getting out of a market.

Many beginning traders mistakenly assume that the commission and fees charged to them depend on the number of order tickets rather than the number of contracts, but this is not the case. If a trader buys 10 crude oil futures contracts at $49.00 and later sells all 10 at $50.00, he has executed 10 round-turns and will be charged 10 commissions. This is true regardless of whether the 10 contracts were purchased and sold on single tickets or whether there were 10 separate orders to buy one contract at various prices and then 10 separate orders to sell one contract at $50.00.

Of course, not all traders are day trading, and it is common for positions to be entered on one day and exited at some date in the future. In this case, a futures trader is charged a half of a round-turn commission on the day the trade is initiated and is then charged the other half the day that the trade is offset. Notice that I specifically noted futures traders; option traders normally are charged the entire round-turn commission when they enter the trade. Therefore, a trader who buys a soybean $9.00 put would be charged a commission to enter the position but would be able to exit the trade without being charged.

Keep in mind that I have been referring strictly to commissions, which your brokerage firm charges. Each round turn is accompanied by exchange fees, minimal National Futures Association (NFA) fees, and possible transaction fees charged by the clearing firm. Transaction fees are charged on a per-side basis, regardless of whether the instrument being traded is an option or a futures contract.

When negotiating a commission rate with your brokerage firm, be sure to confirm that the quoted rates are per round turn. You should also be aware of whether they include the additional fees. Because exchange fees vary from product to product, most firms state commission rates on a round-turn-plus-fees basis. This means that you have to account for any exchange, NFA, and clearing fees in addition to the commission. Some firms, typically deep discount brokerages, quote rates as "all-inclusive," which already account for incremental fees. Many of these firms also quote rates on a per-side basis simply because it "sounds" cheaper and can be an effective marketing tool. In short, make sure you and the account executive you are speaking with regarding your proposed trading account are not talking about apples and oranges.

PRICE SPECULATION

As easy as it is to have the freedom to buy or sell in any order, sticking to the overall goal of buying low and selling high can be challenging. The price of a given asset, whether it be grains, metals, energies, or Treasury bonds, depends on a seemingly unlimited number of factors. Even as a market is making a large price move, it is nearly impossible to determine the driving force behind the change in valuation and whether it will last.

Not only are market prices the result of supply and demand fundamentals, but they can also be swayed by logistical issues such as light volume, options expiration, and excessive margin calls. A primary catalyst for some of the largest commodity plunges in history was the sweeping number of forced liquidations due to the insufficient margin in speculative trading accounts. Remember, commodities are mostly traded by highly leveraged speculators and are, therefore, more susceptible to forced selling than stocks and bonds typically are.

In addition, a seemingly unlimited number of intermarket relationships can be used as a guide but not a guarantee. For instance, a strong dollar often works against commodity prices, but that doesn't mean that if the dollar is down, commodities will always rally. Another example is the negative correlation between Treasuries and stocks. In theory, investors have two major asset classes to choose from, stocks and bonds. If money is flowing into one, it is likely flowing out of the other. This is a useful but simplistic bit of information. Although this relationship tends to exist over time, in many cases, both markets travel together, and stubbornly trading according to the historical relationship could lead to large losses.

This discussion isn't intended to discourage you from attempting to speculate on the price of commodities or to insinuate that it can't be done; it can. However, I want you to recognize that analyses should be done with an open mind and a willingness to adapt to changes in what you consider to be the norm.

FUTURES SPREADS

The practice of buying one futures contract and selling another that is similar in nature is known as *spread trading*— specifically, *futures spread trading*. The goal of a futures spread is to profit from the change in the price difference between the two related futures contracts involved. Simply, a futures spread trader isn't necessarily concerned with the direction of the underlying market. Instead, the trader is

> Exchange-recognized futures spreads involve discounted margin requirements; before trading spreads, be sure you are properly capitalized.

speculating on the relationship (spread) between the prices of the two contracts in question. Two basic futures spreads exist—the *intracommodity* spread and the *intercommodity* spread.

Intracommodity spread. In reference to a futures spread, there are a plethora of interpretations or meanings. However, the most commonly used spread strategy is the intracommodity spread, which is often referred to as a calendar spread. Specifically, this entails simultaneously holding a long position in one contract month of a specific commodity and a short position in another contract month of the same commodity.

For example, a grain trader might buy a July corn futures contract and sell a December corn futures contract. Whether the position is a winner or a loser doesn't necessarily depend on whether corn prices go up or down; instead, it depends on how much more July corn increases relative to the December contract or how much less it decreases. Specifically, it is concerned with whether the spread widens or narrows.

 Intercommodity spread. Don't get intracommodity and intercommodity spreads confused. The prefix *intra* denotes that the spread is between the same commodity; the prefix *inter* indicates that the spread is between two different but related commodities. As you can imagine, due to the less obvious correlation between the components of an intercommodity spread relative to those in an intracommodity spread, intercommodity spreads tend to be much more volatile and expose traders to more risk.

An intercommodity spread consists of purchasing a futures contract in a given delivery month and simultaneously holding a short position in a related commodity market but the same delivery month. An example of popular intercommodity spreads includes the crack spread (spreading crude oil against unleaded gasoline and heating oil) and the crush spread (spreading soybeans against soybean oil and soybean meal).

Similar to an *option spread* that can have its own quote, a *futures spread* can also be referenced in terms of a package. Consequently, exchange recognized spreads are traded via a unique strategy symbol assigned by the futures exchange itself. In short, the spread itself trades as if it were a single instrument. However, these types of exchange- recognized strategies might have volume concerns; most spread trades are filled via a market maker rather than natural market liquidity. The existence of unique instrument symbols enables traders to name the spread price and place the order to execute both sides of the position on a single ticket.

> The term *spread* typically implies hedge. In theory, one or some of the components of the spread will hedge the risk of others.

For example, if July corn futures are trading at $3.70 and December corn is trading at $3.91, the bid/ask spread on this particular intracommodity spread might be $0.20/$0.21. Thus, a spread trader could buy the spread for $0.21 or sell the spread for $0.20, or choose to work a limit order at an alternative price. Alternatively, a spread trader could choose to execute each leg of the spread separately, as opposed to a package, by executing two order tickets—one for the July corn futures and one for December.

A BRIEF INTRODUCTION TO COMMODITY OPTIONS

The theory and practice of option trading are diverse and sometimes complicated. Accordingly, it is impossible to do the topic justice in such a brief mention. The purpose of this section is to merely introduce the subject. Options can be purchased outright, in conjunction with futures contracts, or even as a package with both short and long options of various types. There are no limits to the versatility of options trading. Commodity options provide a flexible and effective way to trade in the futures markets with various amounts of potential risk and reward. For example, through the combination of long and short calls and puts, investors can design a strategy that fits their needs and expectations; such an arrangement is referred to as an *option spread*. It is also possible to use options to hedge futures positions and vice versa.

The method and strategy should be determined by personality, risk capital, time horizon, market sentiment, and risk aversion. Plainly, if you aren't an aggressive individual with a high tolerance for pain, you probably shouldn't be employing a trading strategy that involves elevated risk. Doing so often results in the panicked liquidation of trades at inopportune times and other unsound emotional decisions. If you are interested in learning more about option trading concepts, consider reviewing my books *Higher Probability Commodity Trading* and *Commodity Options*.

WHAT IS AN OPTION?

Before it is possible to understand how options can be used, it is important to know what they are and how they work. The buyer of an option pays a premium (payment) to the seller of an option for the right, not the obligation, to take delivery of the underlying futures contract (exercise). This financial value is treated as an asset, although eroding, to the option buyer and a liability to the seller. There are two types of options: a *call option* and a *put option.*

- Ω   **Call options.** Give the buyer the right, but not the obligation, to buy the underlying futures contract at the stated strike price within a specific period of time. Conversely, the seller of a call option is obligated to deliver a long position in the underlying futures contract at the strike price if the buyer opts to exercise the option. Essentially, this means that the seller is forced to take a short position in the market when the option is exercised.

- Ω   **Put options.** Give the buyer the right, but not the obligation, to sell the underlying futures contract at the stated strike price within a specific period of time. The seller of a put option is obligated to deliver a short position from the strike price if the buyer chooses to exercise the option. Keep in mind that delivering a short futures contract simply means being long from the strike price.

Similar to futures contracts, there are two sides to every option trade: a buyer and a seller. Option buyers are paying for the underlying right, whereas sellers are selling that right. The most important point to remember is that option buyers are exposed to risk limited to the amount of premium paid, whereas option sellers face theoretically unlimited risk. Conversely, option buyers have the possibility of potentially unlimited gains, whereas the profit potential for sellers is limited to the amount of premium collected (see Figure 10).

	Call	Put	
Buy			Limited Risk
Sell			Unlimited Risk

Figure 10: Relationship between the call and put options. Option buyers face limited risk and unlimited reward, but option sellers are exposed to unlimited risk and limited reward.

Traders who are willing to accept considerable amounts of risk can write (or sell) options, collecting the premium and taking advantage of the well-known belief that more options than not expire worthless. The premium collected by a seller is seen as a liability until either the option is offset (by buying it back) or it expires. Believe it or not, option selling is appealing to traders willing to scratch the surface to discover the advantage of favorable odds of success. I go into great detail on option selling strategies and theory in *Higher Probability Commodity Trading*.

OPTION SPREADS

The majority of beginning options traders prefer trading outright options (buying or selling calls or puts), due to their simplicity. However, there are definite advantages to becoming familiar with the flexibility of risk and reward when using option spreads.

An option spread is the combination of two different option types or strike prices to attain a common goal. The term *option spread* can be used to refer to an unlimited number of possibilities. For example, an option spread can involve the purchase of both a call and a put with the same strike prices, or it can be the purchase and sale of two calls with different strike prices. The sheer number of possibilities makes this topic beyond the scope of this book, but if you are interested in learning more on option spreads, you might want to pick up a copy of my book *Commodity Options*.

To add to the confusion surrounding commodity vocabulary, an option spread has its own bid/ask spread. Just as a single call or put would have a price that you can buy it for and a price you can sell it for, a spread is priced as a package and has both a bid and an ask that represent the purchase or sales price for the combination of options.

Fortunately, when dealing with a spread on a spread, most insiders identify the bid/ask spread by its full name and also refer to the option spread by its specific name. For example, if a trader calls the trading desk to get a quote for an option spread, she might say something like this to the clerk who answers the phone: "Will you get me the bid/ask on the July soybean 900/950 call spread?" Similarly, when accessing an option spread quote via an electronic trading platform, a trader inputs the appropriate strike prices and designates the query as a "vertical call spread," or some other type of recognized spread structure.

It is important to realize that when getting a quote for an option spread, it isn't necessary to decipher whether you will be buying or selling the spread. This is because the broker or trading platform gives you the quote for doing each. Therefore the bid/ask spread—the spread can be bought at the ask and sold at the bid.

Once again, option spreads are too complex to discuss in any detail within this text. However, you need to realize that when it comes to option spreads if the price of the long option of the spread is higher than the price of the short options, the trader is buying the spread. If it is possible to collect more premium for the short legs than is paid for the long legs, the trader is selling the spread.

The increasing popularity of electronic trading platforms and the resulting transparent option pricing has encouraged many traders to place separate order tickets on various legs of their spreads instead of entering a single ticket to enter the trade as a package. For instance, an option spread between a long and a short call option could be entered using a spread order in which both legs are executed simultaneously. Alternatively, a trader could simply place an order to buy the desired call option, and then another to sell the other call option to complete the spread. This is known as legging into the spread. To be honest, in the liquid market I execute most orders this way.

Because of the thousands of possible option spread strategies, the market on the particular spread you want to trade can be either non-existent if another trader hasn't traded that exact combination or if it has been traded and, therefore, is listed as a tradable strategy on the exchange it might be illiquid. In short, there is better liquidity in the outright calls and puts than there are the spread markets. Thus, I find that a trader can often get a higher fill quality by entering an order to buy the long legs of the spread at the bid and then enter a separate order to sell the short legs of the spread at the ask. From there, the trader can move the prices in tick by tick to get a fair fill.

Also, option spreads on electronic platforms can be far more complicated than they seem. For instance, in the previous example, we quoted a soybean vertical call spreads. However, some trading platforms give traders the ability to split vertical call spreads into two separate strategies; a bull call spread and a bear call spread. A bull call spread is synonymous with buying a vertical spread, and a bear call spread is synonymous to selling a vertical spread. Thus, it isn't necessary to have two strategy types for vertical spreads. Yet, platforms attempting to cater to inexperienced traders do this for marketing purposes. Nevertheless, the result is mass confusion, trading errors, and frustration. This is because traders assume if they can build a spread on their platform that it will be tradable by the exchange. This is not the case. The exchange requires that option spreads be structured in a specific way (buy side listed first and closer-to-the-money-strikes listed first). In the end, fancy option spread building platforms tend to experience frequent order rejections by bewildered newbie traders.

For margin purposes, option spreads are treated the same whether they are entered on one ticket or multiple tickets. However, some brokers with strict order entry risk policies might prefer traders to enter spreads on a single order ticket so that they know the trader's intention before approving and executing the order. In other words, overactive risk-management features in trading platforms might reject certain orders intended to be a part of a spread due to misunderstood risk and margin consequences. A good brokerage should be able to manipulate the risk parameters of your platform to avoid these types of erroneous order rejections.

UNDERSTANDING OPTION PRICING AND TENDENCIES

Option market liquidity is far less than that of the underlying futures contracts. The typical order flow of each individual option can be spotty, at best, compared to the constant flow of incoming trades seen in most futures markets. Accordingly, most trading applications keep traders informed of the current market quote or bid/ask spread in addition to the last trade. This is important because it is relatively common for an option with a specific strike price in a particular commodity to go several hours without being traded. If this is the case, the last traded price might not be indicative of the current value. Those who have hesitated to progress with technology and are still retrieving delayed quotes from websites will find they are often working on grossly inaccurate option prices.

Because the options markets don't have as many participants as most futures contracts, the bid/ask quote typically represents the price a *market maker* is willing to execute rather than the working orders of other retail traders similar to yourself. Option market makers literally "make a market" by offering to take the other side of a retail transaction at the quoted price. This is absolutely necessary

> Traders shouldn't assume that the last trade of an option contract is the current value.

to create a viable option trading arena. On the contrary, most liquid futures contracts experience trading action nearly constantly around the clock, so market makers are not needed in such an environment. Without market makers in the options markets, we would be forced to rely on the orders of other traders to provide price discovery and the ability to execute. However, take it from me that, in such a scenario, options trading would be extremely inefficient and likely a money pit for anybody who dared to venture in. If you don't believe me, look at option quotes in markets such as gold, silver, and crude oil in the middle of the night. The markets are open, but nobody is home.

On that note, nearly 24-hour electronic trading in most futures markets has also led to 24-hour option markets. Nonetheless, the market being open doesn't guarantee that you will be able to trade options at prices you will be happy with. Each market has different liquidity and execution quality in overnight trading. For instance, the Treasury options have great market makers with fairly priced spreads. In such a market, traders are likely comfortable executing trades around the clock, although there will still be far better fill quality during the official day session. Some of the grain options—namely corn and soybeans—often have competitive market makers throughout the night. Although it is best to try to execute during the day session, in some instances, it makes sense to place trades before the morning open.

On the other hand, some of the options markets traded in New York, such as silver and natural gas, often don't have market makers available during off hours. Accordingly, pulling up a quote on a particular option in either market during the night session would likely reveal a shockingly wide bid/ask spread, or perhaps no spread at all. These markets should not be traded outside the official day session, despite the fact that they are technically "open." By the way, the unmanageable quotes seen during the night session in silver and natural gas are what most option markets might look like without market makers—even during the day session.

For example, if a December corn $4.00 call option last traded three hours ago at 25 cents and corn futures have since rallied 20 cents, the value of the $4.00 call option would likely be much higher. A buyer shouldn't expect to purchase the option at 25 cents because that price doesn't reflect the recent 20-cent rally that would have increased the value of the $4.00 call.

With so many options contracts available (various strike prices and months), it would be nearly impossible for traders and brokers to keep tabs on each of them. Thus, access to live bid/ask spreads is imperative; ironically, knowing the last trade is rather useless. Even if you were provided a time stamp along with the last trade price, determining an estimated current fair value would take some time. With that said, despite having live bid and ask access, during unusually fast-moving futures markets, determining the true market value of a particular option can sometimes be extremely difficult. This scenario occurs as the spread between the bid and the ask balloon due to frenzied volatility, leading to uncertain values and, thus, wide price ranges in each option. Adding to the potential chaos is the tendency for a great influx of options orders during or after a large move in the futures price.

Those attempting to trade electronic options in the E-mini S&P 500 or Treasury futures in August 2015 can testify to this. During this particular volatility shock, seeing options quoted with thousands of dollars between the bid and the ask was not uncommon. For instance, E-mini S&P options were being quoted as 15.00 bid, at 45.00. Each point in the E-mini equates to $50, so traders could have sold this option for $750 ($50 × 15.00) or bought it for $2,250 ($50 × 45.00). Likewise, some Treasury options were quoted 1'15 bid at 3'20. The math is complicated, so I spare the details here, but this equates to a difference of more than $2,000 between the price a trader could buy at and the price he could sell at. To put this into perspective, a more typical spread in either of these markets is less than $50. As this example portrays, despite conventional wisdom, highly chaotic pricing is possible even in an electronic trading environment.

Dramatic option price changes are possible or even likely if a period of low volume and volatility is followed by a sudden burst of sizable volume and high volatility. In such a case, market makers and market participants are no match for the disarray in option pricing. Although these types of hectic periods occur in options markets now that most are executed electronically, the phenomenon was worse during the days of pit trading.

A good example of this phenomenon in open outcry trading was the precious metals crash in April 2006. At that time, electronic options were newly available, but open outcry execution was still preferable and far more liquid. In a matter of minutes, silver and gold violently sold off, causing astronomical losses for long futures traders, and even more so for options traders who couldn't "see" the value of their holdings and, in some cases, were forced to blindly enter market orders to liquidate. Based on my observations, the execution prices of metals options on that particular day were less than agreeable by most but difficult to argue, given the circumstances.

Specifically, traders covering short puts in the midst of the pandemonium might have received fill prices in excess of $2,000 worse than they were expecting, based on estimated theoretical values. The price of silver dropped $2 ($10,000 per futures contract) that day, so losses due to actual changes in market price combined with excessive slippage as a result of frantic conditions led to large losses for many. Imagine selling a silver put for 10 cents, or $500, and entering a market order to buy it back with expectations of a fill near $2,000 (equating to a $1,500 loss) and being reported a fill of $4,000! Such an event is rare, but traders should be aware of the fierce potential of market behavior at all times. On a side note, a trader should never execute an option order at the market price. Only limit orders should be placed on options! We discuss order types in a later chapter.

It is important to realize that some option markets see higher trading volume than others. Likewise, within option markets, some months and strike prices have more liquidity. In general, options with strike prices that are closer-to-the-money will have more players, and months with less time to expiration will also attract more trading interest. When choosing an option to trade, liquidity should play a factor because without it you might find it difficult to get accurate pricing and fair fill prices.

WHAT ARE WEEKLY OPTIONS

The CME Group has vigilantly added weekly options to its array of products. In the past, commodity futures contracts generally had options written against it with monthly expirations. In short, each month nearly all futures contracts would have a corresponding option expiration date. For instance, in the stock index futures there was an option expiration on each third Friday of the month. Thus, there were a group of options that expired in January, then February, March, and so on. Weekly options in the stock indices, on the other hand, expire each week. In other words, every Friday of every month there are a group of options written against the E-mini S&P 500 expiring.

Shorter expiration dates give traders more opportunities to trade with a strengthened ability to narrow their speculation down to a particular week, event, or day. The increased frequency of option expirations has created an environment in which traders wishing to speculate on an upcoming economic announcement can do so using lower- priced options that expire near, or even on the day of, the event. Conversely, when traders were forced to use monthly options for event trading it was generally more expensive and higher risk to buy options for this purpose. After all, the more time to expiration an option has the more expensive it is.

Although weekly options have complicated options on futures trading, and confused inexperienced traders, the CME Group was wise to begin listing them. They are a great way for the futures industry to compete with binary options (which are basically options that can be bought in the morning for expiration that evening). Also, they increase the freedom to customize speculative risk and reward prospects, while increasing trading volume and revenue for the exchange.

THE BOTTOM LINE ON OPTIONS

My intention isn't to deter you from trading options; in fact, I prefer option trading over futures in many cases. Nonetheless, I do feel as though it is my responsibility to warn you of option market characteristics so that you are better prepared and know what to expect in terms of pricing and execution. Keep in mind that I used dramatic examples of inefficient option pricing in this section, but day-to-day trading in "normal" circumstances provides commodity option traders with liquid, viable, and attractive opportunities for speculation. The best way to combat temporary bouts of excessive option pricing is maintaining a low margin-to-equity ratio. For instance, naked option sellers should target 20% to 30% of margin usage, which means they are leaving as much as 80% of their margin funds unused. Consider this a rainy day fund; you will eventually need it and having it will probably be the difference between success and failure as an option seller.

In conclusion, traders are doing themselves a disservice by ignoring the potential benefits of incorporating option trading into speculation. Although option trading can seem complex on the surface, you owe it to yourself to be familiar with all the tools available to you as a trader. After all, taking the "easy road" in life often fails to be beneficial in the end, and this may be no different.

CHAPTER 2: HEDGING VERSUS SPECULATING

As discussed in Chapter 1, "A Crash Course in Commodities," the futures markets were created to facilitate commodity transactions and give producers and end users the means to hedge price risk. In its simplest form, hedging is the basic practice of shifting price risk to

> The futures markets were created for hedgers but are made possible by speculators.

a party that is willing to accept it, the speculator. I don't cover hedging concepts in detail simply because a majority of market participants are speculators. Therefore, being aware of the overall concept and its implications in the marketplace should provide a sufficient background for beginning traders.

HEDGING COMMODITIES

Now more than ever, businesses are looking to the futures markets for an efficient means of mitigating the price risk associated with their operations. However, the opportunity to hedge isn't without cost or even inconvenience. Nonetheless, the excessive volatility in commodity prices has created an environment in which the burden of hedging can easily be justified by the potential detriment of assuming the price risk outright.

WHY HEDGE?

Producers and users of commodities are constantly faced with price and production risk due to an unlimited number of unpredictable factors, including weather, currency exchange rates, and economic cycles. As volatility in the agricultural and energy markets has increased in recent decades, so has the risk exposure to those involved in cash transactions of affected commodities. For instance, during the 2008 energy boom, many major airlines were facing bankruptcy at the direct hand of unhedged exposure to the price of crude oil, which rallied from $50 per barrel to $150 in a year and a half. On the contrary, Southwest Airlines notoriously hedged its price risk and managed to avoid the financial hardship that its competitors endured. Not only was it rewarded by the commodity markets, but its hedge of energy price risk made it possible for the company to keep fees and fares at a minimum to increase its market share.

> Hedging is similar to buying insurance; it is nice to have when you need it, but costly if you don't.

Firms that choose not to hedge their risk are essentially speculators. Many insiders refer to them as "cash market speculators" because they behave as if they are predicting favorable price changes by not taking action to counteract the risk of unfavorable market moves. For instance, many unhedged farmers missed out on several hundred thousand

dollars or more, as the prices of corn and wheat plummeted from their all-time highs in the late 2000s and early 2010s. By choosing not to participate in a hedging strategy, they were indirectly betting on higher prices at which they could sell their crops. Unfortunately, in this case, many farmers lost their wagers.

NOTHING IN LIFE IS FREE

The concept of hedging is based on the same premise insurance companies use. Similar to the purchase of car insurance to protect yourself from the unknown damage that you or others might cause to your vehicle, commodity producers and users find solace in knowing that they have a security blanket when it comes to changes in price and market volatility. Likewise, just as the benefits of car insurance come with strings attached such as premiums and deductibles, users and producers face expenditures to hedging price risk.

It is quite possible that the position taken with the intent to hedge price risk will become a burden. For example, if market prices move favorably (higher) for a producer subsequent to execution of price hedge, the potential cash markets gains are forfeited along with any transactional costs incurred. On the contrary, if a producer undergoes adverse (lower) market prices while being hedged, he will likely be thankful. To clarify, a commodity producer benefits from higher market prices because he can realize a larger profit when the goods are sold in the cash market. Therefore, producers might prefer to hedge their risk of price decline by selling futures contracts to avoid the detriment caused to the cash market sale. I go over this concept in detail in the next section, "Using Futures to Hedge Price Risk."

HEDGING VERSUS SPECULATING

As you can see, the purpose of a price hedge isn't to profit, but to eliminate the price uncertainty that can contribute to potential operating losses. When price uncertainty is removed, it is easy for commodity consumers and producers to properly manage their business affairs to ensure that they are not working for free or even losing money in the process. Simply put, without price risk, it is possible to budget operations and make decisions accordingly.

USING FUTURES TO HEDGE PRICE RISK

The futures market is arguably the most efficient means of hedging commodity price risk. This is due to the trading of standardized contracts on organized and regulated exchanges, and thanks to the market liquidity brought by speculators. In addition, prices in the futures and cash market tend to be highly correlated, meaning that they move up and down together. For that reason, investors exposed to price risk in the cash market have the capability to take on an equal and opposite position in the futures market to shift the price risk to speculators.

Businesses can choose three basic situations to mitigate price risk through hedging: storage, production, and future purchases. In each of these instances, the same course of action can be employed; take a position in the futures market opposite of that being held in the cash market to reduce price risk. Simply put, for those long the cash market (holding the physical commodity), price risk can be largely offset by selling an equal value in the futures markets. Any gains in the cash market will be nearly, completely, or slightly excessively offset by losses in the futures and vice versa. Again, it is important to note that a price hedge is insurance and, therefore, entails an opportunity cost in that any potential cash market gains are forfeited.

> Speculators create the liquidity necessary for hedgers to shift price risk in hopes of earning a monetary reward.

Grain elevators, or those in the business of storing commodities for future use or sale, run the risk of the value of their inventory declining while it is being stored. In other words, if between the time that the grain is acquired and then subsequently sold, the price of the commodity in question decreases significantly, a grain elevator might lose money on the transaction. Had the grain elevator operator in this situation opted to reduce price exposure by selling a futures contract when the commodity storage began, the profit on the futures position would have offset all or most of the loss in the cash market. This is because of the tendency of cash and futures prices to move up and down in tandem.

Similarly, a corn farmer faces a considerable amount of price risk throughout the planting, growing, and harvesting cycle. If a farmer plants his crop in the spring with the intention of harvesting in the fall and selling the proceeds of his efforts in October, a proper hedge could be created by selling a December corn futures contract for each 5,000 bushels of expected crop yield. Doing so eliminates the price uncertainty involved with the cash market transaction and allows the farmer to accurately budget his expenses to ensure an acceptable profit.

EXAMPLE

Again, I don't feel as though it is critical that you be able to calculate profit and loss of a hedge, but you should understand the concept. Let's take a look at a simple example that gives you a broad-based view of the premise behind using the futures market for the price protection of cash market assets and transactions.

A soybean farmer completes the planting in his field in late April, with the intention of harvesting and selling the beans in late September. Based on planted acreage and projected conditions, he expects to yield 50,000 bushels of soybeans. At the time of planting, the farmer considers the market price for the grain to determine his budget and profit margin. Without a price hedge, he stands to benefit from any market price appreciation, but he might suffer considerable financial losses if the price of soybeans falls. Naturally, as a businessperson, it is a luxury to know that, on the day of reckoning, barring any unpredictable adversity, there will be a nearly guaranteed profit. The price of having such comfort is the opportunity cost of giving up any potential price appreciation in the commodity.

It is important to realize that, for a farmer expecting to yield 50,000 bushels of soybeans, each penny in price change affects the overall revenue of the sale by $500. In a market that can sometimes move $1.00 in a short period of time (equivalent to $50,000 in this example), you can see that the stakes are high. Although farmers might have an insider's look at the industry and might believe that they are capable of predicting price movements, they are in the business of producing the product, not speculating in its price. Therefore, in many cases, it is preferential for them to remove the uncertainty involved in their eventual cash market transaction by hedging their price risk.

The farmer in this example has the ability to shift his cash market price risk to futures market speculators by selling an equal position in futures that he holds in the cash commodity. Note that because the farmer owns the soybeans, he is said to be long the cash market and would look to sell futures contracts to hedge his price risk. In this example, the expected 50,000 yield is equivalent to 10 CBOT soybean futures contracts, with a standardized size of 5,000 bushels (50,000 ÷ 5,000 = 10).

At the time of planting and execution of the hedge, September soybean futures are trading at $12.95, and the cash price of the commodity in the farmer's area is $12.70. Before you get excited that the farmer is already locking in a gain of 25 cents, remember that commodities with distant maturity dates trade at a premium to closer-dated futures contracts and the cash market, due to the cost to carry, also known as the contango.

If the price of soybeans declines between the time the hedge is executed and the futures position is offset, and the cash crop is liquidated, the farmer will be profitable in his short futures position but worse off in terms of his cash market sale. For example, assuming that the farmer can sell 10 September futures contracts (equal to a crop yield of 50,000 bushels) at $12.95, if the futures price is $12.20 and the cash market is $11.95 at the time the farmer unwinds his hedge and sells his crop, he will have completely offset his price risk. Ignoring transaction costs, the futures hedge will have been profitable by exactly 75 cents, while he would have given up exactly 75 cents on the price at which he can sell his crop in the cash market (see Table 1). By taking an equal and opposite position in the futures market as is held in the cash market, it is possible to reduce, or even eliminate, the risk of price fluctuation in the cash market.

Table 1: Hedgers are concerned with controlling price risk not turning a profit. They generally lose on one side and make money on the other.

Timeline	Cash Market	Futures Market
At planting	$12.70 (Long)	$12.95 (Short)
At crop sale	$11.95 (Short)	$12.20 (Long)
Results	Loss in cash market	Profit in futures transaction
	-75 cents x 50,000 = -$37,500	+ 75 cents x 50,000 = +$37,500

Keep in mind that this example leaves out consideration of the basis, which is the difference between the local cash market price and the futures price. Yes, various prices are available in the cash market, depending on the locale. In addition, farmers typically don't hedge their entire expected production because there are no certainties that they will yield what is anticipated in terms of crop size. Hedges aren't always this clean cut, but this should help you grasp the overall goal of removing price risk from business operations and shifting it to speculators who are ready and willing to accept the risk in hopes of large profits.

LONG HEDGE VERSUS SHORT HEDGE

The previous example depicts a short hedge because the farmer sold futures to alleviate his cash market price risk. However, it is also possible to buy futures to place a hedge against adverse price movement. Doing so is referred to as a long hedge. You might wonder how farmers determine whether they buy or sell futures to protect themselves; taking a step back and looking at the big picture, the concept is relatively elementary. In a nutshell, commodity users are long hedgers, and commodity producers are short hedgers.

> Leverage gives speculators the potential for abnormal profits and gives hedgers the ability to reduce price risk with relatively little capital tied up.

Long hedgers, those who need to buy futures to shift price risk, plan to buy a commodity at some point in the future and are therefore short the cash market (because they need it but don't have it yet). Some examples of long hedgers are a home builder who needs to buy lumber, a meat packer who must purchase pork, a portfolio manager who must buy stock with future allocations, and a flour mill owner who must purchase wheat.

Short hedgers, those who must sell futures contracts to offset their price risk, plan to sell a commodity at some point in the future and are, therefore, long the cash market (because they own it and would eventually like to sell it). Some examples of short hedgers are a lumber mill owner who needs to sell lumber, a hog farmer who would like to sell his livestock, a wheat farmer who wants to sell his crop, and a pension fund manager who must sell holdings for retirement redemptions in the future.

It is certainly possible for the same firm to be long hedgers in one instance and short hedgers in another. Case in point, a farmer wanting to reduce price exposure of his crop would sell futures to accomplish his goal (because he is long in the cash grain market). The same farmer might be interested in hedging the price risk of gasoline if his expected consumption is material enough to justify the burden. This action requires a long hedge because fuel costs typically are incurred in the future. Simply put, he is short the cash market because he needs fuel to operate his machinery, but he has not yet purchased it or locked in the price. As you can see, the label of a long or short hedge is applied to the action itself instead of the parties making the transactions.

COMMODITY SPECULATORS

If you are reading this book, you most likely fall into the speculator category. Speculators make up the lion's share of the daily trading volume in most commodity futures contracts. They enter the market in hopes of lavish profits—or, at least, hopes of coming out ahead. In return for the profit potential that comes with commodity trading, speculators must be willing to accept a great deal of risk of loss. This is in stark contrast to the intentions of the hedger who comes to the futures markets to manage risk.

Despite arguments against speculation and its place in the commodity markets that shape our economy—and, therefore, our lives—without it, producers and users of commodities would have a difficult time facilitating transactions. Thanks to speculators, there is always a buyer for every seller and a seller for every buyer. Without them and the liquidity they provide, hedgers would likely be forced to endure much larger bid/ask spreads and, in theory, price volatility. Consumers would also suffer in the absence of speculators simply because producers would be forced to pass on their increased costs to allow for favorable profit margins.

Unfortunately, we speculators are not provided crystal balls. Instead, we are left to rely on technical, seasonal, and fundamental market analysis (discussed in *Higher Probability Commodity Trading*) along with their best guess of what might occur next. Consequently, most speculators fail to make money in the markets but don't forget that some flourish.

Unlike some hedgers, speculators have no intention of making or taking delivery of the traded commodity; they will most likely never see or touch the commodity they are trading. Additionally, some speculators, focused on technical analysis, might not have a clue of the harvest cycle, production figures, or supply-and-demand picture involved in the market they are trading. This is because many speculators believe it is possible to be accurate in price prediction without much knowledge of the commodity being traded. Conversely, by nature of their business, hedgers are extremely familiar with the underlying fundamentals of the markets in which they are shifting price risk. Simply being a speculator doesn't require knowledge or skill; the only requirement is the acceptance of risk.

LEVERAGE IN HEDGING AND SPECULATING

It is likely clear by now that speculators in the futures markets enjoy, or perhaps suffer from, a considerable amount of leverage. The source of the leverage stems from low margin requirements set by the exchange to buy or sell futures contracts relative to the actual value of the commodity that is traded. For instance, a Eurodollar trader experiences profits or losses based on the value of $1,000,000 of the underlying asset for as little as $1,000 deposited into a futures trading account. In essence, if a futures trader is correct in price assumptions, he stands to be wildly profitable if the market conditions support such success. However, inaccurate predictions can be just as painful as the winners are triumphant.

What might not be so obvious is the reality that the exchange provides hedgers even more leverage. Assuming that an account can prove to the FCM (Futures Commission Merchant) that the investor is a bona fide hedger, the trader is granted discounted margin requirements. A bona fide hedge is one in which the account holder actually owns the underlying commodity and takes a position in the futures market opposite of the cash market position. With that said, hedgers are subject to margin calls if they lose money on their futures position. Naturally, if this is the case, they are also gaining the difference in their cash market holdings. Nonetheless, the cash proceeds from the sale of the commodity don't come to realization until the sale takes place. In the meantime, the hedger needs to come up with the margin (cash) to continue holding the price hedge. As you can imagine, this isn't always an easy task. Thus, leverage can work for and against a hedger, just as it can a speculator.

CHAPTER 3: THE SLOW DEATH OF OPEN OUTCRY AND THE GROWTH OF ELECTRONIC TRADING

The futures markets are the birthplace of a method of communication between trading professionals known as *open outcry*. Open outcry is an exciting form of trade execution in which shouting and hand signals transfer the details of intent to buy or sell a commodity and in what

> The language of trading floor hand signals is referred to as *Arb*, short for arbitrage.

quantity. You might also hear this method of execution referred to as pit trading, for reasons discussed later in the chapter.

You have likely been exposed to open outcry via the media and in movies such as *Trading Places*. After all, the energy projected from the trading pits is thrilling and can make for good television. Those who have had the opportunity to experience the trading floor will tell you that it is even more electrifying in person.

Beginning in the late 1990s, technological advances greatly altered the way open outcry business was conducted and it eventually killed it, not unlike the way "video killed the radio star." For example, electronic quote boards, handheld computers, computerized order entry, and electronic fill reporting became an integral part of the process and eventually, the technology engulfed the entire process. Split- second electronic order filling in both futures and options, compliments of lightning- fast internet and computer processing feeds, have rendered pit commodity trading obsolete. Nearly all futures and options on futures trading now takes place in these over the counter (OTC) markets in which execution is 100% electronic and, thus, there is no physical trading location. For this reason, many in the industry are speculating on the future of the CME Group's headquarter residence. With most of the trading pits in the CBOT building turning off the lights, they might not feel obligated to continue residing in downtown Chicago where taxes and rents are astronomically high.

As we discuss the topic of pit trading vs. electronic trading, it is important to realize that the difference between open outcry and electronically traded futures and options is based on the location of execution, not the method of order placement. For example, it is possible to use a computerized order entry platform to submit an order that will be executed in the open outcry pit. Conversely, it is less common but possible that you or your broker might call a trading desk, perhaps even on the trading floor itself, to execute an options or futures order for a contract that is executed electronically in the OTC market.

Although nearly all futures contracts and futures spreads are now traded electronically, some options and option spreads are still executed in an open outcry environment. This is because, as mentioned in the previous chapter, electronic trading platforms haven't perfected the art of placing option spreads with the exchange. Nevertheless, even when open outcry trading is completely abolished (by 2020 by my estimation), it is important to know where the industry has been and how commodity trading has evolved with technology.

DON'T JUDGE A BOOK BY ITS COVER

During its heyday, the exchange floor appeared to be unorganized but was far from chaos. Everything was meticulously designed to reduce confusion and propel a proficient trading arena. For example, exchanges require that exchange members, employees, clerks, and brokerage firm employees wear color-coded jackets to assist in role identification. In today's environment I suspect they are all on a first-name basis, but when the pits were bustling things were different. Also, electronic date and time boards are displayed in the corners of the room, and in some cases, a letter or symbol is displayed so that traders can distinguish 15-minute time brackets. In essence, filled tickets are denoted with the appropriate mark to narrow the time of execution to a 15-minute span. Exchanges, traders, and brokers face excessive liabilities regarding timely and efficient order execution. Thus, the ability to pinpoint events chronologically is critical to resolving any issues as they occur; this makes an extremely organized operation a must.

THE PIT

Open outcry trading takes place in what has been dubbed a trading pit. The name likely stems from the shape of the execution venue, which are typically tiered areas, similar to bleachers. Trading pits vary in size but are traditionally in the shape of an octagon. Within this tiered arena, you used to see traders violently shouting and signaling trades with their hands. Now, it is more of a civilized conversation that takes place to execute a trade, but the same language and hand gestures are used. As mentioned, this process is known as open outcry or pit trading. If you are trading large orders or spread orders, you might hear your broker say, "I will take this order to the floor." This simply means that she will be calling the exchange floor and placing your trade verbally with a broker to be executed in a trading pit rather than sending the order electronically via an electronic execution platform. For a few select clients, this is the preferred method to ensure an efficient fill, but for the majority of retail traders, electronic platforms and execution are ideal.

In late 2017 as this book was going to print, all futures trading pits have been eliminated with the exception of the full-sized S&P 500 futures. All other trading pits were for the execution of options only, not futures. In general, each pit represents a different commodity; therefore, traders wouldn't be buying or selling corn and soybean options in the same marked area. Trading in a specific commodity option takes place only within the designated pit on the trading floor. Although corn, wheat, and soybean option trading pits are close to each other, trading them is exclusive to their designated pits. Also, futures and options transactions between exchange members are authorized only within the trading pits. Two members may not facilitate a trade between each other at the water cooler.

"Those who cannot remember the past are condemned to repeat it."
—George Santayana

As you've probably concluded, having an exchange membership and therefore access to the trading floor isn't nearly as coveted as it once was. In fact, even if you were an exchange member you would probably prefer to execute most of your trades online via a trading platform and simply go to the exchange floor for bragging rights or a social session. Few are attempting to make a living standing in commodity trading pits. Those who do still trade in the pits have the luxury of keeping an eye on other futures contracts and stocks around the world. Electronic tickers and display boards line the walls of the exchanges and are viewable from the trading floor. Other electronic displays provide appropriate information such as spot market prices and exchange news. It goes without saying that the vibrant colors and timely information create an exhilarating and addicting atmosphere for traders.

Surrounding the trading pits are workstations simply known as *desks* in which orders are received. Orders arrive at the desk by phone or by printed trade ticket from both individual retail traders and large institutions worldwide. After acknowledged by a desk clerk, the orders are flashed to the appropriate recipients via hand signals or transmitted via handheld computers. From there, the order is said to be working as the executing floor broker attempts to fill it according to the type and price specified. In the case of a market order, it is filled immediately.

When the order is filled, the information is arbed or electronically transmitted back to the order desk to be reported by either making a phone call to the appropriate party or, most likely, entering the fill price into a computer. Obviously, the process can be somewhat challenged in regard to time making it clear as to why the industry has shifted the process to computers.

As we discuss in Chapter 4, "Account Access, Trading Platforms, and Exchange Data Fees," due to the cumbersome nature of open outcry trade execution, subscribing to real-time data in these markets was costly. Luckily, we no longer have to worry about that. The advent of electronic trade-matching environments has greatly reduced the burden of obtaining live market data for retail futures and options traders. In fact, paying for costly price data is no longer necessary for most traders, but in recent years the CME Group has opted to charge a minimal fee to traders deemed to be non-professional for access to real-time futures and options quotes.

ELECTRONICALLY TRADED MARKETS

Once again, domestic futures exchanges have spent the last decade gradually moving away from open outcry execution and into electronic trade matching. In recent years, the execution of futures contracts in trading pits has been eliminated (with the exception of the S&P 500 futures), and the electronic execution of options contracts has dwarfed that of pit traded options as traders enjoy the transparency, instant order execution, and immediate fill reporting made possible by advances in technology.

Electronic trade-matching platforms began as a way to facilitate trading overnight in key contracts during times when the trading pits were closed but the world was still turning and events were unfolding that could affect the price of various commodities. The result was a venue in which traders could manage positions and risk in some of the most heavily

> The markets don't sleep and neither will your positions.

traded commodity markets while they should be fast asleep. Eventually, the overnight electronic sessions extended into the day session and became the norm rather than the exception. Electronic trading is now offered nearly 24 hours per day in most futures markets. Unlike its predecessor, open outcry, electronic trade matching technology gives traders from all over the world inexpensive access to accurate bid/ask pricing, real-time volume data, and price ladders that display the market depth.

If you are unfamiliar, market depth is simply the capability to see the number of orders working at the available bids and offers; you might also hear price ladders referred to as DOM panels (DOM stands for depth of market). Some traders feel as though visual access to the potential trading volume at each price and any possible overweighting on the buy or sell side can provide an edge in speculation. Perhaps this is true in some regard, but the reality is that, in the current environment, all traders have access to the same information. Consequently, it is imperative to realize that despite the amount of work put into studying charts, news reels, and internet forums, there are no guarantees—only educated guesses.

Electronic trade matching is believed to have leveled the playing field for market participants in that it gives retail traders admission to the same information, market access, and fill quality that anybody else might have. Specifically, in the case of the E-mini S&P and a handful of other markets, there are no market makers. In theory, this provides an arena in which traders of all sizes are treated equally in terms of fills; this is true whether they are trading one or 100 contracts at a time. Those who sent orders into the trading pits of the old days know that the bid/ask spreads were wider, the fill quality was worse, and the lack of transparency raised many questions to the fairness of pricing. Further, those standing in the pits were privy to information that the average retail trader didn't have. For instance, they could see the order flow (who was buying or selling and how much), where stop orders were accumulating, and they had a better sense of fear and greed. All of those advantages to being a floor trader in the pit have been mitigated in favor of online traders.

CONFUSING CONTRACT SYMBOLS

Newbie traders might be scratching their heads in regard to the different trading symbols various trading platforms use to identify the same commodity contract. This is because electronic futures and options were created during the heyday of pit trading; further, the two methods of execution existed together side-by-side. The exchange needed a way to decipher between the preferred execution method so they created special symbols to identify the underlying commodity as well as the execution method. For example, the symbol for corn futures executed on the trading floor was *C*, but the electronically traded version of the contract is *ZC*. Corn is a CBOT division product, and in most cases, the symbol for the electronic version of CBOT contracts begins with a *Z*. Likewise, electronic COMEX products were denoted by an *E*, or on some platforms a *G*, before the traditional open outcry symbol. To illustrate, although the symbol for gold traded in the open outcry is *GC*, the symbol for the electronically executed contract is *EGC*, or in some cases *GGC*.

Because most futures contracts are exclusively traded electronically, traders have grown accustomed to the electronic symbols and have nearly forgotten about their open outcry counterpart. If you ask a new trader the symbol for any given futures market, she'll likely give you the electronic version but asking the same question to a long-time commodity speculator will likely yield the open outcry version. Nevertheless, the important takeaway from this discussion is to not allow yourself to panic when you notice there are multiple ticker symbols for the exact same futures contract; this is in stark contrast to the equity market, which is highly uniform.

THE GOOD AND BAD OF ELECTRONIC TRADING

There are obviously more advantages to electronic markets than disadvantages, but there are some drawbacks to futures and options trading moving to the "screens" from the open outcry pits. Further, there were enormous casualties to industry insiders. As the process of trading commodities moved from a specialized human trading arena to a computerized practice available to the masses, futures exchange and brokerage firm personnel were dramatically downsized.

MARKET LIQUIDITY

It isn't difficult to argue that electronic trading has contributed to deeper and more liquid options and futures markets. Not only are traders who wouldn't have been able to, or interested in, trading commodities prior to electronic trade execution doing so, but those who have been trading futures and options for decades seem to have stepped up their game. For instance, electronic access to markets has made it easier for brokerage firms to manage the risk of leveraged clients. Therefore, they are able to offer lower day trading margin rates to speculators and, consequently, the barriers to entry are much lower than they were before electronic trading platforms existed. Also, the hassle of picking up the phone to enter buy and sell orders likely deterred some trading. Yet the ability to trade futures and options with a click of the mouse has likely enticed higher trading volume than would have been the case before computer trading. In any case, electronically traded commodities have led to massive gains in trading volume.

QUICKER AND MORE EFFICIENT EXECUTION

It should also be obvious that electronic trade matching by the exchange is a much faster and cleaner process than using telephones, paper trading tickets, and hand waves to execute a single order. When I started in the business in the early 2000s, electronic trading platforms were already in use but orders placed in them were not directed to electronic trade matching. Instead, an order entered into a trading platform would result in a paper ticket printing out on the exchange floor. From there, a runner would take it to the pit to be executed and then run back to the desk to report the fill into a computer. This process could take as little as a few minutes in a slow market but during a market flurry of volume and volatility, it could take several minutes to receive a fill. In extreme cases, I recall fills taking upward of 30 to 45 minutes.

In one particular day of insanity, I saw an account start a trading session with roughly $6,000,000 in net liquidation value and after a wild day of liquidating short options in the gold and silver trading pits, the end of the day balance was closer to a negative $3,000,000; that is a $9,000,000 swing in equity! Most of the losses were unnecessary and can be attributed to slow fill reporting, which triggered panicked order placement. For instance, out of terror, the trader began entering market orders to exit option trades without knowing the price they were trading at (there were no electronic quotes available and humans couldn't keep up with the open outcry quotes because of the mass hysteria). As you can imagine, fills trickling back at astronomical prices were shocking and heartbreaking. Unfortunately, for the client, better decisions during the liquidation process would have made a dramatically positive impact on the outcome (using limit orders or selling futures against his short puts).

Can you imagine waiting minutes, not seconds, to find out if your order had been filled or not, and at what price? Those trading big portfolios often had a hard time figuring out their new position and true account balance during wild intraday price swings. Also, if you entered an order and wished to modify it to a new price there was a chance of getting double filled (filled twice on the same order). At the time, it seems like a streamlined process but relative to today's seamless execution process it was nothing short of a nightmare. Luckily, those days are over.

STRICTER INTRADAY MARGIN

In the "good ole days" of pit trading, there wasn't any way to enforce day trading margins, nor to keep track of the cash in option trading accounts. This is because orders to buy and sell futures were often placed directly with a broker on the exchange floor. As a result, the only two people who knew exactly which positions a particular client had on intraday was the client and his individual broker—at least until the end of the day, when all trades placed on the exchange floor and through brokerage platforms were reconciled. Thus, some brokers let clients get away with murder when it came to day trading margin or option purchases.

For example, a trader with $5,000 on deposit in a trading account might place several orders to buy options with the total amount spent equating to something beyond $5,000. As long as this trader offset enough of those long options to bring his cash balance to positive, he wouldn't have been hassled by risk managers. I'm not suggesting this was right, or even wise; I am just saying this happened frequently.

In today's world, this is unheard of because technology has enabled brokerage houses to keep much better tabs on traders and individual brokers. All trades are placed through brokerage platforms, many of which communicate with each other. As a result, risk managers have a precise accounting of what positions are in a client's account and what his account stats are at any given time throughout the day and night. In short, traders today will need more than $5,000 in their account to buy options valued beyond $5,000. This is obviously reasonable, but some of the traders who were accustomed to the benefit of smoke and mirrors provided by open outcry trading found it to be annoying that technology acted as an obstacle in their quest to leverage already leveraged option contracts.

Long-term day traders experienced the same disappointment when electronic trading began to dominate the landscape. Open outcry and direct floor access often enabled them to day trade with far more leverage than futures trading platforms allow with electronic trading. Also, it can be frustrating to have a platform reject an order because the account is short $1 in regard to required margin. Even brokerage firms with the strictest risk controls wouldn't have rejected an order because an account was short a buck or two. The bottom line is, there is a new sheriff in town and he is here to stay.

NO SLEEP FOR THE WEARY

Being a commodity broker has never been a typical 9-to-5 commitment. It takes long and hard hours to make it in this business. Nevertheless, in the beginning of my career I slept well at night knowing that although asset values were adjusting to global markets, any positions my clients had open wouldn't have the opportunity to move until the following day when the pits opened. I know many of my clients shared in the same comfort. Times have changed. Electronic trading has made it possible for commodity futures and options to trade around the clock. This means traders and brokers must sleep with one eye open.

OPTION SPREADS DON'T TRANSLATE TO THE "SCREENS"

There are a handful of options on futures trading platforms capable of accepting option spread orders such as iron condors, bull call spreads, etc. However, we've yet to see a platform or exchange solution to execution that matches the flexibility and ease of placing such orders in an open outcry pit. We thought nothing of constructing a complicated custom option spread and phoning it into the trading pits. We could always find a market maker to give us a fair quote for execution. Traders today are free to create custom option spreads in some trading platforms, but getting a market maker to pay attention to it and be willing to take the other side of it is challenging. Further, it can take several minutes to create the spread in the platform. It is an extremely time-consuming and confusing process.

We generally recommend that clients simply leg into option spreads in liquid markets. We've found this to be simpler and come with more efficient fill quality. For example, if a trader wanted to buy a vertical call spread he might simply enter an order to buy an E-mini S&P 2400 call and then another order to sell a 2450 call. The exchange nets each leg of the trade and margins it as a spread...and the trader saved himself several minutes in order entry.

MORE MARKET ACCESS & INFO

Electronic markets have streamlined the practice of accumulating and studying price data. No longer are traders required to purchase expensive historical data from the exchange to analyze the markets. In addition, the live data available to traders far surpasses the quality of data during the days of open outcry trading. The most obvious example is the visualization for the current bid/ask spread for any futures and options market. Prior to electronic trading, traders relied on the last quote, or last trade, of a security. In futures contracts, the last quote is generally accurate; this is true even during the days of open outcry trading (aside from a delay of a roughly 30-second delay in transmitting the quote from the pits). However, the last trade for an option could have occurred hours ago, or it might have even been the previous day's settlement price. Such information is not only useless, but it can be misleading to inexperienced traders who falsely believe *what they see is what they will get* in regards to pricing.

Another positive impact on market information brought upon by electronic trading is the Depth of Market panel. We will talk more about this later in the book in a discussion of trading platforms, but in short, it is a panel displaying the 10 best bids and the 10 best asks in a particular futures or options market. This gives traders the ability to see how many buy and sell orders are working at what prices.

WEEKLY OPTIONS

Without electronic trading, we would probably never have experienced the versatility of using weekly options within a trading strategy. Weekly options are now available in most futures markets; essentially, the CME Group has decided that rather than having options expire once per month in each commodity they can have options that expire each week, and in the E-mini S&P they even list Monday, Wednesday, and Friday options! This means there are options expiring every other day in that market.

If you are wondering what the big deal is, keep in mind options are priced in regards to time, volatility, and demand. Thus, traders can purchase options that expire next week for far less than they could purchase an option that expires next month. This gives speculators an opportunity to dip a toe in the water with less risk as well as pinpoint specific market moving events such as the non-farm payroll report. It also enables traders to better hedge their risk by purchasing cheaper weekly options against their futures positions. In essence, it offers traders more flexibility and potentially lower risk. Also, the exchange also recognizes that weekly options are a great way to boost trading volume (they make money on transaction fees).

Humans likely wouldn't have been able to keep track of, quote, and execute so many different option securities but electronic platforms enable speculators and market makers to easily manage a suite of options expiring multiple times per month.

BETTER CHARTING

Plentiful and affordable market data wasn't available throughout the open outcry era. However, since the explosion of electronic trading matching of futures contracts, trading platforms, and charting services have been able to create powerful charts that can be customized in an unlimited number of ways. It truly has been a game-changer for market analysis and, in my opinion, has done wonders for leveling the playing field for traders with less financial resources to allocate toward commodity speculation.

ORDER FLOW, CHATTER, AND SENTIMENT

The greatest aspect of the open outcry trading pits roaring on the floors of the CME, CBOT, and NYMEX was the constant chatter and visible order flow. Although I was never stationed on the trading floor, I had access to those that were via telephone and instant message. This type of admittance was helpful in that those with eyes on the floor had the ability to convey the feeling of the market (where local pit traders were either sweating or getting excited). What were the big banks' desks doing (was the Goldman Sachs desk going long or short and how aggressively)? And where were the stop- loss orders accumulating? This type of insider information was extremely helpful in judging market sentiment and speculating on future price changes.

When the pits died, so did this source of information. Big players now route their orders through online trading platforms via what are known as iceberg orders. This means not only is their buying and selling activity anonymous, but the ultimate quantity of the orders of the market moving traders is disguised. In short, now that trading activity has moved to the screens, speculators, floor traders, and brokers have been forced to find an edge somewhere other than the pit order flow and floor chatter.

WHERE ARE THE FLOOR TRADERS NOW?

Not unlike manufacturing industries that have experienced the peril of automation, the commodity industry has suffered from computerization. Although these automations are ultimately a positive for the industry as a whole, and more specific market participants, floor traders, trading desks, and many restaurants and bars in downtown Chicago are casualties.

One of my favorite documentaries was a movie titled *Floored*, directed by James Allen Smith. It follows a handful of Chicago floor traders through their journey of transitioning from the open outcry pits to the computers. The movie is gritty; it doesn't sugarcoat the nature of the pits and the vast personalities that navigated them for years. It also accurately depicts the pain inflicted by the commodity markets in various manners to those who either weren't able to find an edge in pit trading or those who were prosperous but later couldn't find the same success trading from the screen.

In previous decades, the commodity trading pits were bubbling with excitement. As a result, even those traders executing orders from the screens opted to rent desk space on the trading floor. Also, market newsletter writers, commentators, etc., all made homes of the desks surrounding the trading pits. All of that is gone. Those who used to occupy those desks have scattered. In my estimation, the majority of them have ventured into other career paths. Without the inside information the pits were providing, many found it difficult to market and sell their trading signal and newsletter services. Those who have managed to succeed in the commodity market information and educational space in a post-pit world are the cream of the crop.

There aren't official stats or data available that tells the story of where pit traders and others who previously made a living on the trading floors have landed. Nevertheless, I keep in contact with quite a few. Floor traders who couldn't find a way to make a living trading electronically took this as a sign that it was time for a change. Those who took care of their money might never have to work again, others have ventured into real estate, driving for Uber, and even delivering pizza. The cannibalism of the commodity industry has been a brutally painful exercise in Darwinism, leaving the industry humbled.

CHAPTER 4: ACCOUNT ACCESS, TRADING PLATFORMS, AND EXCHANGE DATA FEES

The commodity markets are volatile and often unforgiving. Thus, it is imperative that traders receive accurate information regarding their trading accounts and ample market access to react to that information. After all, I believe that the largest component to trading success is psychological, and it is hard to be calm, cool, and collected if you are essentially blind when it comes to market price, account positions, margin requirements and net liquidation balances.

With that said, the phrase "ample market access" can have wildly different meanings among various traders. For instance, a professional trader likely needs analytical software, seasonal tendencies, and data from the COT (Commitments of Traders) report issued by the CFTC, etc. On the contrary, the average retail trader is ecstatic to have access to real-time quotes and charts, point-and-click trading capabilities, and immediate access to current account balances.

In this chapter, we take a detailed look at the process involved in gaining access to real-time futures and options quotes, capable trading platforms, and the cost of acquiring price data from the exchange, or in some cases third-party vendors.

COMMODITY MARKET ACCESS CAN BE COSTLY, BUT IT DOESN'T HAVE TO BE

Unlike the cumbersome and expensive process of open outcry quote reporting and distributing, real-time quotes of electronically executed futures and options contracts are easy to compile and dispense. As a result, technology has granted retail traders access to relatively affordable and accurate streaming futures and options pricing. Nevertheless, the software used to display it and eventually trade it might not be as affordable for those seeking high-end features.

> Trading is a business. Sometimes it takes money to make money. You can't put a price on information.

Further, those deemed to be *professional* traders in the eyes of the Chicago Mercantile Exchange are charged dramatically higher rates for live price data relative to *non-professionals*. Those falling into the *professional* category are generally brokers, money managers, CTAs (Commodity Trading Advisors), and other brokerage employees. In my opinion, charging industry insiders such as brokers and risk managers is counterproductive to a smoothly functioning marketplace because it reduces the manpower at brokerage firms servicing clients and managing their risk, but I have little say in the matter. Similarly, some retail traders are surprised that merely trading an account for a family member might qualify them as a *professional* trader and, accordingly, cost them dearly in the price of market access. Thus, it is important to be aware of the technology available in addition to the logistics of acquiring market information and any exchange or industry rules that might complicate the process. Hopefully, this chapter prepares you for the daunting task.

For newcomers, the amount of money that can be spent subscribing to high-end charting applications, order entry software, and even price data can be shocking. Fortunately, the growing popularity and availability of futures and options trading has attracted development dollars into commodity platforms. This has greatly increased the capabilities of the free-to-use trading platforms offered by commodity brokers. Likewise, the upgraded software packages (those requiring subscription fees or software purchase costs) are now more reasonably priced due to stiff competition and cheaper market data. Before electronic trading, traders looking for fancy setups were forced to pay top dollar for software and were then forced to acquire open outcry data to drive the platform; this quickly added up to several hundred dollars per month. Gaining a similar setup in today's electronic trading environment is relatively affordable. In fact, it can be as low as a few dollars per month for access to a very capable execution platform with streaming quotes, option chains, and charts. If you are unfamiliar with option chains, they are simply grids that include all the listed options available for any given underlying contract with the corresponding price and volume data. The younger generation expects this, but those of us that have been around for a while know we are getting a great deal!

SUBSCRIBING TO COMMODITY QUOTES

There are two ways to access live futures and options on futures prices: via a live trading platform or via a designated quoting and charting service. You might also use an application that acts as both. Regardless of the software you choose, it is in your best interest to avoid using these two types of applications independently because doing so would mean paying two sets of exchange data fees. Additionally, software that is being used for analytical purposes and is *not* being used to enter futures and options trades will not qualify for the CME's discounted data fee rates. This might sound trivial in comparison to the millions of dollars you dream of making in the commodity markets, but it is a heavy burden to carry.

For instance, the cost of data for all four CME exchanges in an active trading account for a *non-professional* trader is anywhere from $3 to $15 per month depending on the amount of data the trader wishes to receive. However, subscribing to the same live data for use in software that is *not* connected to a live trading account can accrue a monthly bill of $340 to $380. Similarly, those who are deemed to be *professional* traders by the CME would be required to pay $340 per month, per device, for access to data on all CME exchanges whether or not that device is connected to a live trading platform. You read that right, per device. If a trader is using three different trading platforms, the total monthly data cost would be $1,020. Keep in mind, this does not include ICE data (the softs).

Obviously, the goal should be to keep devices to a minimum, find an application that can be used for analysis *and* order entry, and avoid being categorized as a professional trader (unless, of course, you truly are one). Being careless in this arena could cost you hundreds of dollars per month. Know the rules and follow them, but don't pay unnecessary fees out of laziness.

CME DATA FEES

On January 1, 2015, the CME Group rolled out a new data fee program requiring all active traders to pay for access to futures and options price data. Thankfully, most retail traders are offered data subscriptions at discounted pricing. The exact cost per trader varies, but it can be as low as $3 per month for top line data on all CME Group exchanges, or as much as $15 monthly for access to multi-tier data on all CME Group exchanges. Multi-tier data displays the 10 best bids and asks, but single-tier data provides traders with the current bid/ask quote without offering any information on proximal working limit orders beneath or above the market price.

Keep in mind, these rates are per platform, not per person. Thus, a trader utilizing a mobile platform as well as a downloaded platform might be subject to multiple sets of fees. Likewise, a trader using one platform for options trading and another for futures might be forced to pay data subscription fees for both platforms. Whether the trader is charged for both platforms depends on the FCM associated with the platform, and whether the order entry server and data service provider are the same. As you can tell, it gets complicated; accordingly, it is imperative to consult with a broker to ensure against making a mistake and causing unnecessary data fee expenses.

At these rates ($3 to $15), the data costs for using one or two platforms are more of an annoyance than a game changer; most traders simply absorb the new costs and carry on as they always have. I hate to admit it, but these low fees are actually good business by the CME because it doesn't hinder anybody's ability to trade while offering the CME a handsome monthly revenue it didn't previously enjoy. Further, the burden of collecting fees from active traders lies in the hands of the brokerage firms themselves, so implementation of this policy enabled the CME to pass administrative costs on to brokers while padding their own bottom line. As an entrepreneur, I respect the ingenuity. However, the CME charges substantially more to anyone categorized as a "professional trader," according to the exchange's definition and stipulations.

NON-PROFESSIONAL CME DATA FEES

According to the CME Group, a non-professional trader is either an individual or natural person, or certain small business entity (limited liability companies, partnerships, trusts, or corporations) that receive and use price data on electronically traded futures and options in a manner consistent with the following capacities:

1. The subscriber must have an active futures trading account.
2. The subscriber must not be a member of a CME Group exchange (or hold a lease).
3. The subscriber does not have a primary business purpose that involves trading.
4. The subscriber must not be registered or qualified as a professional trader or investment advisor with any stock, commodities, or futures exchange or contract market, or with any regulatory authority, professional association, or recognized professional body.
5. The subscriber must not be affiliated with any entity that is or may be considered a professional user.
6. The subscriber use of price information must be solely for the subscriber's personal, non-business use.
7. The subscriber's use of price data information must be limited to managing the subscriber's own property and, for the avoidance of doubt, not in connection with the management of any property of any third party in any capacity, whether as a principal, officer, partner, employee, or agent of any business or on behalf of any other individual, and whether the subscriber receives any remuneration therefore.
8. The subscriber must not be acting on behalf of an institution that engages in brokerage, banking, investment, or financial activities.
9. The subscriber has no more than two means for accessing information from each distributor.
10. The subscriber must view the information only on a device that is capable of routing orders to the CME's electronic Globex.

Any data subscriber who does not meet the aforementioned conditions is categorized as a *professional trader*. This might sound like an inconsequential designation, and maybe even flattering, but I assure you it is highly undesirable.

PROFESSIONAL DATA FEES

Unfortunately, there is a caveat to the CME Group's data policy that has had a substantial negative impact on the commodity industry. In the previous paragraph, I mentioned the discounted data fees that most individual retail traders enjoy. The CME refers to this group of traders as "non-professionals"; yet, for those falling within the CME's distinction of a professional trader, the cost of data access skyrockets. Professional traders don't have the ability to choose top line or bottom line data; instead, they face a single fee of $85 per exchange per platform. For those wishing to access all four of the CME Group exchanges, the total monthly cost is $340. Once again, this is per platform; a commodity broker wishing to assist clients on more than one platform and FCM must pay $340 for each platform. Prior to the data fee policy being employed by the CME, many brokers under an IIB relationship were working with five to 10 trading platforms. If you've done the math, you are aware the monthly cost for price data might range somewhere between $1,700 and $3,400. Despite the implications of high earnings among commodity brokers, I can assure you that is not reality for the majority. Similar to any other sales jobs, 20% of the brokers make "all" of the money and the other 80% would be better off waiting tables at the neighborhood café. Many commodity brokers simply couldn't absorb this new cost of doing business. Soon, we'll discuss the impact this has had on the industry.

AVOID BEING INCORRECTLY CATEGORIZED AS A PROFESSIONAL TRADER

The implications of being categorized by the CME as a professional trader are profound. It is important to understand the steps that should be taken to avoid incorrectly being designated as such. Anybody registered as a member or directly affiliated with a member of the NFA, CFTC, SEC, or any other global financial industry is considered a professional trader for data fee purposes. In addition, any person who makes a living in any other capacity related to the commodity or financial markets will be tagged as a pro trader. However, in some instances, an "average Joe" trader with a day job can unexpectedly trigger professional classification, which is unfortunate.

Generally speaking, aside from a spouse trading an account for a spouse, anytime a trader takes power of attorney trading privileges over an account in which there are funds other than their own, the trader is considered a professional trader. To clarify, if a trader decides to trade an account for his friend or even family members, he will be subject to the CME's professional data fees at a rate of $340 per month. Don't forget, if the trader wishes to have access to live data for ICE products as well, he will be charged another set of data fees. We'll discuss ICE fees later on.

ICE PRICE DATA FEES

A little over a year after the CME Group implemented their controversial data fee policy, the Intercontinental Exchange rolled out their own set of hefty fees levied on commodity traders. Before we talk about the magnitude of the ICE data fee policy, I'll first remind you which markets are traded on the exchange—the softs (sugar, cocoa, coffee, cotton, and orange juice), along with the dollar index.

As of April 1, 2016, the ICE charges each trader, broker, risk manager, and market watcher $110 per month for access to live market data per exchange. This fee will be levied to each user and each platform, making it extremely cumbersome for traders and industry insiders. To illustrate, a trader accessing live ICE US data while trading in the softs, who also subscribes to ICE Europe data, would be subject to a bill of $220 per month. This isn't necessarily a far-fetched setup because one of the most popular ICE products is Brent crude oil, which trades on the ICE Europe division. If the same trader wished to have access to a mobile platform, depending on the arrangement and platform chosen, he would most likely have to pay another $220 for such access. You've probably done the math in your head; this is equivalent to $440 per month! Prior to April 2016, most traders were provided with real-time streaming data for ICE futures and options products at no cost. Thus, there was mass sticker shock across the industry.

HOW THIS DIFFERS FROM THE CME'S DATA FEE POLICY

The distinguishing factor between ICE and CME Group data fees is the CME policy differentiates *professional* traders from *non-professional* traders. The CME's data fees are a negligible burden to retail traders and a heavy burden to industry professionals utilizing multiple platforms or wanting access to all four CME exchanges at a cost of $340 per month. On the other hand, the ICE policy treats all market participants the same and charges unfathomable data costs to the average retail trader. The ICE policy is likely closing the door to their products for most retail traders—$110 per month, or more, is a deal breaker to the majority of small speculators.

CHARTING

For many position traders, access to a premium trading application simply isn't worth the subscription costs or hassles. However, the charting capabilities offered within some free applications can be subpar when it comes to customizing a chart and might be a bigger burden than some realize. The majority of free charting services via the internet or a brokerage firm trading platform often fail to provide traders with extensive drawing capabilities such as a Fibonacci ruler, Gann fans, trend lines, and so forth. Those that do generally don't have the ability to save a trader's work, which requires time wasted redrawing lines and tools. Nonetheless, a handful of free trading platforms offer very capable charting with drawing tools and anything else you can imagine. If charting is important to you, be sure to test-drive multiple applications to ensure your needs are met at a price you can live with.

Even the free applications offering relatively capable charts typically fall short when it comes to charting commodities in the long term. For instance, they might be great at analyzing a daily chart or an intraday chart (10 minute, 30 minute, etc.), but if you seek a weekly or monthly chart, free trading platforms usually don't have the data to support such analysis. In fact, even high-end trading platforms

> Don't trip over dollars chasing pennies; if your trading strategy requires an upgraded platform, it is worth the money.

and charting software require a separate historical data subscription to support longer-term charting. That said, there are great websites such as Barchart.com that do offer long-term commodity charts to visitors for free, but such web-based charts don't allow the drawing of trendlines or tools. In short, if you wish to have access to the whole package (price data supporting weekly and monthly charts and full drawing capabilities), it will be necessary to pay an incremental monthly fee for access to a premium trading platform.

Trading platform offerings, software competence, and the cost of premium features are in a constant state of flux, but I've worked hard to give my brokerage clients access to nearly all available futures trading platforms. You will find a list of price and function specifications at www.DeCarleyTrading.com. Some of the trading platforms popular among our brokerage clients seeking upgraded charting are Track n' Trade Live, Trade Navigator, CQG, eSignal, CTS T4, Multicharts, Sierra Charts, X-Trader, Barchart Trader, and more. The cost of high-end charting platforms varies but most range between $40 and $130 per month. Obviously, it is a good idea to do your homework and demo the platform before committing to a subscription.

As a reminder, falling in love with a charting application that doesn't also moonlight as a trading platform will dramatically enhance expenses. There are multiple strong charting packages with the capability of entering futures and options trades, and therefore offer traders an economical solution.

FREE TRADING PLATFORMS AND MARKET ACCESS

Brokerage firms are in the business of trade execution. Therefore, it is in their best interest to ensure clients have a convenient and reliable means of placing orders on behalf of their trading accounts. For a few traders, this simply means having someone at the other end of a telephone line, email address, or text message to execute a trade; but most traders rely on computerized trading platforms. The method of trade placement that works best for you depends on your trading style and your personality. A good brokerage firm will offer both services and even allow clients to choose some sort of hybrid in which they can trade online using a platform but also have a broker handy to bounce ideas off of and support trade placement from time to time.

In their quest for boosting trading volume, most brokerage firms offer a complimentary order entry platform, and they typically have several upgraded options, most of which involve a monthly fee, a transaction fee, or both. Free platforms characteristically offer marked-to-market data on open positions and orders, but as mentioned, real-time streaming quotes must be subscribed to and adequate charts aren't necessarily standard in free-to-use trading platforms. Therefore, traders must be well aware of the platform offerings and their own needs before making a decision on a brokerage firm or means of order entry.

Thanks to technology and competition, most retail commodity traders, whether utilizing futures or options, find their needs are sufficiently met with their brokers' free trading platforms. Aside from some of the charting challenges discussed, most free platforms are sufficient in delivering timely price data and efficient trade execution. These are critical when dealing with leveraged contracts that stand to create large profits and losses in a short period of time.

PAID TRADING PLATFORMS

Paid platforms give traders access to streaming real-time quotes with deluxe charting and point-and-click order entry capabilities. Although many of the free platforms provide similar functions, paid platforms advertise low-latency execution, more convenient order entry features, more capable user-friendly charting, the capability to automate strategies, and the potential to possibly even develop your own technical indicators. With this in mind, there are now a few free platforms that offer the ability to code technical indicators and algorithmic trading. We offer such a complimentary platform to DeCarley Trading brokerage clients. However, it takes a considerable amount of computer coding knowledge to pull it off, and this is true even when using pay-to-use platforms. On a side note, one pay-to-use platform we offer (Track n' Trade Live) actually enables traders to program automated strategies using drop-down menus, so there is no need for coding skills; however, this is a rare feature.

> "You must automate, emigrate, or evaporate." — James A. Baker, GE

Nearly all pay-to-use trading platforms enable traders to enter entry and exit orders simultaneously. They are also capable of orders stipulating multiple entry prices when trading more than one contract; once filled, they can instruct the platform to place multiple exit orders at various prices and even trail stop-loss orders higher to protect open profits. This type of staggered order entry is known as *bracketing*. Some free-to-use platforms offer *bracket orders*, but it isn't necessarily standard.

Traders might also instruct the platform to enter a trade if particular events occur, such as specific prices being hit or technical oscillators behaving in a certain way. These types of orders are known as *contingency* orders because they are contingent on a specific event occurring. With that in mind, traders should be aware of whether such orders are held server-side or on the trader's computer. We discuss OCO orders in detail in Chapter 7, "Order Types and How to Use Them," but for now, all you need to know is that contingent orders rely on software to execute or cancel an order, based on another event occurring. Therefore, if you will be utilizing them, it is a good idea to choose a platform/broker that is capable of holding the accompanying execution instructions on an offsite server, not on your computer. This is because, in a server-side arrangement, your orders will still be working and executed even if your personal computer loses connection or crashes.

Several premium trading platforms are available to futures and options traders, but not all platforms are compatible with all brokerage firms. If you have your heart set on a particular platform, I recommend confirming that your prospective brokerage firm offers it before you open an account. On the contrary, if you believe that you have found the perfect brokerage firm for you but it doesn't offer a particular trading platform, it likely still can meet your platform needs because many of the popular trading platforms are similar in nature; just ask. Remember, commodity brokers make money only if you trade. Therefore, they do everything within their power to ensure that doing business with them is as easy as possible.

Also, don't let the word *paid* discourage you; this is no time to pinch pennies. If an upgraded platform has any positive impact on your trading results, it will cover the cost of the application, plus some. In fact, in recent years, the costs associated with platform upgrades have come down considerably; you might be pleasantly surprised. In many cases, I recommend using an upgraded platform or choosing a brokerage that offers a nicely equipped *free* platform. Even if you place orders through a broker, a capable and free platform is helpful to gain access to real-time quotes and charts without the hefty exchange fees and quote vendor fees that you could otherwise face. Accordingly, I strive to ensure that all of my clients have access to a fully equipped free-to-use trading platform, along with multiple affordable upgrade options.

PER-SIDE TRANSACTION COSTS VERSUS A FLAT MONTHLY FEE

Many upgraded platforms charge a usage fee on a per-side basis. This simply means that a set fee is charged to the trading account each time a trade is executed. I have witnessed fees ranging from as high as $1.50 per side to as low as 15 cents per side. More often than not, the brokerage firm subsidizes platform costs that fall on the lower end of the spectrum.

Remember that a trade consists of two sides, referred to as a round turn; therefore, a trader being charged a per-side platform fee is charged when entering the market and again when exiting.

> Active traders should avoid platforms that are charged on a volume basis.

I have found that the functionality difference between platforms charging a fee on the high end of the price range relative to one on the low end is somewhat minimal. The higher-priced platforms tend to offer automated system trading and development to justify higher fees. Yet others charge higher transaction fees and claim to offer faster server communication with the exchange. For those who aren't developing and implementing proprietary systems, or scalping small intraday price moves, less costly per-side platforms are often recommended.

Keep in mind that traders who intend to do a considerable amount of volume will likely be better off choosing a trading platform that offers flat monthly fees instead of transaction-based fees. Doing so helps prevent traders from overpaying for market access. A typical monthly fee ranges anywhere from $50 to $350 per month. Fifteen cents per side doesn't seem like a lot of money, but it equates to 30 cents per round turn and $300 for those trading 1,000 round turns per month. Some flat monthly subscription-based platforms fall into this price range, but most of them go for far less and without sacrificing chart capabilities and order entry features. On the other hand, lower-volume traders have the comfort of knowing that they will pay only for what they use.

Keep in mind that platform vendors might have pricing structures that incorporate *both* a monthly fee and a transaction fee. Before choosing one of these platforms, do your research to ensure that the costs will support your overall goal of making money instead of acting as an obstacle to your success.

OPTION TRADING PLATFORMS AND BROKERS

If you intend to trade options on futures, in addition to or instead of futures contracts, the process of finding an adequate platform is more complicated. Believe it or not, not all commodity trading platforms offer options trading. Further, not all brokerages allow its clients to trade options in any manner they wish. Many brokers limit clients to long option strategies; accordingly, option sellers or option spread traders might have far fewer trading platforms to choose from a traditional option buyer or futures trader. Thus, it requires option traders to put in quite a bit of legwork to find the right fit.

Please note, as an option *seller,* it is generally best to find an appropriate brokerage service first, then consider a platform offered by that brokerage as a second step. This is because brokers allowing short options trading are few and far between, so it might be necessary to sacrifice on platform features to find the right option selling environment (my brokerage, DeCarley Trading, happens to specialize in short option trading accounts).

NOT ALL BROKERS ALLOW CLIENTS TO SELL OPTIONS

It is a surprise to beginning traders who wish to sell options to discover the difficulty in finding a conducive brokerage relationship. The practice of option selling is a controversial strategy throughout the commodity brokerage industry. Many brokerage firms outright forbid the practice. Others allow it, but there are often strings attached. For example, some of the big-name brokers limit the particular markets that its clients can sell options in, and they narrow it down even more by limiting the contract months that can be sold. Additional restrictions come in the form of higher than exchange minimum margin requirements, quantity trading limits, and other broker-imposed handcuffs.

There are a limited number of brokerage services recognizing that despite the challenges of option selling, the strategy offers the highest long-term prospects for successful trading. My brokerage service, DeCarley Trading, specializes in optimizing the trading environment for short option traders. Not only can we provide a restriction-free home for option sellers, we are experienced in the strategy and are capable of offering peripheral services such as margin call management, efficient trade adjustments, and so forth. I'm sure there are other brokers out there willing to do similar things for their option selling clients, but it is important to understand they are the exception rather than the rule. If you truly want to give option selling a fair chance at success, it is imperative you find a broker who is on your side. Nevertheless, even with the optimal brokerage relationship, option selling is far from an easy-money venture and sometimes comes with occasionally excessive risk. There is a reason many brokerage firms shy away from option selling.

ACCESSING THE GREEKS, IV, AND OPTION CALCULATORS

Some traders opt for two trading platforms, one that offers advanced charting and order entry for futures contracts and another for their options trading. However, I believe in today's environment it is possible to find an affordable and competent platform offering both futures *and* options trading in a side-by-side manner. In other words, you should have the freedom to buy and sell options to hedge your open futures contracts, or even establish complex options strategies in the same account you day trade futures. Not only is this convenient, but it is imperative to those using options to hedge futures contracts (if you want to learn more about this, my book *Higher Probability Commodity Trading* covers it in detail).

Without the ability to trade futures and options in the same account and the same trading platform, traders face unnecessarily high margin requirements. For instance, the margin to go long a crude oil futures contract might be $3,100 and the margin to sell an at-the-money call option in crude oil might be roughly $2,000. A trader who can buy the futures contract and sell the call option in the same account (covered call strategy) would face a margin requirement of around $1,500. The same trader would pay $5,100 in margin if the two legs were executed in separate accounts on separate platforms. I'm sure you can see the disadvantage in this. Thus, if your goal is to trade both futures *and* options, steer clear of trading platforms such as NinjaTrader, which doesn't offer options trading.

It is rare to find a free-to-use commodity option platform that offers the greeks (analytical equations depicting how option prices are behaving) and option spread order placement. Also, those looking for option analytics (risk graphs, calculators, etc.) will likely need to spring for a paid platform. That said, in my opinion, option analytics are highly overrated. The same general information can be derived by a simple delta calculation.

Delta is the rate of change of an option price relative to a unit of change in the futures price. For example, if a call option increases by 0.5 points after the futures market increases by 1.0 point, the delta of that option is 50%, or 50, as most traders would say. Also, the delta can be used as a rough estimate of how likely that option is to expire in-the-money. Thus, a 50% delta suggests there is a 50/50 chance it will be in-the-money at expiration. Similarly, a delta of 30% would imply the option has a 30% chance of expiring in-the-money and a 70% chance of expiring worthless. A fancy software package capable of calculating probabilities of option trades working out might come up with slightly different figures (29.8% vs. 30%) but it isn't enough to change the reality of the trade. Accordingly, I believe simply looking at the delta of an option is accurate enough to provide the needed information. Further, it is a time saver. In summary, having an option probability calculator built into a trading platform probably isn't as helpful as some believe it to be; consider this before you decide to pay top dollar for this capability.

On that note, green option sellers often find comfort in using option analytics probabilities. Some sell high quantities of options that theoretically have a 95% chance of expiring worthless. On the surface, this seems like easy money but I assure you it is not. An option having a high probability of expiring worthless, and even an option that does eventually expire worthless, can see dramatic price swings between trade entry and the expiration date.

As a result, traders have a tendency to sell such options in high quantities, only to learn this lesson the hard way. An option can explode in value when market volatility increases whether the futures price ever reaches the strike price of the option or not. I go into this concept in far more detail in *Higher Probability Commodity Trading*.

Having the greeks within a trading platform, on the other hand, is something that I believe can be useful. As mentioned, I like to look at the delta to determine option probability estimates. Although I don't put too much faith in the other greeks (gamma, theta, and vega) I do pay close attention to the implied volatility readings in options markets that are generally included in option platforms that offer the greeks. Thus, I do believe that most traders can benefit from a trading platform that displays this information. Nevertheless, it is possible to find such information on the web for free. For example, at the time of this writing, navigating to the "Futures" section Barchart.com and clicking on "Option Quotes," then "Volatility & Greeks" will reveal option stats. This isn't as convenient as having the data displayed within a trading platform, but it is hard to beat free.

The most difficult feature to find in a commodity option platform is the ability to trade option spreads on a single ticket. Again, there are few that offer this within a free-to-use trading platform. And even those that offer it sometimes do a very poor job of making it user-friendly enough for inexperienced traders to successfully place option spreads. As previously mentioned, the exchange will accept option spreads in a specific format; they don't allow platforms to send orders outside of the set parameters. As a result, beginning traders struggle to understand why their platform allowed them to build a spread but the exchange rejects the order once placed. As a reminder, the exchange requires that spreads list the buy side first and the lower strike price first in the case of a vertical spread. Accordingly, entering such orders can be frustrating for inexperienced traders.

PLATFORM RISK PARAMETERS AND ORDER APPROVAL

Before delving into the types of trading platforms and their features we'll discuss a less talked about issue with trading platforms. A commonly overlooked function of a firm's trading platform is its capability to approve or reject entered orders based on margin requirements and account funding. Nearly all trading platforms now approve and reject incoming orders on an automatic basis, whereas in the past the process required human intervention. In other words, trading platforms deem you able to trade a market according to account funding, the appropriate margin requirement, and other risk parameters immediately upon order entry. Whereas during the days of phone orders and even the early days of platform trading, order entry relied on a brokerage staff member for the credit approval process. Each approach has obvious advantages and disadvantages. Although automated electronic order review is instantaneous, it has its drawbacks. You need to understand the possible implications on your trading.

An automated process cannot "think" and will often erroneously reject orders in accounts that are trading option strategies or futures spreads. For example, if a trader wants to buy July corn and sell September corn on separate order tickets, an automatic credit approval system might reject the order because it is assuming margin on both sides of the trade. In reality, a spread between two corn futures is exchange recognized and is provided discounted margin. Similarly, an account that lacks the required margin by a few dollars would experience order rejections with an automatic system due to a mere technicality. In the days of human order processing, such a scenario would have been recognized and incorporated into the order approval procedure. However, this luxury came with the opportunity cost of time.

In today's world of automated order approval, brokers must set up risk parameters for each client. This might include items such as quantity limits on the number of positions an account can hold, clip limits (how many trades can be executed at a time), exchange margin requirements, broker day trading margin requirements, and some platforms even require that each product to be traded by a particular client must be enabled individually. The practice of setting up traders on platforms is time-consuming for brokers, and resulting constraints are frustrating for clients. Particularly when a client with ample margin available experiences order rejections because he hadn't been enabled to trade a certain market, or the risk limits didn't properly account for funds added to the account or realized market gains. On the bright side, the control gained by risk managers at brokerage firms has opened the door for lower margins, lower commission rates, and lower barriers to entry for commodity speculators.

You might be wondering why quantity limits might be necessary. Why wouldn't a trading platform simply approve or reject orders based on the exchange margin requirement? There are a few reasons, but the most prominent is that many trading platforms are not capable of accurate margin calculations for anything other than outright long and short futures contracts. Thus, option sellers or spread traders (options or futures) are subject to quantity limits as a form of brokerage risk management. Also, day traders are generally granted lower margin rates, which are set by the broker, not the exchange. Day trading, often referred to intraday trading, is the practice of entering and exiting positions within a single trading session. Thus, platforms can be manipulated by brokerage firms to allow traders to trade with far less margin than the exchange requires, assuming they will be flat with the market by the close of the trading session. In Chapter 12, "Coping with Margin Calls," I discuss the key differences between a margin charged within a trading session and a margin charged when a position is held into the close of trade. Beginning traders often assume if the platform allows them to enter an order, they must have enough margin to hold the position indefinitely. Because of discounted day trading rates, this is obviously not the case. Positions implemented courtesy of day trading margin rates must be offset by the close if the trader doesn't have the exchange required initial margin.

Another reason brokers use quantity limits in trading platforms to rein in overzealous option trading. It is a well-known fact that exchange margin for deep out-of-the-money short options is notoriously low relative to the true risk of the trade. For instance, with crude oil futures near $46.00 an option seller might be tempted to sell a crude oil put with a strike price of $34.00 for two ticks, or $20 each. The option seller is accepting $20 in premium wagering that crude oil futures will be above $34.00 at option expiration (a month in the future). The trader is probably right. Oil futures would need to drop $12.00 before expiration for this to be a problem. Yet, most traders wouldn't be satisfied with a profit of $20 minus commissions and fees, so to sweeten the deal they would look to sell several of these options. The exchange margin required to sell such an option might be around $80, so this opens the door for a trader under the illusion that this is nearly guaranteed money to sell 100 of them in an $8,000 account. A trading platform approving and rejecting orders solely by exchange margin would allow the trade to occur. The result is $2,000 in collected premium (before transaction costs) in what an inexperienced trader would consider being *easy money*. Nonetheless, this trade poses more risk to the trader and brokerage firm than any other strategy imaginable.

First, the bid/ask spread for such an option will be at least a cent and maybe two. If the trader must exit for any reason, the least he would need to pay is one cent, which realizes a loss of $1,000. More important, an option worth two ticks ($20) can quickly jump to 10, 20, or 30 times its value on a single large down day in oil futures. I am not talking about a rare black swan event, I am talking about something I've seen occur hundreds (maybe thousands) of times throughout my career. It is a common occurrence. Imagine selling 100 of these options for $20; subsequently, crude oil drops $3.50 in a single trading day and suddenly speculators begin thinking $34.00 crude oil is a possibility. As a result, they begin buying these options all the while bidding its price higher. It would take a mere eight cents in option value change to completely wipe out the trading account. If the option value rises to 20 cents, or $200, the trading account would be negative by $10,000 because the loss on the trade would equate to $18,000 and the trader started with $8,000. For those of you bewildered by why your broker won't allow you to sell deep-out-of-the-money options in excessive quantities, this is why. It is an impossible game and *always* ends disastrously (eventually). Option selling should always be done in moderate quantities relative to account size and with plenty of excess margin to spare.

DON'T PANIC OVER REJECTED ORDERS

Unfortunately, in an electronic world, the orders of futures and options traders can and will be erroneously rejected from time to time. Each platform uses different parameters for order approval or denial and there is a nearly unlimited number of things that might go wrong, causing a trader's order to be rejected. However, this is something that is more troublesome for options traders than futures traders.

To illustrate, if a trading platform is valuing options based on the current bid or ask quote, there will be times in which the market makers are temporarily unavailable to quote the particular open option positions in a trading account. Without their price quotes, the best bid and the best ask working for a particular option could be at ludicrous prices. If so, a trading account might show a dramatically lower balance than reality because the options being valued via an unrealistic bid or ask price is incorrectly showing a large loss. If extreme enough, this could lead to the platform erroneously rejecting orders. A similar issue arises when option spread traders are attempting to peel off part of their position, or if a platform incorrectly calculates spread margin (this happens more than you might think).

Further, the rejection doesn't have to come from the platform itself; even if an order is approved by the platform, the FCM or the exchange might reject it. Any, or all three, of these parties, reject orders on a regular basis for various reasons, and while most of them are legitimate, others are not. Some are outside of the brokerage's control and others due to poor programming or glitches, or as is often the case with incorrect order placement by green traders. In any case, it is the trader who is ultimately responsible to continue to manage the trading account reasonably in the best manner possible on the heels of a rejected order. I've been doing this for a long time and I can assure you it is rare for anybody other than the trader to take responsibility for delayed order placement, slippage, or other damage related to a trader experiencing a rejected order. This might seem unfair, but it is stipulated in all FCM account applications (that I am aware of) as a risk of trading. Technology and platforms aren't perfect, nor are the humans setting up risk parameters for individual clients. Also, clients who are pressing their luck are far more likely to run into the hassle and chaos of a rejected order.

When opening a trading account, I strongly recommend that you ask the brokerage what the procedure would be for rejected orders. For example, is there a 24-hour trade desk that could assist with placing a previously rejected order? If you are working with an individual broker, does he receive notifications of order rejections and does he take action immediately to resolve the issue and assist the client in entering the order without additional costs? Is there leniency for order rejections if the margin shortage is minimal? Can any limitations, other than exchange required margin or quantity limits, be negotiated?

Believe it or not, there are several discount brokerages out there that cannot place orders for clients or go around platform risk parameters to enter or exit a position the client is unable to do so himself. In my opinion, this is a recipe for disaster. A good brokerage will have the ability to react, place trades, and alleviate any delay in order placement due to a platform rejection. Markets move fast; this enhanced service will matter because time is money.

CHOOSING A TRADING PLATFORM

Electronic order-entry platforms come in all shapes, sizes, and abilities. Most of them accept order entry in more than one way. For instance, many platforms offer traders access to a price ladder, often called a price DOM (depth of market), in which orders can be placed with a single click. A DOM panel displays the prices and quantities of other traders' limit orders alongside a progression of prices. Traders simply click their mouse on either the buy side or the sell side of the ladder to enter an order. In such an arrangement, a trader's stop and limit orders are displayed in the corresponding columns and can be modified by simply dragging them higher or lower to change the price.

Similarly, most premium platforms—and even some free platforms—offer traders the opportunity to enter orders directly from a price chart. This enables traders to simultaneously chart price and enter orders. As with a DOM, those trading from a price chart can simply drag orders higher or lower to change the price without the burden of typing numbers or even scrolling.

Traders who are uncomfortable with quick-click trading should look for a platform that allows them to enter orders in a more cumbersome but perhaps less error-prone manner. Most platforms have such a capability in the form of an order ticket screen with dropdown menus.

The free-to-use trading platforms brokerage firms provide to clients are often developed in-house and, therefore, are available only at the particular firm offering it. However, premium platforms are developed by third parties whose sole purpose is to generate revenue via platform subscriptions, sales, and fees. Accordingly, these third-party vendors do not benefit from the commission charged, or any other fees you might pay to your brokerage firm.

Some of the most popular pay-to-use trading platforms are Track n' Trade Live, CityTrader, QST (Quick Screen Trading), TradeNavigator, CQG Q-Trader, Cunningham Trading System's T4, and BarchartTrader. Each of these platforms offers to trade both futures and options on futures.

Each of these platforms has significant capabilities with various strengths; consequently, I've arranged to offer all of them to my brokerage clients, along with several "free" platforms. A brief description cannot do any of these platforms justice, but here's a fleeting synopsis.

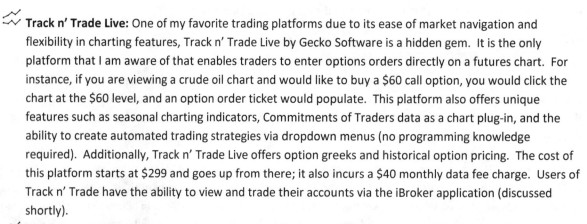

Track n' Trade Live: One of my favorite trading platforms due to its ease of market navigation and flexibility in charting features, Track n' Trade Live by Gecko Software is a hidden gem. It is the only platform that I am aware of that enables traders to enter options orders directly on a futures chart. For instance, if you are viewing a crude oil chart and would like to buy a $60 call option, you would click the chart at the $60 level, and an option order ticket would populate. This platform also offers unique features such as seasonal charting indicators, Commitments of Traders data as a chart plug-in, and the ability to create automated trading strategies via dropdown menus (no programming knowledge required). Additionally, Track n' Trade Live offers option greeks and historical option pricing. The cost of this platform starts at $299 and goes up from there; it also incurs a $40 monthly data fee charge. Users of Track n' Trade have the ability to view and trade their accounts via the iBroker application (discussed shortly).

CityTrader: This platform, created by OptionsCity, is relatively new to the scene. Previously, OptionsCity catered to professional traders seeking uber high-end trading software such as market makers and institutions. They now offer an attractive solution for retail traders, CityTrader, at a cost of $50 per month in addition to a 0.25 cent per contract charge. CityTrader is among the most user-friendly platforms I've seen, it is simple, sleek, and convenient. Because it is web-based, this platform can be accessed from any device including a Mac computer (few commodity trading platforms are Mac-compatible). A unique aspect of CityTrader is an easy-to-use drag and drop spread builder, which can be used to create both futures and option spreads. CityTrader offers a complimentary mobile application. In my opinion, this is a great low-cost option for traders looking for high-end option features in a convenient and simple package.

QST: In my opinion, this is the best all-around trading platform available to those trading both futures and options. QST offers a robust charting package with nearly unlimited choices of indicators, drawing tools, and the capability to create your own indicators. It also enables traders to trade directly from a price chart, enter options orders from an advanced option chain, and provides some option analytics. The only potential downside to using this platform might be the cost. At the time of this writing, the base package started at $50 per month, plus 50 cents per trade, but for those looking for the Cadillac version, the price goes up to $300 per month. To be honest, the base version is relatively limited so traders can expect to pay at least $200 per month to use QST in its full potential. QST offers a mobile application, which is superior to most others available but it comes with a hefty price tag of $60 per month (in addition to the desktop version fees).

TradeNavigator: This platform developed by Genesis Financial Technologies is known for its fantastic charting ability and massive amounts of historical price data. It offers traders access to any trading indicator or drawing tool under the sun, as well as access to several plug-ins to the proprietary indicators and trading guidance from well-known commodity speculators. TradeNavigator has various packages to choose from ranging from a one-time cost of roughly $1,500 to free but with a monthly charge somewhere in the neighborhood of $70. Although it depends on the order entry server being used, those trading with my brokerage generally has the ability to see their TradeNavigator trading accounts and place orders using the iBroker application. Be sure to confirm with your broker whether this will be possible with the access they offer.

CQG Q-Trader: CQG offers a suite of platforms with various costs and capabilities. However, the most reasonable CQG solution for most retail traders is the Q-Trader. At only $40 per month, this platform offers high-end features such as option analytics, option spread trading, and capable charting. It also offers quick and easy point-and-click order entry from a proprietary trading pad. Because the CQG Q-Trader is feature-rich, it is a popular platform. However, keep in mind this is not a platform for newbie traders. It was designed for experienced users and can be overwhelming to those lacking experience in the futures and options markets. CQG offers a mobile application but it requires an additional subscription fee. However, CQG users can log into the iBroker application to see their positions and place trades via their smart phones on the go.

Cunningham's T4: The T4 is a no-nonsense platform for both options and futures traders. It excels in its capability to execute option and futures spread orders and its extremely quick futures order DOM. Some might consider the fact that it offers only one method of order entry, the DOM panel, a negative. Perhaps the most compelling argument for using this platform is ease of account access. The T4 offers traders three ways to log into their trading account to monitor positions or enter new orders: via the traditional desktop version (downloaded software), through a web browser quickly accessible from any computer (even a Mac) with internet without the hassles of downloading a program application, or on a mobile smartphone. The cost of the T4 varies by package, but traders can access the base version (which would likely meet the needs of most traders) for a cost of 50 cents per trade, with a $25 monthly minimum.

BarchartTrader: One of the few commodity trading platforms natively compatible for Mac, and of course also available to PC users, is BarchartTrader. This platform offers traders a plethora of historical data, extensive charting features, and custom order triggers based on price conditions. It also offers option traders access to the greeks and options analytics, grain traders access to cash market quotes, a futures spread matrix, time and sales data, news, weather, and even market commentary and opinions. Further, it is one of the few trading applications configured to be used on multiple monitors. At $129 per month, it isn't necessarily cheap but you get a lot of bang for your buck.

In summary, there are plenty of other pay-to-use futures and options trading platforms, but I believe these to be the most attractive in regards to features and convenience vs. cost. Again, don't overlook the free platform offered by your brokerage; such platforms have improved tremendously in recent years. In fact, I believe many of the platform vendors in business today will be squeezed out as retail traders opt for free-to-use options.

MOBILE APPLICATIONS

As data networks and hand-held technology improves, so does trader access to the futures and options markets. The first mobile trading platforms were slow, inefficient, and unreliable. With real money on the line, this is unacceptable. However, today's marketplace offers traders "on the go" the opportunity to affordably, and confidently, make, place, and monitor trades in an instant from a smartphone or tablet.

In addition to the ability to place trades in your futures account, mobile trading platforms are now capable of charting futures price with popular technical indicators. They also provide live and streaming bid/ask spreads on both futures and options contracts and even integrate into twitter enabling traders to view Twitter feeds on each contract.

Most mobile trading platforms can be downloaded and accessed on any iOS (iPhone, iPad), Android, and Windows Phone device, but if you are still holding on to your Blackberry you will be disappointed. Some trading platforms can be accessed from a "dumb phone" via a WAP (Wireless Application Protocol) browser link. In other words, if you don't have a phone with access to download apps, you can still access a simplified version of the trading application via the WAP link. However, hopefully, anybody wishing to trade commodities from their phone has upgraded to a proficient smartphone.

Naturally, most traders don't use a mobile application exclusively, so futures brokers have worked hard to offer mobile solutions that integrate with other platform offerings. Simply put, if you execute a trade on your mobile device, you will immediately see it in your desktop platform, and vice versa. This sounds obvious, but in the beginning of this technology, there was a lot of money lost erroneously as traders had difficulty determining their net position due to synchronization delays between the mobile and desktop platforms.

POPULAR MOBILE FUTURES PLATFORMS

There are several futures and options mobile platforms available. The right choice for one trader might not necessarily be the right choice for another, so be sure to consult with your broker or at least do your homework.

For full disclosure, my brokerage service (DeCarley Trading) offers access to each of the mobile platforms listed below. There might be applications offered by other brokerage services that I am not familiar with, and therefore are not listed here.

- **iBroker**—This is arguably the best option for the casual trader because it doesn't involve a monthly subscription fee. Instead, traders are charged on a per-trade basis for using it; depending on the brokerage firm, any trade placed through this application comes at an additional cost of 25 to 50 cents. However, in the high-stakes game of futures and options, the luxury of mobile trading execution is far more valuable than a few cents per trade. iBroker can be used at multiple differing brokerage firms due to the ability to connect to the CQG API and is a preferred solution for traders on the go.

- **CityTrader**—Traders can access the CityTrader mobile application at no additional cost ($50 per month for the suite of products). This app strives for simplicity while delivering on function; with trading access on all devices and types of computers, CityTrader delivers for traders of all types.

- **BarchartTrader**—Access to BarchartTrader's mobile platform is included in the subscription cost of the desktop platform discussed in the previous section, which runs about $129 per month. The feature that sets BarchartTrader apart from other mobile applications is its analytical capabilities.

- **QST Mobile**—At $60 per month this is a premium mobile platform, but as usual you get what you pay for. QST Mobile is a high-end mobile platform in that it has brought a lot of features from the full-blown desktop version into its mobile platform. For instance, QST Mobile offers option chains, price ladders, block trades, and news feeds. These features are relatively unique to mobile trading applications. Further, QST Mobile is one of the few mobile solutions that can be used with a Blackberry; thus, those who have refused to give up their keyboards can still have access to their futures trading account on their phone via QST Mobile.

- **T4 Mobile by CTS**—This mobile platform is quick and easy to use with fast loading times and instant execution (really, it is shocking how fast orders can be submitted and filled). The T4 Mobile platform doesn't require an additional platform subscription; it is included in the CTS T4 suite (previously discussed), which also offers a web-based platform and a downloaded desktop version. One of the drawbacks of this platform is its inability to display a clear account summary in the mobile version.

- **Oak Mobile**—This mobile platform can only be used by traders using ADMIS to clear trades. Unlike the T4, this mobile platform excels in offering traders an account summary that includes their margin status. Because of the complications of margin calculations, this is a rare and impressive feature on a mobile platform.

I wouldn't recommend using a mobile application as the sole means of order entry or market analysis, but it is certainly a great way to keep tabs on things while you are away from the computer. Also, on a side note, mobile applications have been a massive blessing to the brokerage industry. Prior to such technology, the typical commodity broker spent the majority of the trading day answering phone calls from clients to give live quotes, position tallies, and market updates. Now, clients have this information accessible at their fingertips at any time.

ORDER DESK ("THE DESK")

Most brokerage firms offer traders a 24-hour live order desk in which clients are free to phone in their orders and verbally place them with a desk clerk in the absence of their full-service broker or in the case of a malfunctioning trading platform. Depending on the brokerage firm you deal with, such a service might have additional fees. I've found that the days of free order desks are largely gone.

Because of dramatic reductions in the average commission rate charged to clients for trade execution and as a means of encouraging clients to place orders via online trading platforms, brokerage firms can no longer justify offering the luxury of a complimentary order desk. After all, if the brokerage is entering the orders the risk of an error shifts from the client to the brokerage. Consequently, most firms charge clients a dollar or two per contract for orders called into a trading desk; this fee does not apply to orders called into a full-service broker. If you are using a full-service broker, you won't be charged a desk fee as we are discussing but you will be charged a relatively higher commission rate. Be sure you know exactly what you will be charged to use an order desk for trade placement. Some deep discount brokers charge outrageous fees to use this service. For example, there are some deep discount

> An order desk is just that; don't expect to call an order desk and get free quotes or advice on a regular basis. That's what your broker, trading platforms, and mobile apps are for.

brokerage firms that offer bottom basement commission rates but if for any reason a trader needs to place an order with the trading desk, they are charged a fee of anywhere between $25 and $60 per contract! Imagine if you are a 10-lot trader, the fee could be into the $600 range, which quickly diminishes any benefit of the lower commission rate. This industry is full of smoke and mirror tactics, so be on your toes. Traders seeking the lowest commission rates generally end up paying the most.

IS IT WORTH PAYING PLATFORM FEES?

Each trader has different needs and desires; therefore, there isn't a simple answer to this question. The decision to subscribe to a pay-to-use platform should be made after considering factors such as the chosen trading strategy, psychological factors, and informational needs.

> If you don't know yourself, the markets will be an expensive way to learn.

To illustrate, a long option position trader might not consider having access to live charting and a premium depth of market panel a necessity, whereas a day trading scalper likely couldn't function without it. Likewise, a trader strictly trading futures probably wouldn't find any value in subscribing to a platform with option greeks and a spread builder.

Another commonly overlooked aspect of choosing whether to use an upgraded platform is the mental turmoil that extensive market access might cause. Some traders simply aren't capable of remaining objective and patient, with the excitement of the markets flashing in front of their eyes with in-depth data and an array of technical oscillators in their grasp. Some are better off doing their research, placing their orders, and walking away from what might happen next, and it is much easier to do this on a basic platform with no frills. Access to high-end platform features often prevents traders from accepting their fate and could lead to panicked decision making as they watch each price tick pass.

In many cases, I recommend that traders use an affordable platform upgrade if the free platforms provided by their brokerage firm lack something in particular that their trading style requires. Don't forget, it is dramatically cheaper to subscribe to real-time data within a live trading platform than it is to do so in a freestanding quote and chart service. Thus, if you need certain data and access you are best off attaining it in a software package that can be used to trade a live account as opposed to using a free-to-use trading platform in addition to some sort of subscription based analytic and charting service.

> "Knowing others is intelligence; knowing yourself is true wisdom. Mastering others is strength; mastering yourself is true power."
> – Lao Tzu

Again, when it comes to gaining access to the proper market information to fit your needs, being "cheap" isn't a good idea. You should be willing to open your pocketbook if it is necessary for your situation. On the flip side, don't be foolish; if you can get away with a Civic, there's no need to buy the Cadillac.

CHAPTER 5: CHOOSING A BROKERAGE FIRM

Deciding on a brokerage firm is often taken lightly, but I argue that this decision can have a large impact on the bottom line of your trading. You probably have already spent, or intend to spend, a massive amount of time studying market theory and strategy. Apply the same intensity to choosing the firm that will be responsible for executing and clearing your trades and handling the incoming and outgoing funds from your account. Most important, choose a firm that you trust will follow appropriate regulations set forth to safeguard client funds. Furthermore, the brokerage firm you trade with should display healthy financial standing and a relatively clear regulatory record.

> If you think commission is expensive, try getting what you pay for.

Before committing to a brokerage firm, it is essential that you conduct the proper research into its services. This includes experience, trading platforms, margin policies, and commission structure. Perhaps more important, determine whether your trading style and personality are compatible with the services the firm provides. For example, beginning traders shouldn't look to a deep discount online brokerage firm—they likely won't get the guidance they need as a novice. In this case, saving a bit of money in commission can mean costly errors in judgment and order placement. Similarly, a seasoned trader wouldn't want to choose a firm that focuses on high-end service with a hefty price tag because there is no reason to pay for services that aren't needed. In this case, the commission is "baggage" and could have a slightly negative impact on overall performance. However, it is important to realize that the real differences between success and failure generally lie in the trading itself, not the transaction costs. In fact, it is the trader himself who ultimately decides how much commission is paid to a broker when choosing how many contracts to trade.

Ideally, most traders are best off working with a firm that offers services on both sides of the gamut. This makes it easy for full-service traders to migrate to online trading while staying with the same broker. Also, discount online traders might want to employ strategies developed by a full-service broker within the same trading account to diversify risk.

A lot of talk among retail traders centers on the differences between trading with an Introducing Broker (IB) and a Futures Commission Merchant (FCM) and there seems to be a lot of misconception surrounding the topic. Hopefully, I can set the record straight and aid you in choosing the type of firm that best fits your needs as a trader and gives you the best value for your buck.

WHAT IS AN FCM?

The CME defines an FCM as an individual, association, partnership, corporation, or trust that solicits or accepts orders for the execution of a commodity transaction pursuant to the rules of a futures contract market and that accepts payment from or extends credit to customers. To the average trader, that means the primary function of an FCM is to represent the trading interests of individuals or firms who do not hold membership in the exchanges. Simply, an FCM is a futures brokerage firm.

> The primary difference between an FCM and an IB is the FCM's ability to accept and hold customer funds.

Briefly, FCMs accept money for deposit in a segregated account that clients can use toward the margin and capital required to buy or sell futures and options. As the world learned from the dramatic collapse of two prominent FCMs in 2011 and 2012, requirements to keep client money separate from brokerage firm money in a segregated account aren't guaranteed to be honored. However, following these events, the Commodity Futures Trading Commission (CFTC) and the National Futures Association (NFA) scrambled to improve the protection of customer money and institute auditing procedures to ensure proper execution of the regulations. I believe the actions taken by regulatory bodies were effective in mitigating the risk of another breach of the broker's fiduciary obligation and the client's trust when it comes to money management. Unfortunately, for the victims of these two events, it felt like too little, too late.

FCMs are also responsible for executing trades on behalf of their customers; clearing those trades with the exchange; and then communicating fills, statements, and margin requirements to customers. Most of this is done electronically and instantaneously.

You might have also heard an FCM referred to as a wire house, brokerage house and, my favorite, commission house. Some FCMs conduct business strictly in options and futures; others are involved in all types of financial investment transactions, including but not limited to stocks, bonds, and forex. Naturally, trading products and markets might play a role in the firm you choose. Firms offering stocks and bonds are known as broker/dealers and are subject to additional registration, licensing, and regulatory requirements. We discuss these types of firms later in the chapter, but I'm compelled to mention that the convenience of a "one-stop shop" is not necessarily the most efficient arrangement. In fact, I believe traders are likely better off working with firms that specialize in the particular asset they are trading, whether it be stocks, bonds, futures, or forex. This might mean maintaining more than one trading account at various brokers.

FCMs are required to become "registered member firms" of the futures exchanges and registered members of the NFA before handling or trading accounts in the corresponding markets. Most exchanges allow only individual memberships instead of firm membership. This usually means corporate officers or the like registering on behalf of their stated firms. As a means of achieving accountability, the named individual is responsible for the actions of the firm and its employees in terms of exchange regulation.

WHAT IS AN IB?

The textbook definition of an IB is a firm or person engaged in soliciting or accepting orders for the purchase or sale of futures contracts. In today's high tech world, this often means providing access to an appropriate futures trading platform and ensuring everything runs smoothly for the trader. IBs are subject to the rules of a futures exchange and regulatory bodies, but they do not accept money or securities to margin trades or contracts—that is the distinguishing factor between an IB and an FCM. The IB is associated with at least one correspondent Futures Commission Merchant and must be licensed by the CFTC; likewise, the IB must be a registered member of the NFA.

> Introducing Brokers are often thought of as small firms, but some have grown to be much larger than some FCMs.

The relationship between an IB and an FCM can most easily be described in terms of a subcontractor. An IB is, in essence, a miniature brokerage firm that is in business for the sole purpose of soliciting accounts for an FCM. The IB is then paid as a subcontractor and issued a Form 1099 at the end of the year. This is in contrast to a broker working directly for the FCM and paid commission; at the end of the year, the broker is issued a W-2. Not all IBs are small, though—some are very large, and many have even surpassed the size of some registered FCMs.

> Despite what your account statement suggests, if you trade with an Introducing Broker, your account is with the IB; the FCM clears your trades and holds your margin funds but generally won't provide one-on-one services or be familiar with your needs.

Simply put, an IB brings clients to an FCM. The FCM holds client funds for margin and executes and clears trades ordered by the IB or its clients. As briefly mentioned, an IB doesn't accept client money in its own name. Those trading with an IB are asked to make checks payable to the FCM or to wire funds directly to a segregated customer fund account in the name of the FCM. This requirement is a measure taken to prevent "rogue" IBs from accepting client money without actually delivering trading services and execution. To illustrate, if IBs were able to accept client funds for margining, it would open the door to a fraud in which the IB could pilfer funds from unknowing clients while issuing "fake" account statements or a similar style of deception. Thus, the stipulation of all funds flowing through the FCM prevents dishonorable brokers from becoming the focus of an episode of *American Greed*. It is also important to note that the CFTC and NFA regulatory bodies prevent FCMs from accepting ACH (Automated Clearing House) transfers to commodity trading accounts for the purpose of preventing money laundering. This is a distinct disadvantage of commodity trading accounts relative to stock trading accounts that are overseen by the SEC (Securities and Exchange Commission) and are granted permission to accept electronic bank transfers other than official Federal wires.

An IB often relies on the FCM for back-office operations including handling requests for outgoing funds, end-of-year tax form preparation for each trading account, execution solutions (trading platforms), fill reporting, and so on. Because customer statements and end-of-year tax reporting (1099s) are issued directly from the FCM, retail traders are often confused about who their broker actually is and where to go for help if an issue arises. A quality IB can efficiently assist you in many of the day-to-day activities, so make it a rule to refer to your broker (IB) first and your brokerage firm (FCM) second. Because your IB knows you personally and what your needs are, they are generally capable of offering more efficient and helpful service. Only after you are unsatisfied with the response or resolution of your IB should you escalate your concerns to the FCM.

Without fully understanding the relationship between an IB and FCM, brokerage statements can be especially confusing for those trading with an IB. A client account statement always includes the name, and likely the logo, of the FCM handling the account. The only reference to the IB is normally in relatively small text labeled with "Business Introduced By."

Justifiably so, beginning traders or those simply not familiar with the futures industry assume that they have an account with the FCM, when, in reality, they have an account with an IB in which margin funds are held at the FCM. In turn, the IB clears trades through that particular FCM. Keep in mind that your introducing broker is free to change the FCMs in which client trades are cleared and statements are issued, with only moderate hassles. If your IB decides to switch clearing firms, your account travels to the new firm in what insiders refer to as a *bulk transfer*. Unless you specifically object, your account stays with your broker and begins clearing trades through the new FCM. Simply put, you are the client of the IB and not the FCM, unless, of course, you want to change brokers.

If you are part of a bulk transfer, aside from having a different logo on your statement and perhaps a change in trading platform, you might not notice much of a difference in how your account is handled.

In some cases, it is actually possible for your IB to clear trades through more than one FCM. This type of IB is known as an Independent Introducing Broker (IIB) and is a much more popular arrangement in the aftermath of the demise of PFGBEST and MF Global because it offers IBs a way to diversify their business and enables clients to diversify their funds on deposit while working with an individual broker. Simply put, if a brokerage firm has clients dispersed among various FCMs, in the unlikely event of a brokerage failure to uphold segregation rules of customer funds, the impact on the IB and the clients will be less significant than it would be if the broker were an IB dealing with a single FCM. Accordingly, traders with larger accounts might find it comforting to spread their funds among different brokerage firms as a means of spreading risk against the unthinkable (a repeat of MF Global or PFGBEST).

Clients of an IIB also tend to have a much larger selection of trading platforms, relative to those of an IB exclusive to a single FCM. This is because each FCM typically has a suite of software for electronic trade execution, so simply having access to multiple FCMs opens the door to a nearly endless list of platform options. Similarly, most FCMs have some sort of specialty offering or areas in which they excel. A good IIB can guide clients to the appropriate FCM based on platform access and margining needs. In other words, using an IIB saves the client the hassle of doing the footwork and research required to find the best fit; because an IIB does this for a living they will be able to offer simple and effectual guidance to an otherwise overwhelming task.

I can personally vouch for the difficulty and frustration of determining the optimal FCM for each type of trader. Following our forced departure from being an IB of PFGBEST, we opted to join an already established IIB operation. This was a great way to give our clients flexibility and options, but we also learned that there is no such thing as a perfect FCM for all trading strategies. Instead, it took a considerable amount of research and bargaining with risk managers at each FCM to find a suitable home for various clients. For example, most FCMs prohibit or at least deter clients from selling options, while others charge high day-trading margins to prevent aggressive intraday trading, and yet others cater to the aforementioned clientele. Using an FCM that doesn't effectively accommodate a particular strategy will have a massively negative impact on trading experience and profitability.

I suspect that the average retail trader would have a difficult time determining the best arrangement and, more important, negotiating the terms in his favor. This is a good example of why it typically is not advantageous to open an account directly with the FCM. Despite conventional wisdom that suggests cutting out the middle man will reduce costs and simplify your experience, an IIB has more negotiating power than an individual trader. This might translate into more competitive pricing, fewer peripheral fees, priority support, margin call leniency, discounted margins, and the ability to trade strategies others are prohibited to partake in. This isn't unlike the ability for employers to get better insurance rates in a group plan than individuals can get on their own. In most instances, the convenience of using an IIB to shorten the learning curve in shopping for an FCM can be done without incurring higher fees or commission. So why not utilize such a service?

Going forward, we'll use the term "IB" to refer to both types of IBs.

WHAT IS A BROKER/DEALER?

By definition, a broker/dealer is an organization that trades securities such as stocks and bonds for itself or on behalf of its clients. When the firm is executing trades on its own behalf, it is said to be acting as a dealer; when it buys or sells securities for its clients, it is said to be acting as a broker. Although the primary business of such firms is dealing with traditional investment and trading vehicles, many have begun offering a limited array of futures and options on futures. Therefore, unlike IBs and FCMs, broker/dealers are also regulated by the SEC in addition to the NFA and CFTC.

I have found that some broker/dealers offering futures products are limited to a handful of the most popular futures and options contracts. They typically don't offer products outside the mainstream offerings, such as the E-mini S&P, the Euro, and crude oil. You might find trading agricultural futures and options either difficult or impossible and options traders will discover that not all expiration dates listed on the exchange are available to them. Broker/dealers often offer trading in the first two or three expiring options contracts but restrict trading beyond that.

Similarly, if you are interested in selling options on futures, a broker/dealer likely will require a substantial amount of funding above and beyond the margin requirement. I've heard of some instances in which a broker/dealer charged double or triple the exchange minimum margin for a short futures option. After all, commodities aren't their primary business, and for all intents and purposes, futures are offered to complement their bread and butter. Accordingly, in my opinion, most serious commodity traders are better off trading with a capable firm that is highly familiar with the futures and options trading arena. With that said, broker/dealers are popular for offering a convenient way to trade commodities alongside stocks. If you strongly feel that you are prepared to trade on your own, you won't be trading options, and you intend to trade the most commonly traded futures contracts, this *might* be a viable alternative to opening an account with a commodity brokerage.

FILL QUALITY

Despite what you might have heard or read regarding the disadvantages of trading with an IB instead of an FCM, I believe that the quality of service lies in the individual broker that you deal with rather than the compensation arrangement that your broker has with the clearing firm. As an online trader, orders are collected and routed in trading platforms identically regardless of whether your account is with an IB or FCM, but it is the individual broker who ensures everything is working smoothly and, for those trading on a full-service basis, will be in charge of efficient order execution.

All else being equal, aside from the talent and disposition of the individual broker you deal with, as a retail trader, you shouldn't see a significant difference in terms of service between working with a broker employed by an FCM or an IB. Again, the primary distinction between the two is as simple as the difference between a W-2 employee and a 1099 subcontractor. Electronic trade execution has done wonders for fill efficiency, and the benefits aren't rooted from the FCM; all traders enjoy them, regardless of their brokerage arrangement. After all, clients with an IB are placing orders on the same platform and via the same data server that a client trading directly with the FCM would.

> As long as you are trading liquid contracts through a reputable brokerage, market success and failure will be determined by client speculation, not a possible split-second difference in fill time.

Hypothetically, if you placed a market order to purchase an E-mini S&P futures contract at the market through the trading platform of an IB and simultaneously placed the same trade through an FCM, chances are, you wouldn't see a significant difference in the execution price. Any discrepancy in price would likely be better explained by your inability to pull the trigger at exactly the same time than by which brokerage firm services your account. However, significant differences in trading platforms might arise due to margin approval issues, as discussed in Chapter 4, "Account Access, Trading Platforms, and Exchange Data Fees." In reality, perhaps the most important aspect of being aware of fill quality only comes into play when something goes awry, not necessarily when things are going right. For instance, a brokerage that can quickly correct erroneous order rejections or place the rejected order immediately on the trader's behalf without incurring hefty fees can save clients far more money in the markets than they could ever save pursuing the lowest commission rates.

BEHIND THE SCENES OF TRANSACTION COSTS

A common assumption is that an IB is not capable of offering commission rates competitive with those of an FCM. This is often argued by the logic that an IB is essentially a "middle man" between the client and the FCM. Conventional wisdom suggests that more hands in the cookie jar will translate into higher costs to the consumer. On the surface, this seems to be a reliable argument; after all, brokers and brokerage firms are in business to make money, not donate services. If there are more mouths to feed, chances are that costs will be higher. However, this argument overlooks the fact that there might be more internal parties to be paid in an FCM, leaving a far smaller cut for the broker working at an FCM relative to an IB. Accordingly, FCM brokers might have an incentive to charge higher rates to clients relative to a broker working for an IB.

> Scratching beneath the surface, it becomes clear that brokers employed at an FCM often have incentive to charge higher fees that those of an IB.

As a retail broker who has worked under both arrangements, I argue that IBs might have the ability to offer lower transaction costs to clients than many FCMs, or more specifically, brokers employed at FCMs. I believe this to be the result of the common business practice of FCMs giving brokers the ability to set their commission schedules within preapproved boundaries, combined with the premise that FCM brokers are, in my opinion, often provided inferior commission payouts on a percentage basis relative to an IB.

The payout of a broker working directly for an FCM is typically predetermined and often involves a percentage structure in which the higher the rate charged, the more income for both the broker and the brokerage firm. In theory, the increased exposure and name recognition of being employed by an FCM should outweigh the difference in payout, but that argument is well beyond the scope of this chapter.

On the contrary, an individual who opts to become an IB is required to pay the clearing firm a predetermined flat fee for every transaction executed but isn't required to pay a percentage to the house, as an FCM broker is likely to do. In other words, for every commission charged to the client, the FCM receives an agreed-upon clearing fee, and the IB is paid a rebate in the amount of commission charged above and beyond the clearing fee paid to the FCM. This type of structure paves the way for more competitive commission rates for IB customers than FCM brokers would be able to offer.

I have found that IBs with multiple members have payout structures similar to that of an FCM but seem to be more broker-friendly. Keep in mind that this is simply an observation and is open for debate. With that said, a broker who receives a higher commission payout might be willing to negotiate more competitive rates without giving up his income potential. Accordingly, you might find that many IBs are very competitive in terms of transaction costs and even much cheaper relative to trading directly with an FCM.

In my opinion, there are no benefits to trading with an IB over an FCM or vice versa. The true value is in finding an individual broker who meets your needs; handle your account efficiently; and is capable of offering quality strategy reports, news feeds, and market analysis. Whether they realize it or not, even clients entering orders online have a broker assigned to their account. If you are an online trader and do not know who your individual broker is, he might not be earning his keep.

DISCOUNT BROKERAGE OR FULL-SERVICE SPECIALIZATION?

Not all brokerage firms are created equal. There are those that are in the business of providing clients with a blended array of services, to be a one-stop shop for futures and options traders. Yet others are dedicated to being extremely efficient at meeting the needs of one specific type of trader. Perhaps the most common focus of specialized firms is the distinction between full-service and deep discount brokerage services.

> Knowledge is the most valuable commodity.

To avoid the costly mistake of choosing a firm that isn't capable of providing the desired service, it is imperative that traders be honest with themselves. This requires a subjective look at skill level, market knowledge, and the necessities based on trading style. Being candid with yourself is sometimes difficult, but it is a must. How can you possibly choose what services are best for you if you are making the decision on something other than reality?

After you determine what you are looking for, you need to keep a few things in mind. Based on my observations and assumptions, I have found that as you move down the commission scale (from high rates to low rates), the adage "You get what you pay for" becomes more appropriate, but as you move to the extreme highs you are likely getting far less than what you are paying for.

In other words, paying $100 per round turn doesn't necessarily mean that you will receive extraordinary service or trading results. In fact, I believe it would be the opposite. A broker charging extravagant commission rates is likely sub-par and must charge higher rates to make up for his lack of clientele. Conversely, if you are paying 99 cents per side, you will likely get what you pay for, which is very little; a platform and a support phone number with a long hold time and a clerk at the other end with few answers or problem-solving skills.

Paying next to nothing and receiving a level of service appropriate with the costs isn't always a negative. Experienced traders with adequate market knowledge, familiarity with trading platforms, a reliable internet connection, and no day job, might be comfortable without having someone to lean on. If this is the case, there is no reason to pay for service that you won't use. Yet, I believe traders are best off seeking a brokerage with reasonable rates attached to significant value rather than simply seeking out the lowest rates. There will come a time in which even the most experienced traders will need speedy support from their brokerage services (internet outages, flash crashes, etc.). Without a competent broker, such an event could cost a trader hundreds, or even thousands, of dollars.

A deep discount brokerage is often staffed with less than experienced brokers who might not have the knowledge or network of contacts (risk managers, platform vendors, etc.) to help you through your predicament. However, history suggests that this can be a painful lesson to learn and, in many cases, can be avoided by simply using a full-service broker until you're properly acquainted with the markets, or at least trading online with a firm that is capable of backing you up in dire predicaments.

Internet connection failures can and do happen. Envision yourself without internet access. After calling your deep discount brokerage firm, you find yourself on hold waiting for a representative. Meanwhile, your open positions are quickly eating away at your trading account. Finally, after the clerk on duty offsets your trades, you discover a desk fee of $25 to $60 per contract for placing a phone order. This is a rather extreme circumstance, but it is important to realize that it is a realistic scenario and it happens repeatedly. Depending on your needs, it might be worth paying slightly more in commission in an attempt to avoid "paying" far more in market losses.

If you do not fit the description of an experienced and self-sufficient trader, I strongly recommend that you seek services that might be slightly more expensive in terms of commission but potentially much cheaper in regards to trading mishaps or a lack of helpful strategy guidance and research. In essence, saving a minuscule amount of money on a round-turn commission doesn't compare to a large amount of money at stake if you make an error in judgment, trade placement, or experience a technology failure.

In addition, being correct in market speculation is only half the battle. The commodity markets are full of intricacies that create landmines for inexperienced traders. For example, imagine inadvertently entering a highly illiquid market and experiencing trouble offsetting your trade. Exchanges will reject market orders if there isn't anyone to take the other side of your trade; it can be helpful to have a broker to get you out of a jam by calling the exchange floor to locate someone to make a market for you and offset your mistake. Unfortunately, I have seen this scenario play out on several occasions. A common trap that beginners fall into is placing a trade in one of the NYMEX soft contracts instead of the much more popularly traded ICE versions, or entering the wrong contract month or year. Just one false click of the mouse or stroke of a key can mean disaster for your trading account.

In conclusion, you need to be aware that your broker earns a living through the commission. During times of high volume, volatility, and stress, brokers are sometimes forced to consciously choose which issues to conquer first. It is irrational and naïve to believe that a broker will approach the situation with anything else but the intention to take care of those that "take care of him" in the form of commission. For the best experience, you should be prepared to pay a reasonable rate based on the level of service that will be required to give you the best probability of success—nothing more and nothing less.

WHAT YOU SHOULD KNOW ABOUT COMMISSION STRUCTURE: BLANKET OR VARIABLE RATES?

A concept that many beginning retail traders overlook is the burden of risk that a brokerage firm and even an individual broker face simply by opening a client trading account. Aside from the normal business risks such as litigation or economic drawdowns, a futures and options brokerage firm faces the risk of client default. The risk primarily stems from the fact that, in the world of commodities, it is possible for clients to lose more money than is on deposit in their account. As a result, opening a futures trading account is a lot like applying for a credit card or an auto loan.

Before you can effectively determine what is and isn't a fair commission rate based on your personal characteristics and service needs, you need to understand a side of the business that you likely haven't taken the time to consider. Little, if any, written resources cover this aspect of commodity trading, but as an industry insider, I feel that understanding what goes on behind the scenes is crucial.

CLIENTS ARE RISKY

Like a majority of brokers in this industry, I have gotten to experience the anguish of a client account going negative (losing more than is on deposit). The experience might be psychologically devastating to a trader but is equally stressful to a brokerage firm and the broker personally responsible for the debit account balance, at least until the client sends funds to cover the deficit. Broker liability is the dark side of the industry that most are unaware of. Before you make the decision to trade beyond your means, think twice about the damage that you could do to innocent parties, along with the pain and suffering that you might cause yourself.

The brokerage firm is expected to cover any negative balance with the exchange immediately, and this often translates into commission withholding from the individual broker in the amount of the negative balance. As you can imagine, large debit balances can mean several months without pay to a commodity broker. In essence, brokers are potentially responsible for the trading decisions that their clients make, regardless of whether they played a role in the demise of the account. It isn't necessarily fair, but we all know that nothing in life is fair. With this known, it is easy to see that any commission charged is partly attributable to the risk of a negative account that the firm is facing by taking you as a client.

After the client refunds the account to bring it to a positive balance, the brokerage firm typically releases the withheld commission. In extreme cases, such as those in which the client cannot pay the monies owed, the broker might find that the sins of her client were permanently paid by her commissions. This liability remains even though the broker wouldn't have shared in the profits had the outcome been different. Simply put, the ultimate risk is put on the party that doesn't stand to share in the glory if it occurs.

> Along with servicing client accounts, brokers are compensated in the form of commission for accepting the brokerage firm's risk of carrying that account.

Naturally, the broker and the brokerage firm will do everything within their power to prevent a client account from suffering a negative balance. This is simply because when an account loses more money than is on deposit, the client is essentially trading with money "borrowed" without permission from the brokerage firm. Likewise, when an account loses more money than it was funded with, a client who refuses to pay the balance to bring the account into good standing with the exchange should expect legal ramifications from the brokerage firm.

On a side note, if a brokerage is charging bottom basement commission rates they have no tolerance for risk and behave accordingly. Thus, traders using such a service should expect trading restrictions and forced liquidations should positions go against them. Charging clients a reasonable commission rate will act as a buffer to risk management and enable the brokerage to give clients more freedom in their trading strategies and risk appetite. Again, when it comes to commission you will get exactly what you pay for, and sometimes the cheapest commission is the most expensive in regard to market losses.

COMMISSION SHOULD BE BASED ON CLIENT RISK AND NOT A PREDETERMINED FLAT RATE

With the risks posed on the brokerage firm and individual broker, the commission charged to clients should depend on the deemed level of risk that an account poses. As with any other industry, risk and reward are highly correlated. Along with this premise, reckless and undercapitalized traders should be charged a relatively higher commission rate. Although a brokerage's firm's primary business is executing trades and the firm welcomes business and traders of all types, it should also think like an insurance company.

> Flat-rate commission structures enable low-risk traders to subsidize the transaction costs of high-risk traders.

To prevent low-risk policy holders from subsidizing high-risk policy holders, insurance companies collect the personal data and characteristics of each applicant to determine an appropriate premium according to the perceived risk. In short, this practice creates an environment in which each policy holder is paying for the coverage rendered, nothing more and nothing less.

In the absence of risk profiling, blanket premiums would create a socialistic system in which all participants carry the same costs, regardless of their potential claims. To illustrate, if this were the case, a devoted smoker would be paying an identical amount of money for an identical health insurance policy provided to an avid jogger. The smoker would be getting a great deal and would be paying less than his policy was worth, based on the inherent risks to the insurer. The jogger, on the other hand, would be overpaying the actual worth of the policy to compensate the insurer for the risk of others. I believe that resourceful brokerage firms, whether an IB or an FCM, should create a similar model in determining the commission schedule of a firm. Rewarding negative behavior is an inefficient business plan for futures brokers and, in the long run, will have a negative impact on the firm and the firm's clients.

Unfortunately, the characteristics of a trader aren't always black and white; they most often come down to verbal claims instead of concrete evidence. However, brokers should casually collect certain pieces of information before determining what they believe to be an appropriate commission rate.

Account size is often a large contributor in determining an appropriate commission rate. All else being equal, a trader with a large account poses less risk and is more valuable to the broker than a trader with a relatively small account. Therefore, in most circumstances, a trader with a larger account deserves a lower commission rate than one with a smaller account. However, this isn't a clear-cut rule. I have witnessed traders with large accounts trade in a manner that poses a great deal of risk to the broker and the brokerage firm. Again, highly aggressive traders should face higher transaction costs due to the danger they present to the firm.

Trading style is another component often used to determine commission structure. This is often something that might be determined after the account has been open and trading. For instance, a trader who has a well-funded account and typically uses approximately half of the available margin on a given day is a relatively low-risk client. On the other hand, a trader who is constantly pushing the limits in terms of margin exposes the trading firm to a substantial amount of risk. Similarly, long option–only traders are exposed to limited risk, and so are their brokers; they should be provided a discount commission accordingly and short option traders should pay a relatively higher commission rate to compensate the brokerage for the unlimited risk the strategy poses.

Understanding these basic concepts of commission and how brokerage firms assess risk, it should be obvious that, in most cases, trading with a firm that offers a flexible rather than fixed commission structure is preferable. Fixed commission structures lead to inefficient policy in which some clients subsidize the risk of others, and vice versa.

REAL-TIME ACCOUNT STATS, TRADING PLATFORMS, AND MOBILE DEVICE ACCESS

The options and futures markets move quickly, making it imperative that traders have efficient logistics in trade execution. What exactly this means is dependent on the time horizon and strategy of the trader, but traders should think about it long before it comes time to begin speculation.

If you are a position trader using options or futures, fancy trading platforms shouldn't be a high priority, but online account access should be. For position traders, simply having the means to easily place trades and monitor the account and market prices is sufficient (preferably on both a computer and a mobile device). There is no need to complicate things unnecessarily.

On the contrary, as discussed in Chapter 4, if you are scalping or doing any other form of day trading, the front-end platform that you use to enter trades becomes important. Not only must the platform be quick and easy to use and understand, but it also can't be so quick and easy that mistakes are highly probable.

It is highly recommended that traders test-drive a prospective platform. Most platforms are offered in live demo versions in which you can practice order entry and trade monitoring to determine which is more suited to your needs before you commit real money.

Market access is most convenient when it is available on any device anytime. This can be achieved if the brokerage offers traders the ability to execute trades and keep tabs on their accounts via a web-based trading platform, a mobile device, and a downloaded desktop application. With such a setup, a trader can easily trade on the go. The web platform makes it easy to access the market on vacation from any computer and the mobile device is great for viewing markets from the car, at work, or even in bed. In my opinion, this type of widespread market access is not only ideal but necessary.

MARGIN POLICY

Many traders fail to realize that although the exchange sets minimum margin requirements, individual firms and brokers have the right to ask clients for additional funds to be on deposit. As mentioned previously, brokerage firms and brokers are subject to a considerable amount of risk for each client they accept. This liability can sometimes be incentive to increase margin requirements above and beyond what the exchange specifies. This process is known as *padding margin* and is particularly true of brokerages whose commission rates are highly discounted and simply cannot afford to accept standard client risks.

With that said, futures and options traders are attracted to this arena by the availability of leverage without the costs of borrowing securities or funds as you would need to do in a stock trading account. Therefore, retail traders should be concerned with finding a brokerage firm that can margin their account based on exchange minimums. Even traders who use the leverage granted conservatively can find themselves in an adverse market move; whether a brokerage pads margin or not might be the difference between receiving a margin call and squeaking by without one. In Chapter 12, "Coping with Margin Calls," we revisit the concept of margin and leverage in greater detail. Nevertheless, I'm compelled to mention two areas concerning margin in which the brokerage firm you choose will make an immense difference in your trading results.

> Margin is something that you want if you need it. However, just because you have it doesn't mean that you should use it.

DAY TRADING MARGIN

In Chapter 12, we discuss the fact that traders who offset their positions before the close of trade each day face lower margin requirements than those who hold positions beyond the close of a trading session. Most traders assume that trading with a brokerage firm that is willing to offer lower day trading margins makes sense. After all, they are giving you the freedom of more leverage without additional costs. However, this is flawed logic simply because things are not always as they seem on the surface.

Beware of firms that advertise ultra-low day trading margin rates; smoke-and-mirror tactics often are in play. For instance, some deep discount brokers focused on attracting high-volume day traders advertise $300 to $500 margin rates on some products (usually stock index futures). However, the same firms often shave client positions as they see fit if the firm's risk management team gets "uncomfortable" or, worse, outright liquidate the entire account at their discretion. Trust me, the risk-management department isn't concerned with the price they liquidate your trade. They simply enter a market order to exit without considering anything else. Some brokerage firms go as far as to blindly liquidate their clients' accounts, regardless of the trader's wishes, near the close of each trading session to avoid any overnight risk and ensure margin calls aren't triggered.

These types of firms might also have a knockout policy. A knockout occurs if a client loses a stipulated percentage of the trading account in a single session. For example, if the knockout is 60%, a client who started the day with $10,000 and draws down to $4,000 would be automatically liquidated and locked out of the account. This might not be such a bad thing, but it shifts control away from the trader and to the brokerage firm, and that is always undesirable.

In essence, the risk-management tactics used by firms that advertise highly discounted margins completely mitigate any potential benefit the additional leverage offers. To sum it up, ultra-low margin rates are simply a ploy for brokerage firms to increase trading volume; in the end, the increased brokerage commission revenue is at the expense of the trader. Although they are a luxury, when choosing a brokerage firm, ultra-deep margin discounts for day traders should not be on the top of the list of priorities.

SHORT OPTION TRADING MARGIN

Short option margin policies can be highly complex, making it unfeasible to discuss details within this book. Nonetheless, if you plan on trading options at all, the first question you should ask prospective brokers is whether they have any restrictions for short option traders and option spread traders beyond the exchange minimum margin requirements. For instance, several commodity brokerage firms have developed strict—and, in some cases, unreasonable—margin policies to deter clients from participating in a short option or spread strategy. Other firms outright forbid the practice and some go as far as to not offer options trading in any form.

In my opinion, such firms are foolish. I believe that option selling has the potential to provide traders with the highest probability of success while facing far less overall risk than most other strategies. Accordingly, it is in your best interest to choose a brokerage firm that will allow you to sell options at your discretion, as long as you are obeying exchange margin requirements. Even those who do not intend to sell options early in their trading careers should ensure that they have the freedom to do so simply because the markets are dynamic, and your trading approach should be also.

BEYOND YOUR BROKER

Having non-trading issues with your account can be provoking. After all, trading itself is a high-stress endeavor; the last thing you need to worry about is a mishap with your wire, your statement, or your trading platform. Trading is a game of emotions, and a good brokerage will do everything possible to keep anxiety factors of its clients at a minimum. Their ability to minimize unnecessary problems and quickly alleviate those that do occur can make a difference in your bottom line.

CUSTOMER SERVICE AND BACK-OFFICE OPERATIONS

We all know fear and greed are the two biggest emotions in trading, but another one is often overlooked: frustration. Expecting to be unaffected psychologically by an unorganized, inefficient, or simply incompetent customer service department is unrealistic. Unfortunately, difficulty in handling the behind-the-scenes aspects of your account can easily have an adverse impact on your ability to focus on trading and, ultimately, the results of your efforts.

A well-functioning customer service department enables you to focus on trading simply by being well informed and capable of meeting your needs in a timely manner. The trick is to determine whether a customer service department is efficient before your account has been open long enough to experience its capabilities or shortcomings.

It is a good idea to browse internet forums and message boards in search of ratings and comments on a prospective brokerage firm. Those looking to trade with an IB should be looking for information on the quality of customer service provided by the FCM *and* the IB. As the client of an IB, you will primarily be dealing directly with your broker, but the FCM must be able to deliver when called upon.

You wouldn't commit to purchasing a car without taking it for a spin. Similarly, consider test-driving the support staff. Simply call and/or email with general questions about services. A great way to do this is through a simulated trading account. As you work your way through the trading demo, you probably will find yourself wanting to ask questions, and this is the perfect time to do just that. Doing so can give you a good idea of the extent of the staff's knowledge, the promptness of their replies, and their ability to problem-solve.

TECHNICAL SUPPORT

In a day and age of electronic everything, it is absolutely crucial that traders have access to a properly staffed and knowledgeable tech support staff. Without the ability to resolve technical issues in a timely and effective manner, you can find yourself in an extremely frustrating situation.

> Time is money, especially when you are on hold.

Put yourself in the shoes of a trader who, minutes after entering a market, experiences a frozen (inoperable) trading platform. Most firms offer 24-hour trade desks, making it possible for you to simply make a phone call to exit the trade; if you are with a firm that doesn't offer this service, or does but implements an unreasonable fee to use it, I strongly recommend that you reconsider your business there. However, upon exiting your trade, you would want an immediate resolution to your issue; without it, you might be missing opportunities in the markets, and this can be both financially and psychologically devastating. Trading is difficult enough; the last obstacle that you want in your way is an ineffectual technical support staff.

As with customer service, determining the quality of a tech support staff is a challenge without having an open trading account to experience the service in real time. However, you might want to go as far as to ask your prospective firm approximately how many people make up its tech support department.

You might be taken aback by the answer. I have known sizable firms to have small technical support departments. One- or two-member staffs might be adequate for smaller firms, but this is likely not enough to meet the needs of a considerably large firm.

I recommend opening a simulated trading account with a firm to access its technical support department and experience what it has to offer. A common symptom of a small technical support staff is long hold times while trying to reach a representative by phone. Delayed responses to email inquiries also might be a red flag.

CONCLUSION

Choosing the right brokerage firm is a big step toward success and should be treated as such. However, whether you are an online trader or a full-service client, your ultimate experience might be largely influenced by the individual broker that handles your account. An experienced broker can deliver efficient execution, recommend proper trading platforms, and provide excellent service regardless of whether she works for an IB or FCM. With that said, don't forget that IBs, specifically IIBs, generally offer clients more platform, clearing, and margin choices. Although it isn't as fulfilling, you should be researching brokerage firms and prospective brokers nearly as much as you research the markets. In Chapter 6, we talk about some of the most important factors in determining which broker best fits your trading needs.

CHAPTER 6: FINDING A BROKER THAT FITS AND CHOOSING A SERVICE LEVEL

> The broker you choose could have a profound impact on your trading results.

Too many beginning commodity traders focus on trading platforms, margins, and commission when it comes to choosing brokers to service their accounts. Unfortunately, the quality of information provided, such as newsletters and educational material, comes in at a distant third. Worse yet, most traders never even consider inquiring about the hours their broker is available to answer questions, place trades, or provide account maintenance services; further, nor do the traders question their ability to do so efficiently and effectively. Believe it or not, these aspects are critical even for those who enter their orders online without the help of a full-service broker.

Leaps and bounds of progress forged in trading technology, combined with an improved flow of information, have many beginning traders overlooking the benefits of a full-service broker. As a result, most new trading accounts are opting for self-directed online service. In other words, many traders prefer to bypass the broker and enter their orders directly through an online trading platform. However, I argue that an experienced and competent broker can make a profoundly positive influence on the trading experience of beginning traders and should be considered for those who simply aren't comfortable with placing trades on their own, prefer to have someone to offer a second opinion, or simply aren't adequately familiar with contract symbols and market characteristics. Of course, as time goes on and a trader becomes familiar with the commodity markets and becomes more comfortable with the process of placing orders directly through a platform, it makes sense to downgrade the service level and become an online trader.

Despite what you might have been led to believe, full-service commodity brokers are not obsolete and probably won't be anytime soon. Yet, their role has changed dramatically. The differences in commodity point values, exchange procedures, trading hours, and such among the various commodity contracts surround the markets with a cloud of mystery that can be best unraveled with the help of an experienced broker.

> Lower commissions and online trading access haven't improved the odds of success that retail traders face.

Likewise, those who choose to open a self-directed online trading account can likely benefit from having a proficient broker available in emergencies as a backup plan, an occasional opinion on strategy, margin help, or for quick and easy support. Many traders assume that if they trade online, they don't have a broker. In most cases, this is untrue. The brokerage business is a commission-based industry; accordingly, even online traders were brought to the firm by a broker in some capacity even if it is merely the person who happened to answer the phone when a trader called to establish a trading account. That person is likely earning a commission every time a trade is executed and, under most circumstances, is responsible for meeting the needs, wants, and desires of a trading account (within reason, of course) in exchange for a piece of the commission. Naturally, the better equipped this person is, the better the experience will be for the client.

With this said, traders of all types and desired service levels want to make sure that they have a knowledgeable broker to rely on, not necessarily one who is willing to agree to the lowest commission rates. Choosing a broker is a good example of "You get what you pay for," and sometimes saving money now might mean paying more down the road in the form of trading mishaps or improperly handled tech support and customer service issues. While trading, time is literally money!

Supporting my claim that less service at a cheaper rate isn't always better is the fact that the retail trader hasn't managed to improve his odds of success over the years. Based on my research and assumptions, I have found that the average retail trader has consistently been a net loser in the world of options and futures trading. Unfortunately, lower commissions and self-directed trading haven't improved the success rate. Some might argue that it has made things worse for the retail trader. Lower transaction costs tend to encourage overactive trading. Trading too much dramatically lowers the odds of success and, ironically, it wracks up a substantial commission bill a few dollars at a time.

Whether you open a full-service or self-directed online trading account, it is necessary to take the research one step beyond commissions, margins, and trading platforms. As mentioned in Chapter 5, "Choosing a Brokerage Firm," traders must choose a brokerage firm that can meet their needs based on the parameters discussed; however, the decision-making process doesn't end there. It is even more critical that an individual broker is chosen based on the feasibility of efficient communication, the trader's comfort with the experience of the proposed broker and, most of all, faith in the broker's ability to help the trader on his journey to being successful.

Once again, choosing the person you will be relying on for properly executing your trades, acting as the backup for your online order entry, and handling your account isn't a decision to be taken lightly. Several key points, including the background of the individual, are critical in the decision-making process. Here is a closer look.

UNDERSTAND YOUR BROKER'S BUSINESS

The media often paints a different picture, but believe it or not, being a futures and options broker has few perks...unless, of course, you are at the top of your game. Because the brokerage industry is commission-based, no limitations constrain how much or how little a broker can make. Those willing to put forth the effort can make a respectable living; those who aren't would likely fare better on unemployment benefits.

> Be sure your broker works for you, not just the commission.

For many brokers in the commodity industry, the hours are long, but it is easy to see how people can become addicted to the excitement of the markets. Being a successful broker entails an open mind, a constant yearning for information, and a commitment to provide unparalleled service. Not only that, networking with FCM support staff, research providers, margin departments, and other industry insiders to ensure proper execution, the flow of information, and leeway on margin calls for clients is imperative to success in this field.

A big concern facing the industry is that brokers are provided incentives in the form of commission. Those brokers who are short-sighted and fail to employ a long-term business plan are tempted to churn commission paid by

> "Goodness is the only investment that never fails."
> – Henry David Thoreau

clients by encouraging them to overtrade their accounts, without always holding to the best interest of the client. Naturally, you are venturing into futures and options in hopes of your own success, not your broker's. It is my goal to provide you with the knowledge you need to avoid the frustrating and costly mistake of hiring a broker with ulterior motives. On a side note, many of the most egregious examples of churning I've witnessed have been self- inflicted by online traders and have nothing to do with the broker on the account.

THE 80/20 RULE

In the world of commodities, and perhaps most incentive-based industries, roughly 20% of the brokers make 80% of the money, and vice versa. This is an opinion, not a proven fact, but I can tell you that I haven't seen any evidence to prove otherwise. It is my guess, and hope, that the 20% of the brokers who do enjoy success are doing so by providing their clients with the service they deserve at a reasonable price.

Ironically, I have found that many of the brokers who approach their clients aggressively in terms of promoting high volume or implementing a high commission rate in an attempt to generate excessive revenue fall into the 80% of brokers who struggle to survive. You can take a few steps to evaluate whether your broker fits your needs as a trader and is qualified to earn your business.

WHAT IT TAKES TO BE A COMMODITY BROKER

You might be disappointed to discover that the only requirement to becoming a commodity broker is a passing score on a proficiency exam administered by the Financial Industry Regulatory Authority (FINRA) and written by the National Futures Association (NFA). The exam is known as the Series 3. Don't get me wrong; the test is somewhat challenging and does require some market and regulation knowledge, but the hurdle seems to be low, considering the responsibilities that come with passing the test.

| Lack of knowledge breeds risk. |

With the bar set so low, many new commodity brokers have made their way to the industry from completely unrelated career paths and backgrounds. For example, I have witnessed people ranging from chiropractors to window washers enter the commodity brokerage business with no formal training. Even more surprising, I've seen Craigslist ads published by deep discount commodity brokerage firms seeking "experienced sales people" with "no market experience necessary" to fill their broker seats.

Granted, coming from unrelated fields doesn't mean that they aren't capable of brokering in options and futures. In fact, some of the most honest and hard-working brokers that I have known started out as inexperienced in finance and trading. However, it does mean that you should pay attention to their background and judge their ability to service your needs accordingly.

I am not providing this information to trigger doubt in the system, but as a potential commodity trader, I feel that this is an important realization. After all, you have likely seen the movie *Trading Places*; the film paints a much different picture.

GET TO KNOW YOUR FUTURES BROKER

You probably wouldn't choose a business partner if you haven't established the potential for efficient communication, don't have confidence in that person's ability to bring something positive to the relationship and, most of all, don't have mutual trust. Why would you think of choosing a broker without considering these things? Even online traders should be asking themselves this question. Trust me, if you ever need to bypass the platform and go to your broker for execution, guidance, or margin help, you will be glad you did your homework. Fast-moving markets are merciless; time is money and each second counts!

Becoming familiar with your broker before you ever begin trading is a significant step in the right direction. The vital areas of concern are educational background, experience in the industry and, most important, general market knowledge. A college degree in finance isn't necessarily a reason to open an account with someone, nor is the fact that a broker has been in the business for 20 years. Considering these factors in conjunction with a well-rounded grasp of market characteristics and proper lines of communication is key. For instance, I provide clients with access to me via phone, email, instant message, and SMS text message 15 or more hours per day during the week and, in most cases, on the weekend. The markets don't sleep, so having access to proficient support personnel is key to mitigating collateral damage caused by technical issues or an inability to understand market specifications. The ability to email a broker to quickly confirm the positions and working orders in your account is immeasurable.

You should be able to determine whether a broker fits your needs and personality with a 20- to 30-minute conversation. During this time, don't be shy. If the broker wants to do business with you, she must answer your questions, assuming they are sensible.

USE AVAILABLE RESOURCES

After you identify a possible candidate for a brokerage firm and individual broker, I encourage you to visit www.NFA.Futures.org to research your choice. The NFA is a regulatory body of the futures and options industry and offers investors complimentary background information on brokers and firms. Unfortunately, many traders are simply unaware of this valuable resource.

> "If a man empties his purse into his head, no man can take it away from him. An investment in knowledge always pays the best interest."
> – Benjamin Franklin

The NFA's website offers access to a database known as BASIC (Background Affiliation Status Information Center). BASIC contains CFTC (Commodity Futures Trading Commission) registration and NFA membership information, such as the length of a broker's time in the business as a registered member of the regulatory bodies and a list of any regulatory actions. Listed actions include NFA arbitration awards and CFTC reparation cases involving the broker. The same information exists for a brokerage firm.

It is important to realize that listed CFTC reparations do not infer guilt. A displayed claim might have been settled, dismissed, or withdrawn but will be on the BASIC record of the broker for as long as the database is available. As you can imagine, although the intent is to protect investors, it can sometimes result in false assumptions about the ethics of some industry insiders.

I recommend that you confront your broker to discuss any possible infringements of regulation or ethics. After all, it is your money, and you deserve to fully understand the caliber of person that you will be hiring to help you find your way around the futures and options markets.

The NFA's online BASIC database also provides traders with information on any NFA arbitrations. Unlike the previously discussed CFTC reparations that involve a possible infraction of regulation, NFA arbitration is a dispute resolution forum. Naturally, you want to know whether your broker might have been party to questionable practices in the past. However, again, it is only fair that you get your broker's side of the story; simply being part of an arbitration hearing might not translate into any wrongdoing.

WORK ETHIC

Having convenient access to your broker is an important step toward successful trading. Even if you are an online trader, if something goes wrong, you don't want to go through the stress of being unable to reach a knowledgeable party to straighten out the situation.

As a prospective client, you want to test the broker by simply communicating via telephone, email, instant message, and maybe even SMS text. If she is hard to get hold of or slow to return your inquiries, consider shopping around for another broker. Many brokers take long lunches and consider themselves off duty when the closing bell rings and they leave the office. However, this doesn't make themselves available for their clients. In my opinion, traders paying anything other than bottom-basement commission rates deserve better. I'm not picking on traders who opt to do business with deep discount brokerage houses, but the reality is, if the broker is making a nickel or less each time you trade as deep discount brokers do, he cannot afford to answer your questions; he will be too busy trying to bring in other clients.

WORK EXPERIENCE

When shopping for a broker, I believe that it's a good idea to put yourself in the role of an employer. To fully trust the person you will be working with, you can't have any looming uncertainty. If you were managing a restaurant, one of the first things you would require applicants to provide is a list of prior employers. Why wouldn't you extend the same scrutiny to the person you will be hiring to aid you in trading your hard-earned money? I believe that judging the quality of a broker's skill is difficult without also knowing his employment background.

Naturally, you don't want to be irrational in your quest for information. A general idea of work experience is enough to properly evaluate the service you will be paying for. Remember, the only requirement to being a commodity broker is passing the Series 3 exam. Again, although the proficiency exam is challenging, the standard isn't set incredibly high. I am not trying to discourage you from having faith in the industry; I simply want you to keep your eyes open to the realities and encourage you to know who you are dealing with.

TRADING BACKGROUND

Don't be afraid to ask prospective brokers how long they have been involved in trading. Don't assume that your prospective broker's experience is equivalent to the NFA registration data displayed on the NFA's BASIC database. It is highly possible that a broker has been involved in the markets before registration and is relatively distant to the markets while being registered.

Don't be immediately turned off if your prospective broker isn't currently trading a personal account; many currently registered brokers are forbidden to trade accounts in their own name and maybe even for friends and family. For obvious reasons, a personal trading account is seen as a conflict of interest. As a result, brokers often have to take a back seat in their trading. It is also important to realize that your broker is often left slightly behind the curve when it comes to trading. For example, preferable fill allocation on a bulk ticket (a single order with multiple contracts to be allocated to multiple accounts) always goes to the client, leaving the least favorable fill to the broker. Similarly, brokers not entering trades on a bulk ticket must always execute client orders before their own. Clearly, this rule is in place to protect the client, and I don't think that anyone could argue that the intention is flawed. Nonetheless, these and other rules and regulations act as deterrents for brokers to trade. Further, a broker's income is in many ways tied to his ability to provide clients with successful trading ideas and guidance. Accordingly, in an indirect way, a broker's income is always at risk and, therefore, similar to a large and never-ending "trade."

I do choose to trade a personal account but I do so on a small scale to ensure my emotions aren't interfering with my ability to service my clients. Nevertheless, I participate in the recommendations I make to clients via our trading newsletter, *The DeCarley Perspective*. In my view, it is only fair that I have some skin in the game if I am going to call out trades.

TRADE EXECUTION

Speculation is a difficult venture, and many obstacles to success are beyond your control. Yet, increasing your odds of proper trade execution is one aspect that you can dictate if you do the proper research when choosing a broker. Ideally, you want to choose a broker who offers execution through

> Trade online, but do it with competent backup!

multiple methods, including a capable suite of trading platforms offering market access via downloaded desktop software, a web application, and a mobile application.

Recognize that, with electronically traded contracts, very little, if any, difference exists in fill quality between brokerage services—assuming that the platform used to enter the trades is reliable, of course. Yet, it is beneficial to have an experienced order taker available, who preferably accepts orders by phone and electronically (text message, instant message, email). Such a luxury is priceless when dealing volatile and leveraged markets; it should not be overlooked.

HELP IN CHOOSING A TRADING PLATFORM

The greatest part about technology is that it gets cheaper, faster, and better with each day that passes. As a result, the futures and options on futures industry has bred a seemingly endless array of execution platforms for traders. Unfortunately, with choice and features comes confusion. Most trading platforms have a specialty in that they cater to specific types of traders such as day traders or options traders. Other platforms are sufficient for all traders but don't necessarily excel in any particular area. Adding to the anxiety, each trading platform is backed by an FCM (the brokerage firm that handles your money, levies margin policy, and issues statements) or, in some cases, a platform is compatible with several FCMs and the client chooses which arrangement is appropriate.

Most beginning traders might not be capable of choosing the platform and clearing arrangements. Even those who think they've done their research and know what they want will likely discover unintended consequences of their decision. For instance, a day trader choosing a platform because of fancy features, low margin rates, and low commissions might discover the brokerage firm "shaving" contracts off their position size at their discretion, or flattening the trading account at 3:00 p.m. Central sharp, with no regard for price or the trader's opinion.

Having access to an experienced broker, as opposed to a salesman or clerk, when it comes to choosing a platform can do wonders for reducing frustration and improving the bottom-line results.

MARKET RESEARCH

Collecting and analyzing market fundamentals, seasonal tendencies, and technical factors can be a time-consuming and overwhelming process. I've found that traders might be better off letting their broker do the legwork for them. For instance, several brokers and brokerage firms publish daily market commentary and trading strategy reports. This type of convenient research can cut the workload of traders considerably while simultaneously exposing them to market news and trading ideas. Although these types of informational sources are highly beneficial for traders, it is important to be an objective reader. Even the best trading newsletters can be wrong in price predictions at times. Similarly, access to all the fundamental statistics available doesn't guarantee success; the market doesn't always comply with common sense.

> "In this business if you are good, you are right six out of ten. You are never going to be right nine out of ten." – Peter Lynch

CONSIDER THE FUTURE

The commodity industry is known for its transient nature. Make sure your prospective broker is in it for the long haul before you invest too much time in the relationship. Unfortunately, the opportunities in the futures and options markets attract attention from individuals with a get-rich-quick mentality. Those privy to the industry understand that this perception is the furthest possible from reality. Nonetheless, traders, system vendors, and even brokers often insist on learning the hard way. Accordingly, many commodity brokerage careers are cut short by the harsh realities of the business.

If your broker leaves the firm or the business, your account will be assigned to another executive. You might or might not have a choice in the matter. Thus, you want to be sure that you choose an established broker who intends to remain in business for quite some time.

FULL-SERVICE BROKER OR SELF-DIRECTED ONLINE TRADING?

The decision to trade either online or through a full-service broker will undoubtedly make a large impact on your bottom line. However, the impact might or might not be what you had in mind. If you aren't ready to begin placing your orders online on your own, despite saving money on commission, it could be the most costly mistake you ever make.

Although commission expense is baggage, paying a slightly higher rate might be worth every penny, assuming that your broker is truly giving you what you are paying for: reliable and efficient execution, along with quality guidance in strategy and analyses.

Hopefully, this section opens your eyes to the realities of transaction costs. Although experienced traders should look for reasonable rates with quality service, novice traders can benefit greatly from the hand-holding of a good broker. In this case, commission paid can be thought of as an investment rather than an expense.

> If paid to the right broker with the right motives, commission is an investment rather than an expense.

If a broker guarantees that you will make money trading with him, I recommend that you hang up the phone. There are no guarantees in options and futures trading, yet an ethical broker will provide exceptional service at an equitable price to ensure that you are provided the best opportunities and odds of success. Additionally, in many circumstances, the amount of commission paid, or not paid, doesn't normally have an impact on whether you are profitable in the long run.

SOMETIMES LESS ACTUALLY IS MORE

If you are an experienced trader, there is no reason for you to pay hefty commissions for a service that you may not need. Placing self-directed trades online is economical and efficient, and if you're ready, you should take advantage of every opportunity to do so. With that said, on occasion, you will need support and having a contingency plan is imperative.

Sometimes you are away from your computer, out of cell phone coverage, or are experiencing technical difficulties and need assistance in placing your trade. A quality brokerage firm will enable you to place your trade through a broker or trade desk during such times with little or no financial consequences. Deep discount brokers deter clients from placing phone orders by charging excessive "desk fees." In some cases, a trader could easily spend more on desk fees during the infrequent times he needs assistance than he saves by opting for a "cheap" commission rate in the first place.

Although most brokerage firms specialize in either full-service or discount online accounts, several well-rounded firms enable traders to enter trades via an electronic platform and also allow them to contact a broker if they need trading, margin, or strategy advice from time to time. This type of hybrid arrangement is essentially the best of all worlds: It provides traders economical and efficient execution without making them give up the benefits of a full-service broker. With that said, firms that pride themselves in offering the cheapest commission won't have the manpower or experienced staff to offer such a service. Therefore, unless you are proficient in all things markets and believe your network and computer equipment are indestructible, it is often a good idea to avoid choosing a firm simply because it can give you the lowest transaction cost. You would be surprised how far a little trading support can go toward happy and profitable trading.

FULL SERVICE DOESN'T HAVE TO BE EXPENSIVE

People tend to assume that full service is synonymous with expensive. Although this is sometimes true, it doesn't have to be. Some brokerage firms charge excessive commissions and fees; however, a good brokerage firm understands that higher transaction costs detract from the client's ability to profit and, in turn, prevent the client from becoming a long-term customer.

Be wary of firms that offer set commission rates to all clients, regardless of size, experience, volume, and account size. As discussed in Chapter 5, doing so results in a scenario in which certain types of clients are indirectly subsiding the trading practices of others. This logic can be compared to an insurance company that collects the same life insurance premium for a 60-year-old smoker and a 30-year-old athlete. Just as insurance firms realize that this type of practice isn't equitable to its policy holders, brokerage firms must adopt a similar policy. A quality brokerage firm understands that the needs of each client differ, and the cost of trading should reflect these discrepancies. In addition, firms that offer blanket commission schedules are likely cutting corners in other places, too.

Only you can decide how much commission is too much to pay. However, you can't argue with the bottom line. If you rack up a large commission bill and your account isn't making progress, you might question whether it is worth it. On the other hand, you must also be aware of how much of your account drawdown is due to commission and how much can be attributed to trading losses sustained by your own hand. More important, are the excessive commission costs due to high round-turn charges, or is your trading volume simply out of hand? The easiest way to lower your trading costs is to trade less!

Be honest with yourself about whether the trading might have been better or worse without the help of your broker. This is difficult to do. By nature, we are always looking for someone or something to blame for poor trading results, and your broker is an easy target. Conversely, if you were able to negotiate a low commission rate at a discount broker but are losing money, it is fair to say that you might be better off paying a little more for better service and support.

IS YOUR BROKER WORKING FOR YOU OR FOR YOUR COMMISSION?

There's a big difference between a broker who works for you and one who is simply looking to collect a transaction cost. If you feel as though your broker is putting his best interests ahead of yours, don't be afraid to confront him. It is your money, and you should be completely comfortable with how you and your account are handled. This premise goes for online trading accounts as well (with the exception of deep discount brokers who make a penny or two per trade and have no reason to offer clients anything other than access to a trading platform).

Unfortunately, because the brokerage industry thrives on commission, it can be easy for account executives to succumb to the pressures of generating income *now*. After all, they have bills to pay, too, but I think we all agree that your broker's financial stability shouldn't have an effect on the trading in your account. I would like to think that brokers with this type of mentality are the exception rather than the rule, but it is important to fully understand the potential motivations behind the industry to avoid, or at least recognize, a compromising situation.

WHY USING A BROKER'S ASSISTANCE MIGHT BE A GOOD IDEA

Many traders have a propensity to avoid commission without considering the consequences beyond saving a few dollars or cents in transaction costs. For instance, I have witnessed inexperienced traders lose several thousand dollars in the markets without blinking an eye but argue over 50 cents in commission. Similarly, I have been approached by traders who have offered to write a check to me for several thousand dollars in exchange for tutoring, yet they weren't willing to open a brokerage account with me because they could save a dime per trade somewhere else. Some quick math reveals that it would take a lot of trades to equal the money saved in commission that they were willing to pay me up front to teach them. Being knowledgeable and wise about the choice you make in terms of service and commission is commendable, but don't be foolishly stubborn. You get what you pay for—if you pay the right person, slightly higher transaction costs in the short run might actually save you money in the long run.

Always remember, the goal of trading is to make money, not to save it.

AVOID OVERTRADING AND PANIC LIQUIDATION

Working with a broker might mean having someone to bounce ideas off and hold your hand through good times and bad. Under most conditions, the trading decisions made in your account should be yours, but you can't deny that your broker will have an influence. If you are with the right account executive, it should be a positive influence.

> "I wish it grew on trees, but it takes hard work to make money."
> – Jim Cramer

This isn't to say that a good broker will always be right; remember, there are no crystal balls. Nevertheless, a second opinion from seasoned professionals can be priceless. They have the luxury of keeping fear and greed out of the decision-making process and hopefully have the market experience that you are paying for through commissions to aid in their advice.

Additionally, online traders are often tempted to trade unnecessarily by executing orders in multiple contracts or simply lacking the patience to wait for a proper opportunity. Those who choose online trading to save money in commission often end up paying far more in transaction costs due to a higher trading volume—often destructive trading. I've worked with some traders who have found placing orders by phone with an experienced broker to be an effective tactic in preventing them from succumbing to the human tendency to overtrade and take on too much risk. It might also work against the emotional toll of decision making because having someone to talk to keeps traders grounded.

SHIFTING RISK OF ORDER PLACEMENT

You have likely heard the old adage, "Don't trip over dollars chasing pennies." This is the best way I can explain the idea of traders pushing themselves to trade using a trading platform without the help of a broker before they're truly ready.

One of the biggest benefits of using a broker is that it shifts the risk of error in trade placement from yourself to your brokerage firm—or, more specifically, your broker. Too often a trader placing orders online does so to save a minimal amount of money in transaction costs, but the result can be expensive errors that can dwarf any potential transaction cost savings. After all, the minimum price tick in most futures contracts equates to several dollars while potential commission savings from firm to firm is a mere fraction of this.

If you aren't completely comfortable in your knowledge of the markets and trades, trading without the help of an experienced broker isn't wise. I can't emphasize enough that mistakes can be costly. I have seen online traders lose hundreds or thousands of dollars simply because they were unprepared for online trading but insisted on saving a few dollars in commission. Examples of common mistakes are unknowingly executing trades in extremely low-volume markets, buying or selling the incorrect number of contracts, selling instead of buying (or vice versa), placing a stop order when it should have been a limit (or the other way around) and, most destructive, overtrading.

Many of the mistakes that inexperienced online traders make stem from a lack of emotional stability. Whether looking to get out of a trade gone badly or seeking to take a profit on a well-speculated position, exiting a market can be psychologically challenging. I have witnessed many traders mistake wheat for corn (yes, it happens) or confuse buying and selling when it comes to verbally or electronically offsetting holdings. It sounds strange that anyone would mistake a buy order for a sell order, but it happens frequently. Beginning traders often equate selling with exiting the trade; if the trader is long, he would sell to offset his position. However, if the trader is short, he must buy back the contract to exit, not sell it.

A trader with a large profit or loss can often become disoriented in the heat of the moment. A good broker can't save you from yourself, but he might eliminate some of the risks by being aware of your positions.

Conversely, if you call your broker and ask her to buy July corn at the market and she inadvertently sells a contract, she is responsible for making your account whole again. In other words, your broker must liquidate the accidental position, execute your order properly, and compensate you for any damages incurred, including the commission charged on the mistaken trade. Of course, if you tell your broker to buy July corn at the market and she does, the rest is left to your ability to speculate, the timing of your exit, and fate.

MARGIN CALLS

Although most retail traders don't fully understand the exchange's method of margining short options and option spreads known as SPAN (Standard Portfolio Analysis of Risk), a seasoned broker should. Putting a monetary value on the ability to relieve a margin call without wiring money or completely liquidating positions is difficult, but take it from me, it is substantial. Possible margin adjustments might include buying or selling options as a hedge against current positions, or it might involve purchasing or selling futures to do the same. If you are unaware of the mechanics of SPAN, working with a broker will be well worth the commission paid if you ever get into a tight margin situation.

COMPANIONSHIP

This might sound corny, but many traders find that the people they are closest to have either no interest in, or no knowledge of, the trading world. Thus, having a full-blown trading conversation with friends and family can be hard, but your full-service broker will always be there for you.

CONCLUSION

The commodity industry has something for everyone; as a retail trader, you are free to choose your own transaction costs through both trading behavior and broker selection. Keep in mind that when you choose a commission rate, you are also choosing a service level. Absolutely nothing is wrong with negotiating an affordable commission rate, but be sure you are prepared to operate with the associated level of service.

Saving money in commission can actually be more expensive in the long run than paying a full-service broker or paying a slightly higher discount online commission than the basement rate. This is because a substantial amount of risk is involved in trade

> "Things may come to those who wait, but only the things left by those who hustle." – Abraham Lincoln

execution and market speculation. If you aren't comfortable with your knowledge of the markets and trading platforms, as well as your psychological stability when it comes to trading, you and your account might be an accident waiting to happen. Nevertheless, if you are an experienced and well-informed trader, you should be looking to trade online at a reasonable rate; don't pay for service that won't help you reach your goals.

CHAPTER 7: ORDER TYPES AND HOW TO USE THEM

Being familiar with order types and when to use them can make a profound impact on trading results. Market prices and dynamics are ever changing, making every second count. Regardless of whether you trade online or through a broker, knowing the type of order you need to place and placing it accurately is vital.

Later in this chapter, I discuss proper phone order etiquette when placing trades with a broker or a trading desk. Whereas an experienced full-service broker can typically translate the intent of his clients, an order taker at a trading desk can't—and it isn't a good idea to leave anything to chance. Knowing exactly what you want and how to communicate your wishes is critical.

ORDER TYPES

If you've done your research, you have likely come across excessive lists of "exotic" order types but not all order types are accepted in all markets, nor are they appropriate. For all intents and purposes, order types that you should be comfortable with are a *market order*, a *stop order,* and a *limit order*. Generally speaking, the others are more useful in academics than they are in reality. However, I go over some of the others for the sake of being thorough.

MARKET ORDER

The *market* order is likely the most commonly used because of its convenience and the lack of uncertainty involved. A *market* order is a request to execute a trade at the best possible price at that particular time. In other words, the trader is agreeing to sell at the bid, synonymous with taking the other side of the best buy limit order. If the trader's intention is to buy, a *market* order agrees to pay the ask, which equates to taking the other side of the best available sell limit order. We discuss the details of limit orders later in the chapter.

In most cases, a market order guarantees that you will receive a fill, but it doesn't guarantee that you will enjoy the price. Sometimes the best possible price at the time of the order isn't the best price for your trading account. Beware of markets with low volume and large bid/ask spreads; in such markets, a market order can result in an unfortunate fill price. Also, if a market is so thinly traded that nobody is willing to take the other side of your market order, the exchange will reject it.

This happens only in extreme cases of illiquidity and is a sure sign that you shouldn't be trading that particular market anyway. The exception to this rule is options trading; nearly all options markets will reject *market* orders placed to buy or sell a particular option. Option traders should always place limit orders to enter and exit a position.

If a *market* order to enter a *futures* trade is rejected for this reason, it is a blessing in disguise. If it were an order to exit an already open position, it would be an unnecessarily stressful and a potentially expensive predicament to be in. Once again, I don't recommend trading in futures markets that aren't capable of providing the liquidity necessary for seamless entry and exit via *market* orders.

Traders who place market orders have little control over the fill, but they do control the timing. In electronically executed markets such as the E-mini S&P, fills are instant. As you can imagine, the lack of transparency in open outcry trading environments caused a considerable amount of anxiety for those entering *market* orders. Nevertheless, most exchanges and contracts abided by a policy stating that a *market* order must be filled within three minutes of reaching the floor broker's hands. Even then, sending a *market* order into the trading pit was an uncertain and stressful event.

WHEN TO USE MARKET ORDERS

Although they should not be used in markets that have low levels of volume and open interest, *market* orders are useful when time is of the essence. Specifically, the trader feels as though ensuring that the order is filled is more important than stipulating the fill price. If a trader feels strongly about being long or short a particular contract, a *market* order might be the optimal entry choice because missing the trade isn't an option.

LIMIT ORDER

A *limit* order is often called an "or better" order because it is a request to initiate a trade at a specific price *or better*. The phrase "or better" is meaningful in many ways, some being less than obvious. First, *or better* has a different meaning for buyers than it does for

> A *limit* order is synonymous with an "or better" order.

sellers. A better price for a buyer is a lower price, whereas a better price for a seller is a higher price.

Don't make this simple concept more difficult than it is. Many beginning traders I speak to unnecessarily confuse themselves when it comes to *limit* orders. From the buyer's perspective, using a *limit* order in the futures or options market is no different than putting in an offer to buy a car or a house.

As a buyer, it would be better for you to pay less for the car. Therefore, after you issue your final offer, you are claiming that you will pay the stated amount or less, but no more, to purchase the car. You are probably thinking to yourself that it is rare to purchase a car for less than your offer, and you are right to be suspicious. Similarly, it is also relatively rare for a *limit* order to buy a futures contract to get filled at a better price than what is asked for, but it does happen from time to time.

From a seller's standpoint, the more he can sell the car for, the better. Therefore, the final offer that a salesman puts on the table is an agreement to sell the car for the stated price or more, but no less. As you would expect, the seller typically doesn't have the opportunity to sell a car for more than the named price but is happy with the offered price.

> "When I have to depend upon hope in a trade, I get out of it." – Jesse Livermore

Let's go back to a commodity example: If a trader places a *limit* order to buy a September soybean futures at $9.95, the order states that he is willing to accept being long only from $9.95 or less. In other words, the trader would be happy to receive a fill price of $9.95 and would feel rather lucky to receive a better price. If the same trader wants to place a profit target after being filled in the previous example, he might place a *limit* order to sell September soybeans at $10.05. In this case, his instructions are to fill the order if it can be executed at a price of $10.05 or more, but not less.

Thus far, I have ignored an important point about an "or better" order. Contrary to what many assume, if the market reaches your price but never surpasses it, you are not owed a fill. If this happens, you might or might not receive a fill. This is because the bid/ask spread typically prevents an order from being filled at the *limit* price without the market trading beyond it. Using the previous example, if the high of the day in September soybeans were $10.05, the trader might have been filled on the *limit* order, but if he wasn't filled, he has no grounds for a complaint because he isn't owed a fill. In other words, the trades at that price might have been buys, not sells, in which a market maker was on the other side, or perhaps only a few contracts traded at that price and there weren't enough to go around to fill all working orders. *Limit* orders are typically treated on a first-in, first-out basis, so if a trader is last to enter an order at a specific price, he would be the last owed a fill. However, if the market ticks higher to $10.05'2 ($10.05 and one-quarter of a cent), he is owed the fill, and most likely it would have been reported. It is often said in the business that it "has to go through it to do it."

WHEN TO USE LIMIT ORDERS

Limit orders can be useful, but you need to understand that their purpose shouldn't be greed. I recommend that traders use *limit* orders as profit targets, or as entry prices, if they are looking for the market to travel a significant distance from the current price at which they would like to enter, or if they are trading a market with considerable bid/ask spreads such as options on futures.

In my opinion, *limit* orders should not be used as an attempt to save a small amount of money. With the exception of scalpers, if a trader truly wants to be long or short a market, saving a tick on the entry price likely won't have a profound impact on the overall result. On the other hand, missing the trade altogether can.

Imagine thinking that the E-mini S&P is going to rally sharply in the near term. With the market trading at 2,405.25, you place an order to buy a futures contract at 2,405.00, assuming that the natural ebb and flow of the market will allow you to enter the market at a slightly discounted price and, in turn, cover the cost of commission and fees. Now imagine the gut-wrenching feeling that overcomes you as you watch the market soar to 2,425.00 without you because your limit buy at 2,405.00 wasn't filled—or "went unable," as insiders would say. In this example, you would have missed a potential profit of 20 points, or $1,000, while attempting to save a few dollars.

The moral of the story is that if a tick—in this case, $12.50—isn't going to make a large difference in the profitability of your trading strategy, then it isn't worth the risk of not getting filled on a *limit* order. Simply put, if $12.50 will keep you out of a market, you likely aren't comfortable enough with the position in the first place and should look elsewhere for opportunities. Options traders, on the other hand, might find *limit* orders much more useful due to the breadth of the bid/ask spreads. In some option markets, the bid/ask spread is a substantial cost of executing a trade. Therefore, a practice known as splitting the bid is common. When traders split the bid, they place a *limit* order at a price between the bid and the ask, hoping that the market maker will budge in price and fill the order; in many cases, this does happen.

One of the most illiquid and difficult markets to trade options in is copper. For example, if a trader attempts to purchase a $3.00 call option in copper, she might find that the bid/ask spread is 2.00 bid at 4.00—in other words, it would cost 4 cents in premium to buy the option, and the seller would receive two cents in premium. With each penny representing $250 of profit and loss to the options trader, you can see that the intrinsic transaction costs are large. For this trader, it seems worthwhile to enter a *limit* order at 3 cents (splitting the bid) as a means of potentially reducing the cost of entering the market. In doing so, he will accept the risk of not getting filled. However, the potential savings of $250 might be substantial enough to justify placing a *limit* order instead of paying the market price. Nevertheless, markets with significant bid/ask spreads such as this are often better left untouched.

STOP ORDER (A.K.A. STOP LOSS)

A *stop order*, often referred to as a *stop loss* or simply a *stop*, is an order to execute a contract at the market price when a specified price is reached. This might mean that the market trades at the *stop* price—or, more specifically, when the price falls within the bid/ask spread, at which time the ticket essentially becomes a market order.

Contrary to popular assumption, a *stop order* can be placed as a means of either entering or exiting a position. In most cases, stop orders are used to defend open positions from losses beyond the stated point or simply an attempt to lock in profits up to the stipulated price. However, some traders use *stop* orders as a method of entering a market after it has broken some sort of price barrier, with the anticipation of a continuation of the move.

Unlike a *limit* order that requires the price to become favorable before a fill is owed, a *stop* order requires that a market price become unfavorable before the trade is executed. For instance, a *buy stop* order would be placed at a price that is above the current market price, and a *sell stop* order should be placed below the current market price. As you can see, the buyer of a contract on a *stop* order will be filled only if the price goes up (unfavorable), and the seller of a contract on a *stop* will be filled only if the market goes down (unfavorable).

Because *stop* orders become market orders after the listed price is reached, the possibility of undesirable slippage on the fill exists. In other words, your fill price can be different than the *stop* price you originally named. In theory, the slippage can be favorable or unfavorable, but throughout my experience, I have found that *stop* order slippage almost always works against the retail trader.

WHEN TO USE STOP ORDERS

As mentioned, *stop* orders are most commonly used as a means of exiting a trade gone badly or to lock in open profits in an existing trade. Imagine a trader long a December corn futures contract from $3.45; he may decide that it would be prudent to place a *stop loss* order at $3.10 to liquidate the position if the market goes against the original speculation in the amount of 35 cents. Assuming that this trader was actually filled on his *stop* at $3.10, the total loss would be $1,750: (35 × $50).

Many traders rely on *stop* orders to remove some of the psychological anguish involved in pulling the plug on a bad trade. Without a working *stop* order, some traders don't have the ability to take a loss and can end up letting a small loser turn into an account-devastating trade.

On the contrary, a *stop* order can also be used to enter a market. This strategy is often used by breakout traders who are anticipating the market to continue to move in the current direction following the penetration of technical support or resistance. Let's take a look at an example.

Markets generally spend most of their time trading in a range; many traders believe that the best time to make money is during the time when markets break out of their price envelope. In Figure 11, a trader might have recognized a tight trading range in crude oil futures and opted to place a *buy stop* order above the price channel at

$55.60 and a *sell stop* order beneath it at $53.40. This trader doesn't have a preference in the direction of the market; he simply wants to catch a ride if it breaks either support or resistance. The trade will only get filled on an order if the price of oil surpasses either of his working *stop* orders.

Figure 11: Breakout traders often use stop orders to enter a market, in hopes that the underlying move will continue. (Chart courtesy of QST)

Keep in mind that when one of the stop orders is filled, the trader must cancel the other order to avoid confusion and accidental fills. Most electronic trading platforms are capable of orders in which you can instruct the platform to cancel one order if another is filled. A full-service broker also would likely be willing to do this for you. These types of orders are known as OCO orders, or "One Cancels the Other," and are discussed next.

TRAILING STOP

A trailing stop order is a stop loss order that moves in specified increments as the underlying futures market moves in the desired direction. Such an order is designed to help a trader either reduce risk or lock in profits without the hassle of manually canceling the original order and replacing it with a stop order at the new price. After all, not everyone can stare at the quote screen all day long. This automates the profit of revising stop loss orders.

Each platform is slightly different in regards to how trailing stops are placed and carried out, but they all have some sort of buffer or delta increment that trails the stop with favorable price movement. To illustrate, if you enter a trailing stop loss in the E-mini Dow Jones futures contract at 21,375 and a buffer of 10 ticks to protect an existing long position. Each time the mini Dow moves higher by 10 ticks, the stop will also move higher by 10 ticks.

If the mini Dow declines, the stop will not be adjusted. Thus, if the market moves from 21,385 to 21,395 the stop would move to 21,385 (10 ticks above the original stop price), but if the E-mini Dow declined back to 21,390 the stop loss order would remain at 21,385. The order would not trail again unless the mini Dow moved 10 ticks above the previous high (21,405); at that time the new stop loss order would become 21,395.

Traders should always be aware of how their platform treats trailing stops. Particularly, where the instructions of the trail are housed. For instance, if the trailing stop order is housed on the trader's local computer it will not trail if the computer loses internet connection, is shut down, or the trader logs out of the platform. If the trailing instructions are held server-side (on the server of the platform vendor or broker), they are operational regardless of whether the trader's computer or platform is running.

WHEN TO USE A TRAILING STOP

Trailing stops are most useful to day traders wishing to continually reduce risk and lock in profits as their position moves favorably. Such traders might set their trailing stop to adjust higher with every tick of positive price movement. On the other hand, position traders with "day jobs" might also find trailing stops handy in that they are likely unable to monitor the markets on a constant basis. Having a trailing stop can prevent a scenario in which a market makes a largely favorable move while the trader is out of touch and reverses before the trader can react. In short, this order type reduces the chances of a winning trade turning into a losing trade due to a lack of constant supervision. That said, it is important to clarify that position traders must confirm the platform they intend to use to implement trailing stop loss orders holds the instructions to trail stops on the server, not the local computer. As a reminder, if the software holds the trailing stop on the local computer, it must be online for the trail to occur. As a result, internet or power outages, or even accidental log-offs, could result in unfortunate surprises. In such an instance, the stop order wouldn't cease to exist but it would cease to trail.

STOP/LIMIT ORDER

The "stop/limit order" is perhaps the most confusing order type there is. The name implies that it is somehow both a stop and a limit order, but that isn't the case. It is actually a stop order with a catch. Essentially, this is a stop-loss order in which the trader states how much slippage he is willing to accept. This might seem like a wonderful idea, but it has the ability to cause plenty of heartaches.

An example of a stop/limit order might be to sell gold at $1,185.00 on a stop/limit of $1,183.00. This is a stop order to sell gold at $1,185.00 but only if the order can be filled at a price above $1,183.00. Generally, this order would be filled at a price much better than $1,183.00 anyway, but the trader is stating he won't accept slippage beyond that point.

WHEN TO USE STOP/LIMIT ORDERS

Never, *never* use stop/limit orders trading futures. If the futures price trades through the stop/limit price without the possibility of filling it within the trader's stated slippage "limit," the order dies. As a result, the trader who attempted to limit his stop order slippage by placing it as a stop/limit suddenly has no stop order working at all and is, therefore, subject to theoretically unlimited risk. You can imagine the horrified surprise of some traders when they check their account after waking up in the morning to find complete carnage. This order type is the equivalent of picking up nickels in front of a moving steamroller. That said, the futures exchanges stipulate the maximum slippage a stop loss order, or even a market order, can experience. Thus, in essence, all stop orders are stop/limit orders but the amount of possible slippage is dependent on floating ranges based on market volatility. Nevertheless, interfering with the optimal slippage limits by placing a stop/limit order is asking for trouble.

ONE CANCELS THE OTHER (OCO) OR BRACKETS

An *OCO* order is referred to as a contingency order because it requires that the broker—or your trading platform—cancel one of your orders if the other is filled. An OCO order can consist of a combination of any order type but most often involves a stop order and a limit order intended to exit an existing position. For instance, a trader long crude oil from $44.00 might enter an OCO order consisting of a stop loss at $43.75 and a limit order at $45.25. This creates a scenario in which the trader is stopped out with a loss if crude oil falls to $43.75 or takes a profit at $45.25 if oil rallies to the noted level. In any case, once one of the two orders is filled, the other is canceled. You might also hear this referred to as a bracket order. Although bracketing the market is the most common use of an OCO order, there are several possible combinations of linked orders such as the futures strangle (see Figure 11).

It is worth noting that most platforms are only capable of accepting OCO orders in the same commodity and expiration month. In other words, a traditional OCO order might involve a bracket as previously discussed but it would not be possible to place an OCO order consisting of an order to buy natural gas or sell crude oil, but not both.

WHEN TO USE OCO ORDERS

An OCO order makes trading more convenient and helps to avoid erroneous fills resulting from failure to cancel working orders that you no longer desire to be executed because another order has been filled. As mentioned, they are typically used by traders who want to manage an existing position by placing a profit target (limit order) and seek protection against an adverse market move (stop order). Let's look at a detailed example.

Using the previous example, a trader short crude oil from $53.40 as the result of an OCO futures strangle (a buy stop and a sell stop in the same market in hopes of entering the market on a breakout) might enter a bracket OCO to exit the new short futures position (Figure 12). Had the trader placed an OCO consisting of a buy *limit* order at $49.00 to lock in a profit and a buy stop order at the entry price of $53.40 to limit risk, he would have been filled at $49.00 to lock in a profit of $4,400 before transaction costs. The buy *stop* order at $53.40 would have been automatically canceled once the buy *limit* was filled. Had the trader failed to enter the order as an OCO and, instead, placed it as two separate and free standing orders, the buy *limit* would have been filled first at $49.00 but failure to cancel the buy *stop* would have resulted in an unintended long position from $53.40, which could have been catastrophic to the trader if he was unaware of the trade. Crude oil later fell to $45.00; this would have been a loss of over $8,000!

Figure 12: OCO orders prevent traders from becoming unintentionally long or short the market due to failure to cancel orders working to exit a position that no longer exists. (Chart courtesy of QST)

On a side note, because an OCO order is an instruction to a broker or a capable platform to automatically cancel the unfilled order, a broker assumes a substantial amount of responsibility with this type of order and will likely do so only on either a full-service basis or a not-held basis via a trading platform. This simply means that, in extreme market volatility, if the platform is unable to cancel the appropriate order in time, traders cannot hold their brokerage responsible. Such instances are rare but worth being aware of.

ONE SENDS THE OTHER (OSO)

An OSO—or *One Sends the Other*—order is similar to an OCO order in that it stipulates that the platform, or the broker, initiate an order based on the status of another order. Not surprisingly, this too is referred to as a contingency order because its execution is contingent on a certain event occurring. Unlike the OCO order, which cancels an order if another is filled, an OSO order sends an order for execution if another is filled. For instance, a trader wishing to enter a market on a sell stop order in hopes of a continuation of a price decline following a break below a specific price level might place an OSO order instructing the platform to enter a buy stop order to mitigate risk should prices reverse higher.

WHEN TO USE OSO ORDERS

A trader entering a position using a limit order can simply place their corresponding stop loss order at the same time as the limit order is placed. This is because a trader wishing to buy a futures contract at a price lower than the current price knows that he could not possibly be filled on a sell stop order below his trade entry price unless his limit order was filled first. To illustrate, a trader wishing to buy corn on a limit at $3.90 and to place a stop loss order for risk management at $3.85 knows he cannot possibly be filled on the stop loss order unless the entry order is filled. Thus, both orders can be placed simultaneously without any stress or risk of being filled on the stop order before entering the trade. However, a trader wishing to buy corn with a stop order working at $3.95 to enter the market with a risk-management sell stop at $3.85 would use an OSO order to avoid being filled on the sell stop before actually entering the trade. Only when the entry order buy stop is filled will the risk-management sell stop be placed.

MARKET IF TOUCHED (MIT)

This order is similar to a stop order, in that it becomes a market order when the specified price is "touched." However, it is also similar to a limit order because a sell order is placed above the current market price and a buy is placed beneath. In other words, this is a special type of limit order. The trader isn't simply asking for a price or better; the trader simply wants to be filled at the best possible price if the market hits the stated MIT price.

WHEN TO USE MIT ORDERS

Many platforms accept limit orders, but few accept MIT orders. This is because, unlike limit orders, MIT orders are subject to unfavorable slippage. Nonetheless, if you are provided the opportunity to take advantage of MITs, they can be useful if you're looking to buy at a lower price or sell at a higher price and are more interested in getting a fill than getting an exact price. Remember, with a limit order, the market must go through it to do it, reducing the odds of a fill but MIT orders are filled if the stated price is simply touched.

FILL OR KILL (FOK)

These orders are limit orders submitted to be executed immediately and in full, or canceled. With this order type, traders are unwilling to accept a partial fill. Either all contracts requested are filled, or the order dies.

WHEN TO USE FOK ORDERS

I have been in this business for a considerable amount of time and can count on one hand the number of times I have placed an FOK order. Accordingly, many online trading platforms simply don't support this order type. However, for traders who are day trading—or, more specifically, attempting to scalp market prices—this might be a viable option, assuming that the performance of the strategy being utilized can be significantly altered by a tick or two in the fill price and, of course, the trading platform supports this order type. For example, a trader who enters the market with the objective of gaining only two ticks in price but is trading large multiples of contracts to make the two-tick profit substantial might find FOK orders useful. Such a trader might wish to buy or sell 100 contracts but isn't interested in being filled on a quantity less than 100.

FOK orders are sometimes used by option traders who attempt to execute a trade by placing a limit order to split the bid/ask spread. In a sense, they are telling the market maker, "Here is the price I am willing to pay—take it or leave it." This might also be a viable order in extremely illiquid futures markets with a wide bid/ask spread.

IMMEDIATE OR CANCEL (IOC)

An *Immediate or Cancel* (IOC) order is nearly identical in nature to the FOK order. The primary difference is that a trader who enters an IOC order is willing to accept a partial fill, whereas a trader who placed an FOK does not accept partial fills.

WHEN TO USE IOC ORDERS

Similar to the use of FOK orders, IOC orders are normally used by extremely short-term day traders. Because their intention upon entering the market is for very modest gains, a single tick in the entry price or missed entry might have a significant impact on the performance of a trade. However, those interested in using IOC orders might be trading high numbers of contracts. For instance, a trader wanting to buy 100 E-mini S&Ps might rather get a fill on some or most, as opposed to none of them.

MARKET ON OPEN (MOO)

A *Market on Open* (MOO) order is an order to buy or sell a named contract at the best possible price on the open of trade. In open outcry markets, MOO orders were executed in the opening 3 minutes of trade but in electronic markets, trading platforms simply enter an order to buy or sell at the market price in the opening seconds of trade.

Keep in mind that with the advent of 24-hour markets, "the open" of trade can be left to interpretation and those placing MOO orders should clarify with the broker accepting the order. For instance, most markets open for trade in the afternoon for what is considered to be the next day's business, but the official day session open is considered to take place at a noted time in early morning trade. You should confirm the opening and closing time your trading platforms use to execute MOO orders beforehand.

WHEN TO USE MOO ORDERS

Many commodity traders prefer to use MOO orders as a means of eliminating some of the guesswork in entering a market. If they had conducted an extensive amount of research in the evening or over a weekend and feel confident in being long or short a market, they might use a MOO order to execute a trade. Such an order takes away the risk of not being filled on a limit order or the agony of staring at a quote board deciding when to pull the trigger.

On the other hand, many traders are reluctant to use MOO orders due to the potential price volatility that can occur during the first few seconds of a trading session. MOO orders might be subject to volatile and unexpected fill prices. However, it seems as though, in the end, favorable and unfavorable fills might end up being a wash relative to attempting to time trade entry in early trade.

MARKET ON CLOSE (MOC)

A *Market on Close* order, most often referred to as a MOC order, is one in which the trade is executed within minutes, or seconds, of the close (usually the last 30 seconds). If you wish to execute a MOO or a MOC order in a platform that doesn't offer this order type but does have the ability to enter timed execution orders, simply place an order to execute the trade about 30 seconds before the close of the session; or in the case of an MOO order, 30 seconds after the open.

WHEN TO USE MOC ORDERS

We now know that 24-hour markets have blended the boundaries between trading sessions. Nonetheless, futures traders most often use MOC orders as a method to avoid overnight risk. Because many of the commodity markets trade virtually 24 hours per day, many traders are not able or willing

> When a trader becomes a prayer rather than a player, the odds of a positive outcome are slim.

to hold positions and the corresponding risk beyond the confinement of a single trading session. Similarly, several brokerage firms that specialize in high-leverage day trading force-liquidate all client positions before the close. In other words, they do not allow their clients to carry overnight risk and utilize MOC orders to exit their client's trades at the end of each day.

Some traders, although perhaps not wise traders, use MOC orders to liquidate positions necessary to meet margin calls. Frankly, when they become over-leveraged and under-margined, they hope that any incremental exposure to the market will improve their position and, thus, their margin deficit. However, I have found that this type of wishful thinking often does more harm than good. Waiting until the last possible minute to exit a position to satisfy a margin call usually implies that the trader has gone from being a player to a prayer, and nothing good can come of that.

CANCEL (STRAIGHT "CAN")

Canceling an order completely eliminates a previously placed order. In today's electronic markets, the cancellation takes place immediately, but in open outcry markets, it took a considerable amount of time to confirm order cancellation and some orders were reported as filled because it was "too late to cancel." Most traders now will likely never encounter the challenges of trading open outcry, but those who trade options might, so it is worth noting.

Electronically traded markets provide traders with instant fills and fill reporting. Thus, barring any technical glitches with the exchange or your trading platform, any order placed in an electronically executed market that has not been reported a fill can generally be canceled. That said, market orders are filled and reported so quickly that the only possibility of a trader canceling the order would be during a period of internet or platform connectivity issues; that is the only instance in which the order might not immediately reach the exchange, giving the trader a short amount of time to cancel the order.

Brokers typically confirm whether you are straight-canceling a ticket or canceling a ticket and replacing it with an alternative order. If it is an outright cancel, you might hear your broker refer to it as *canning* the order or a *straight can*.

WHEN TO STRAIGHT-CANCEL AN ORDER

A trader who wants to completely eliminate a previously placed order, whether it a stop order or a limit order, straight-cans the ticket. When the trigger is pulled on a market order, the trader is forced to live with the consequences because quick execution times leave no time to cancel the order.

A trader wanting to cancel the existing order and place a new but similar order might be better off using a cancel/replace, otherwise known as modifying the order, instead of straight-canning the original and placing a new ticket.

CANCEL/REPLACE (MODIFIED ORDER)

A *cancel-replace* order is exactly as it sounds; a trader who wishes to cancel an existing order and replace it with a revised order would use this order type. Some platforms refer to this as a *cancel/replace* order. A *cancel/replace* order eliminates the possibility of double fills on a changed modified order. The primary premise behind using a cancel/replace orders instead of straight-canning an order is to avoid being double filled, but it is also a great feature for streamlining the process of changing orders on the fly. For instance, if a trader has a limit order working to buy corn futures at $4.25 and wants to change the price to $4.24 [1/2], a *cancel/replace* order is necessary to avoid the possibility of being filled at both prices or missing the trade. Manually canceling an order and then placing a fresh limit order price involves a timely additional step that could lead to missing the trade altogether. That said, futures traders generally enjoy the ability to cancel/replace orders with a click or two. Those trading via a chart trader or a depth of market panel simply needs to drag and drop their order to a new price to *cancel/replace* an existing order. As you can imagine, such technology has created a far more efficient and less error-prone manner of revising existing orders.

> A cancel/replace or modified order eliminates the possibility of double fills or missing fills due to the time it takes to manually cancel an existing order and replace it with a new order.

WHEN TO CANCEL/REPLACE AN ORDER

Traders use a *cancel/replace* as a means of changing the price or quantity of an existing order. However, most brokers, exchanges, and platforms will not allow a cancel/replace to be used to modify the order type, commodity, or contract month. Traders wanting to change these characteristics of an order need to straight-cancel the previous ticket and enter a new order. This makes sense because, in these circumstances, double fills are not possible and the order must be routed to a different division of the exchange.

GOOD TILL CANCELED (GTC)

Good Till Canceled (GTC) orders, often called open orders, are always considered active until filled, canceled, or replaced using a cancel/replace or modify feature in a trading platform. A GTC can be any order type but most often is a stop or limit order.

> GTC orders really are good until canceled. Don't forget about them after you have placed them!

WHEN TO USE GTC ORDERS

GTC orders reduce the number of conversations with the broker or the number of times you must enter the trade online if you are a self-directed trader. In each of these cases, a GTC order reduces the probability of error in trade placement.

Those who have determined their strategy in advance and would like the benefit of not watching the market on a constant basis might place GTC orders. However, beginning traders have been known to place GTC orders and forget about them, only to find that disaster has struck while they weren't watching. If you want to use GTC orders, make sure that you properly monitor them and cancel them when appropriate.

MULTIPLE ENTRY, MULTIPLE EXIT (MEME)

Most order-entry platforms enable traders to enter *MEME* (Multiple Entry, Multiple Exit) orders, or multi-bracket strategies. A bracket strategy, when correctly entered into a computerized trading platform, is a collection of user-defined rules that create and manage a set of entry and exit orders applicable to a trading position. MEME orders can be simple entry orders with automatic profit targets (limit orders) and stops (stop-loss orders). They can also be highly complex orders in which traders enter the market with multiple contracts and automatically place various target prices and stop orders for each individual contract. In the case of a strategy, or MEME order, the platform is "intelligent": It is programmed to automatically cancel the stop order if the limit is filled, or vice versa.

WHEN TO USE MEME ORDERS

Traders habitually buying and selling multiple contracts at a time (any number greater than one) can benefit from bracket, or MEME, orders, in my opinion. This is because it is nearly impossible to pick a market high or low with precision, so scaling in and out of trades will almost always yield better results. For example, a trader wishing to be long a total of five contracts will almost certainly obtain a better average fill price by entering one contract at a time from better price levels. Although he might not be guaranteed a fill on all five contracts it is a better outcome than buying five contracts at the market and watching prices drop. The same theory applies to exiting the market, which validates the advantage of MEME orders. A trader long five futures contracts can peel one position off at a time, hopefully at sequentially higher prices, to obtain a favorable average exit price.

PLACING STOP ORDERS ON OPTIONS

The CME doesn't accept stop loss orders on options because it could result in ridiculously horrible fill prices during volatile market conditions. In fact, in some less liquid commodities, a stop order would almost guarantee a frightening fill price even in normal market conditions. However, you can place stop/limit orders on options as day orders only. As previously discussed, a stop/limit order is basically a modified stop order.

As a reminder, a *stop order* becomes a market order once the price is reached; a *stop/limit* order also becomes a *market* order but it allows traders to name the amount of slippage they are willing to accept. The downside of a *stop/limit* order is it runs the risk of being rendered useless if the price of the option explodes beyond the stated limit price. In short, when using a *stop/limit* order, if the futures price trades beyond the stated stop price but the exchange cannot fill the order within the stated limit price, the order is canceled to leave the trader without any stop order at all.

To illustrate, an S&P trader who is short a naked put option with a strike price of 2300 might have collected 35.00 points in premium (sold the put). If that trader wishes to try to limit his risk to 10.00 to 15.00 points, he could place a buy *stop/limit* at the beginning of each trading session. If so, he would identify the buy stop price at 45.00 with a limit of 50.00. This order tells the exchange to buy the short option back if the bid/ask spread reaches 45.00, but only if the order can be filled at 50.00 or lower. If for some reason the option price explodes and cannot be filled at a price between 45.00 and 50.00 the order simply dies to leave the trader with no risk management at all. Traders can reduce the odds of this happening by stating a wider *stop/limit*, for instance, STP 45.00 LMT 60.00 but of course that leaves the trader open to a wide amount of slippage.

WHEN TO USE STOP ORDERS ON OPTIONS

Quite frankly, never. Stop/limit orders are subject to either being filled at catastrophic prices or being canceled at precisely the time that risk management is needed most. Unfortunately, their existence tends to lure traders into a complacency that doesn't acknowledge their true risk; this is a dangerous combination.

A DISCLAIMER TO STOP LOSS AND MARKET ORDERS IN AN ELECTRONIC TRADING WORLD

In earlier chapters, we have discussed the death of the open outcry pits and the implications to commodity traders. Because electronic trade matching on platforms such as the CME's Globex or on the Intercontinental Exchange differs considerably from the logistics of open outcry trading, the exchanges have altered the way stop loss orders are executed to accommodate the new environment. Further, they have gone as far as to modify the definition of such orders.

Traders sending orders to the open outcry pit for execution knew that a *stop loss* order became a *market* order once the stated price became part of the bid/ask spread. They also knew a placed *market* order was guaranteed a fill, but they might not necessarily like the price.

Although the process wasn't necessarily transparent, they knew the filling broker working on their behalf in the pit would accept the best bid or ask being quoted by other floor traders handling the orders of *their* clients. In most circumstances, the stop order would be filled at a reasonable price at, or near, the stated stop loss price. However, in fast market conditions, it was possible to experience painful slippage without any real limits to the deviance from the original stop price. For instance, a trader with a buy stop in soybeans at $10.50 might get filled at $10.50, $10.51, $10.52, or even much higher. In extreme situations, the slippage could be several cents causing hundreds of dollars in losses beyond what the trader had intended his risk limit to be. However, because there was a human touch there was generally a good effort made by floor brokers to limit or prevent slippage. After all, if clients aren't happy with the performance of the open outcry execution team they had the option to take their business to another brokerage.

In electronic trade matching, there isn't the same amount of accountability nor is there cognitive ability by a brokerage to massage stop orders to obtain reasonable fills. Instead, in the beginning, in an electronically traded market, a stop loss order simply became a market order and sometimes the fill prices were horrific. Accordingly, the CME and the ICE implemented some price protections to prevent the stop orders of traders from becoming traditional market orders without regard to price. You might recall the infamous 2011 flash crash; these new price protections are aimed at preventing a repeat of the fiasco by ensuring triggered stop loss orders aren't filled at unintended extreme prices. Under normal trading conditions, these protections go unnoticed and even unneeded. However, there are rare occasions in which market prices are shocked, causing these protections to come into play.

For example, the grain markets can move 20 to 30 cents nearly instantly on mornings that USDA reports are released and every Wednesday morning crude oil can rally or fall a dollar or two should the weekly inventory figures surprise the market. If you have a stop loss order working during a highly volatile market condition such as these, your stop order is no longer guaranteed to get you out of the market if your stated stop loss price is hit. On the bright side, if the order is filled it is guaranteed to be within what the exchange has deemed to be a reasonable price.

This reasonable price is set by a calculation that yields what is referred to as a *protected range*. The *protected range* varies from market to market and is determined by the exchange and updated from time to time to account for market conditions. At the time this book was going for publication, the *protection point* in the E-mini S&P was 3.00. Thus, at any given time a triggered stop loss order fill could not exceed 3.00 higher than the best ask or 3.00 lower than the best bid at the time of trigger. The 6.00-point range between these two points is known as the *protected price band*.

Beginning traders sometimes fail to remember, their order can only be filled if someone else is willing to take the other side of the trade. Thus, just because your buy stop price is reached and the order is triggered doesn't mean there will be another trader's limit order waiting to be filled at your desired price. The trade matching software must seek the next available sell limit order and match it against your buy stop order. However, in the case of the E-mini S&P 500, if the next available offer is 3.00 higher than the best offer, your stop loss order will be rejected because it was not possible for the exchange to fill the order within the *protection point* or predetermined *price band*.

To clarify, if a trader places a buy stop order in the E-mini S&P 500 at 2450.25 while the market is trading at 2445.00, the order will be triggered if the E-mini futures contract rallied to print a trade at 2450.25. Once the stop is elected, a market order is automatically submitted to buy a futures contract at the best possible price at that time (usually the lowest sell limit order placed by another trader). However, for the new market order to execute, the best available price must be no more than 3.00 above the trigger price of 2450.25. If the exchange's trade matching software cannot buy an E-mini at a price of 2453.25 or less, the order is rejected and then placed as a *limit order* at the *protection point;* in this case 2453.25. If you've traded E-mini S&P futures you realize that the odds of there not being another contract available within the 3.00 protection limit is slim. The market is deep and liquid, leaving these added price protection limits only necessary in highly unusual market conditions.

The good news is, the exchanges' price protection measures reduce the odds of an insanely unfavorable fill. Over the years, I've seen losses in the thousands at the hands of an aberrant move in an illiquid market and it also works against a cascading market move such as the flash crash. Yet, similar to most things in life there is an opportunity cost of such luxury. Traders can no longer assume that a *stop loss* order will guarantee a market exit if triggered. Further, even a *market* order placed in extraordinary market conditions might not guarantee a fill. Although it is rare and unlikely, it is possible for a futures market to trigger a stop order but fail to fill the order within the protective price band then subsequently run away from the resulting limit order to exit the trade. In a nutshell, the market might jump right over the stop order and continue moving against the trader with no limits, hedges, or protections!

For this reason, and many others, I prefer using short options for hedging and long options for limiting risk, as opposed to stop loss orders. If you are interested in learning more about such a strategy, I go into great detail in using options rather than stops for futures trading in my latest book, *Higher Probability Commodity Trading*.

PLACING A TRADE WITH YOUR BROKER

Now that you are familiar with the types of orders that are available, you must effectively communicate your intentions to your broker or efficiently enter the trade into a platform. In either case, being properly prepared could make the difference between profitable trading and the contrary. Aside from possible miscommunications or online errors, being knowledgeable and confident in your desires will help to mitigate the nerves and emotions that can work against the mental stability of any trader.

Even if it is your intention to place and execute trades through an online trading platform, sometimes you will need to place trades over the phone due to technical difficulties or other unforeseen events.

> Timing is everything, in more ways than one.

Before you even pick up the phone, you should have a good idea of what you want to do. Clearly, if you are working with a full-service broker, you are paying for the ability to ask questions and gather the broker's opinion on strategy and market speculation. Be sure to get your money's worth—that's what brokers are there for. However, don't assume that because someone is a broker, he is somehow a trading genius; relying solely on your advisor's advice isn't a good idea. After all, it is your money, not your broker's. You need to have an opinion and a plan of your own.

You should also have a good idea of the current market price. I realize that this isn't always possible; in fact, one of the primary reasons to use a full-service broker is to have the ability to call in to stay in touch with the markets. Thankfully, most brokerages offer access to account stats and market data via smartphone applications. Nevertheless, not knowing where the market is trading sometimes leads to erroneous orders. For example, if a limit order names a price at which the market has already "traded through," either it will result in the equivalent of a market order that is executed immediately or, in some markets, the exchange will simply reject it.

A good broker generally notices an error before placing the trade on a client's behalf, but this isn't guaranteed. Additionally, if you made the call to a discount trading desk or a courtesy night desk, the order will be handled by a clerk, who will likely not offer the hand-holding that a full-service broker would. In any case, the client is responsible for the consequences of the order and should be properly prepared to communicate efficiently.

As a trader, you should also be aware of the opening and closing times of the markets that you place trades for. As an industry insider, I realize how difficult this can be due to constant revisions and various trading hours in each contract. Even so, you need to be aware for the purposes of placing and monitoring positions. If you place orders on off-market hours or when the market is closed, you are at risk of being exposed to gapping prices on the reopening of trade. Further, some platforms reject orders placed while the markets are closed, but others accept them, and this opens the door for surprises on fill prices. Being attentive to small details does matter!

CALLING YOUR BROKER OR A TRADE DESK

Confusion caused by miscommunication between you and your broker can be costly for both parties. A full-service broker will happily clarify your intentions and coach you along the way; however, it is a good idea to be aware of the proper procedures to avoid compromising situations. Also, a clerk at a trading desk will enter orders exactly as the trader states; he will not be equipped to help traders avoid errors and shouldn't be expected to be.

Most full-service brokers can interpret your order in alternative formats, and that is fine, but it is in your best interest to know the proper format. This is the sequence of information that you should communicate to a trade desk clerk or broker.

- Ⓢ State your name and account number.
- Ⓢ If the order will be a futures or option spread, make that known in advance.
- Ⓢ Specify whether you will be buying or selling.
- Ⓢ State the quantity.
- Ⓢ Identify the expiration month.
- Ⓢ Identify the futures contract.
- Ⓢ State the strike price (if applicable).
- Ⓢ Specify the price and order type (*limit, stop, market*).
- Ⓢ Clarify the time horizon (*good until canceled, day order*).
- Ⓢ State any contingency orders, such as OCOs, or place a limit after the primary order is filled.

A verbal account of placing an oral order with a broker might sound something like this:

"Hi, this is Robin B. Good. For account 79700, I would like to place an order to buy one June T-note at the market with a stop order at one-thirty-one-eleven (131'11)."

This is a market order to enter a long position in the June 10-year note with a stop loss to exit the position at 131'11, and it is implied that this is a day order only. If the trader wants the stop to be *GTC*, she must specify because it is assumed a day order if there is no mention.

"For account 79700, I would like to place an order to sell five December gold on a stop at twelve-seventy-five ($1,275.0) for the day only."

This trader is placing an order to sell five futures contracts of December gold if the market drops to the price of $1,275.00. The trader also specifies that this order is good for the day only, meaning that if it is not filled during the session that it is placed, he wants the order to "die." Again, if a trader does not state whether an order is good for the day or *GTC*, it is assumed to be a *day order*. Therefore, if you enter a market and place a *stop order*, be sure to state that it is intended to be *GTC*. Otherwise, you could be in store for an unpleasant surprise.

"For account 79700, I would like to place an order to buy five July corn 360 puts for five cents or better GTC."

As you should recall, a *limit order* is the same as an "or better" order. Therefore, the preceding order instructs the broker to try to buy five July corn puts with a strike price of $3.60 at five cents on a *limit good till canceled*. Note that the execution price denoted in an order with multiple contracts is based on the individual contract price, not the cumulative price. Simply put, this trader is buying 5 options at five cents per option, not five options at one cent per option.

"For account 79700, I would like to place an order to buy two March orange juice at 98 cents (98.00)."

This trader is instructing his broker to purchase two March orange juice futures on a *limit* at 98 cents. Even though a *limit order* was not specified, nor were the words or better used, any time a price is mentioned without a specific order type, it is assumed to be a *limit order*.

PLACING A TRADE ONLINE

Experienced traders might determine that placing orders through an online trading platform is a great way to increase efficiency; after all, doing so saves time and lower transaction costs. However, this can be a detrimental scenario for those who aren't mentally capable of controlling their trading or simply aren't knowledgeable enough about the markets to take on so much responsibility.

When it comes to actual trade placement through an online platform, the procedure varies widely from application to application; many of them even offer multiple ways to enter orders. Almost all futures and options platforms offer dropdown menus to guide traders, and many advanced trading environments provide point-and-click capabilities in which orders can be placed with a few quick clicks. For example, some platforms enable you to place trades directly from a price ladder or a chart, whereas a right-click triggers a buy order and a left-click triggers a sell. As convenient as these functions are, they can be too convenient for those who are restless or, worse, careless.

Order entry with dropdown menus is designed to guide traders and reduce errors, but there is a downfall. Many have default settings that reset in between orders or after minimizing a trading window, and so on. In other words, traders must be careful to ensure that the contract, month, and price are as they want them to be before placing the order. I have lived through the horror of having a platform default to a December S&P futures while I was trading the June. These types of blunders are scarring from both a monetary and a psychological standpoint.

Some platforms even enable orders to be entered by typed text. This might sound cumbersome, but I actually prefer it. After you learn the format, and assuming that you have strong typing and 10-key skills, this can be a fast and efficient way to place trades. To give you an idea of how it works, the following text would instruct some platforms to buy a December 2018 electronic bond futures contract at the market:

B 1 ZBM18 M

Similarly, the following text is a command to buy a June Euro currency 115 call for 30 ticks:

B 1 6EM18 11500C 30 O

You might be wondering what the *O* at the end of the command stipulates. For options trades, many platforms require that you disclose whether you are attempting to enter or exit a trade. Therefore, the *O* indicates that this order is to open the position. If it were a closing order, the command would have a *C* at the end.

The purpose of denoting option orders as "open" or "close" is to aid the brokerage firm's risk-management department in approving client orders. This is because option sellers face unlimited risk, but the risk to buyers is limited to the premium paid. Consequently, it is helpful for the brokerage firm to know whether a trader is selling an option to get out of an existing long position or is selling to enter a new short options trade.

Keep in mind that each platform has a slightly different format and maybe even contract symbols. Unfortunately, if you want the benefits of trading online, you have a lot of learning to do before you can start.

CHAPTER 8: MAKING CENTS OF COMMODITY QUOTES

Too many stock traders or aspiring commodity traders are discouraged from participating in the futures markets by the complexity of the pricing. Even worse, others venture into the markets relying on their trading platform to calculate their trading results *after* they execute the trade.

> "Risk comes from not knowing what you are doing." – Warren Buffett

I believe that becoming comfortable with commodity quotes and calculating profit and loss in each market is even more critical than accurate market speculation. In fact, until you are proficient in determining position and contract value, you shouldn't be risking money in the markets. After all, if you can't measure your reward, how can you possibly manage your risk?

Unfortunately, quoting and calculating commodities is also the most frustrating aspect of trading commodities. Unlike stocks, in which all securities and options are calculated in the same manner, each commodity contract has its own set of rules.

Even though each futures contract is standardized, comparing commodities to those with differing underlying assets reveals that the values and corresponding calculations involved are worlds apart. As you can imagine, this can be extremely overwhelming for beginning and even seasoned traders. To complicate matters, many of the quote vendors use slightly different formats to display futures prices and option premium. The ability to quickly and accurately sift through the chaos to derive the information and figures desired takes a considerable amount of experience. The following explanations will hopefully lessen your learning curve as you begin your journey into the challenging yet potentially lucrative trading arena known as commodity futures and options.

> The futures industry is notorious for a lack of uniformity. Mergers of the CBOT, CME, COMEX, and NYMEX have improved continuity among various commodity markets, but quoting and calculating in futures will always be a challenge for newcomers.

Some of the differences in quoting and calculating among commodity contracts stem from the underlying product itself. However, a substantial number of discrepancies in price format and quoting methods have occurred due to differences in the creators of the contracts.

Until the early 2000s, the US commodities industry was dominated by four individual exchanges, all with four individual views on how to conduct business. Failure of the industry to adhere to congruent policies led to mass confusion among the trading public. Even brokers had a hard time keeping up.

Inconsistencies between exchanges and products included (and, to a lesser extent, still include) opening and closing times, accepted order types, order-handling policies, price limits, expiration dates and delivery rules, and holiday trading hours. A handful of exchanges working independently of each other created an environment in which traders found it unwise to assume anything. Luckily, the creation of the CME Group has resulted in a single entity controlling four of the major exchanges.

Although the mergers of the CBOT, CME, COMEX, and NYMEX brought a sense of uniformity to the industry, the complexity surrounding contract size, point value, and quoting format still exists. Regrettably, reading and calculating commodity prices will likely never become easier. For example, some commodities are referred to in fractions, whereas others use decimals. In addition, some decimals depict the difference between dollars and cents—others between cents and fractions of a cent.

RULE #1: USE MULTIPLIERS, NOT CONTRACT SIZES

Most of the futures trading literature encourages beginning traders to calculate contract values and profit-and-loss figures via the contract size. However, I feel that using contract multipliers results in a simpler calculation. This is because doing so typically involves smaller numbers, less confusion over decimals and fractions and, hopefully, less room for error.

A multiplier is simply the dollar value of a specific price move in the underlying commodity. Any change in price can be multiplied by the multiplier to find the value of the price change per contract. A similar calculation can be made to determine the risk between the entry price and the stop order placed or the entry price and the profit order (limit order) placed. Most commodities use a penny as the multiplier, but others use a dollar in price change as the multiplier. This distinction will become clearer with a few examples.

Also supporting our assumption that beginning traders will be more comfortable using multipliers, remembering a multiplier is generally easier than remembering the contract size. For example, you might remember that a one-penny price move in corn is worth $50 before you can recall that a corn futures contract represents 5,000 bushels of the underlying commodity. After all, you trade commodities in hopes to make money, not make or take delivery of corn.

With that said, it is necessary to realize that each of the conclusions reached using multipliers could also be achieved through alternative calculations that involve contract size. Using the corn example, it is easy to see that the $50 multiplier is the result of multiplying the contract size by one cent (5,000 × 0.01); therefore, you can determine the value of a futures price change using it. However, for reasons that we soon point out, doing so seems to create confusion, not solve it.

RULE #2: STAY POSITIVE

This might sound elementary, but you need to have a full grasp of the concept. I believe that traders benefit from working with positive values; negative figures often create confusion and breed calculation errors. Accordingly, traders should always be subtracting the smaller number from the larger number to derive a positive value. However, this means that before a calculation begins, you should determine whether it was a profit or a loss.

Any time that a trader can buy low and sell high, whether with an option or futures contract, it is a profitable venture. On the contrary, selling an option or futures contract low and buying it back at a higher price always results in a net loss. This is true regardless of the order in which it is executed.

Knowing this, determining which trades are losers and which are winners is easy at a glance. From there, it is possible to easily subtract the smaller price from the larger price to determine the magnitude of the position and apply that number to the win or loss column.

CORN, SOYBEANS, WHEAT, AND EVEN OATS

Luckily, most of the grain futures and options contracts are quoted and priced in the same format. Accordingly, determining contract value along with calculating profits and losses is done in the same manner by corn traders as it is soybean traders. Even wheat and oat traders can utilize the same math.

As we have learned, the US futures trading industry began in Chicago and was formed to facilitate grain trade. Speculation in the grain complex has been popular throughout the years, and participation and interest are growing. Much of the appeal of the grain complex is the cyclical nature of the markets.

Grain prices fluctuate on what is often referred to as a crop year. Each grain has a specific time of the year in which planting and harvesting normally take place and traders are aware of the time frames the crops are most vulnerable to damage. For instance, during the spring planting of corn and soybeans, too much rain can delay field work or, in extreme cases, make it impossible. On the other hand, too little rain during summer months can have a negative impact on proper germination of the crop and lead to sharply reduced production. In anticipation of something going wrong with either planting or harvesting, the grain markets tend to trade higher in the spring. The increase in prices is known as a *risk premium* and tends to deflate as harvest approaches in late summer or early fall. Despite what seem like obvious and tradable price cycles, grain trading continues to be challenging. After all, timing is everything, and that is all but certain. Early entry or late exit could turn somewhat accurate price projection into a losing proposition. Due to the difficulties involved, market participants must have a solid understanding of what is at stake before putting their money on the line.

> Grain prices are seasonal, but don't mistake this for "easy." Cyclical price patterns are evident in agricultural markets but guarantees are not.

UNDERSTANDING GRAIN MARKET FRACTIONS

In regard to math, the grain complex is the easiest of the commodities to work with simply because four of the major contracts included are similarly calculated and quoted. In the next section, "Calculating Profit, Loss, and Risk in Grain Futures and Options," I discuss the fact that wheat, corn, soybeans, and oats are all referred to in cents and fractions of a cent per bushel. This holds true for both the futures contracts and the corresponding options and should be a breeze for anyone comfortable in adding and subtracting fractions.

Because corn, soybeans, wheat, and oats are quoted in cents and eighths of a cent, the fractions always use 8 as the denominator. Grain fractions are never reduced, despite the fact that they could be. This helps to create continuity and avoid some confusion among traders.

The minimum tick is the smallest increment of price movement allowed in a particular contract. In the case of the grain futures previously listed, the minimum tick is one-quarter of a cent, or 2/8. Options, on the other hand, can move in increments of 1/8, although they are typically traded in quarters, similar to the underlying futures.

Commodity quotes generally refrain from showing the denominator of the fraction because it is always assumed to be 8. Thus, if corn were trading at four-fifteen and a quarter cent ($4.15 1/4), you would see it displayed on a quote board as 415'2, where the number 2 represents the unreduced fraction 2/8. Note that the cents and fractions of a cent are separated by an apostrophe or, in some cases, a hyphen (-). Less commonly, you might see grain quotes in terms of a decimal, for example, 415.25, but this is not the industry norm.

Knowing this, you have probably realized that half of a cent is denoted by 4/8, and three-quarters of a cent is displayed as 6/8. Of course, if you were looking at a quote board, you wouldn't see the denominator of 8. Instead, you would see a 4 or a 6, respectively. This is in contrast to how you verbally state the price. To demonstrate, corn trading at 341'4 would be stated as "three-forty-one and a half," or $3.41 1/2.

Similarly, if wheat futures were trading at $5.50 3/4, it would be displayed as 550'6 and verbally expressed as "five fifty and three quarters"; wheat futures at "five seventy and a half" would be listed as 570'4 ($5.70 1/2). If you are the type of person who cringes at the thought of fractions, you might want to simplify your calculations by replacing the fractions (2/8, 4/8, and 6/8) with 0.25, 0.50, and 0.75, respectively, and simply punching the digits into your calculator.

CALCULATING PROFIT, LOSS, AND RISK IN GRAIN FUTURES AND OPTIONS

Corn, soybeans, wheat, and oats all share the same multiplier because they also share the same contract size (see Table 2). Accordingly, despite having differing underlying commodities and the corresponding value that the market places on them, each of these grain futures contracts trade identically.

Table 2: Identical contract sizes and point values for corn, soybean, wheat and oat futures and options are identical.

Contract	Multiplier	Contract Size	Min. Tick Value	Quote Terms
Corn	$50	5,000 bushels	$12.50	Cents per bushel
Soybeans	$50	5,000 bushels	$12.50	Cents per bushel
Wheat	$50	5,000 bushels	$12.50	Cents per bushel
Oats	$50	5,000 bushels	$12.50	Cents per bushel

With the exception of US Treasury options trading on the CBOT division of the CME Group, all commodity options are valued and calculated in the same manner as the corresponding futures contract.

The multiplier in the grain futures discussed (corn, soybeans, wheat, and oats) is always $50. This is because each contract represents 5,000 bushels of the underlying commodity; one penny multiplied by 5,000 is equal to $50. In other words, each penny of movement in the futures price of any of these grains is worth $50 to a futures trader. For example, a trader long a December corn futures contract from $4.40 would be profitable by $50 if the price of corn increases to $4.41. Conversely, if the price of corn drops to $4.39, the same trader would be losing exactly $50 on the position. Thus, the minimum tick of a quarter-cent (2/8) results in a profit or loss of $12.50 ($50 × (2/8)). When you are armed with this knowledge, computing profit, loss, and risk in terms of actual dollars in your trading account is relatively simple. Let's take a look at a few examples.

A trader who is long March soybean futures from 1020'4 ($10.20 1/2) and later decides to offset his position by selling a March soybean futures at 1054'6 ($10.54 3/4) would have netted a profit of 34'2 cents, or $1,712.50 before commissions and fees. We know that if a trader buys low and sells high, the trade is a profit. Thus, the profit is figured by subtracting the entry price from the exit price and multiplying that number by $50. Note that if this trader had been short beans from 1020'4 and bought the futures contract back at 1054'6, the trade would have been a loser by the same amount.

In the same way, as portrayed in Figure 13, a wheat trader who buys a September contract at a price of 441'6 and sells a September wheat contract at 561'4 is profitable by $5,987.50, or 119'6. This is figured by subtracting the buy price from the selling price and multiplying by $50 ((561'4 − 441'6) × $50). We know to add this to the winning column. Buy low, sell high, remember?

Figure 13: Wheat prices struggled to hold below $4.40 in mid-2017. A position trader seeking value might have gone long wheat hoping the mantra "the cure for low prices is low prices" would eventually force wheat higher. It would have worked! (Chart courtesy of QST)

The same result could have been figured through the use of contract size. Knowing that the preceding trade was profitable in the amount of 119 3/4 cents (561'6 − 441'6), you could have multiplied the contract size, 5,000 bushels, by $1.1975 (119 3/4 cents expressed in decimal format), to arrive at a profit of $5,987.50. As you can see, using the contract size instead of the

There's more than one way to skin a cat and the same applies to calculating profit, loss, and risk in the futures markets.

multiplier requires converting the fraction by shifting the decimal point two spots. You can probably also see that although this version of the equation yields the same result, it creates confusion and opens the door to errors.

An options trader faces the same math. If it is possible to purchase a March soybean call option with a strike price of $11.00 for 15 cents, or $750 ($50 × 15), and later sell the option for 21'4 cents (21 1/2), the net profit would be 6 1/2 cents. Converted to a dollar profit, it would equate to $325 before commissions and fees.

NOT ALL GRAINS ARE CREATED EQUAL

Not all grains share the same convenient contract specifications as corn, soybeans, wheat, and oats. Although they are less talked about and less traded, two futures contracts are written on byproducts of soybeans.

> A "crush spread" involves a speculative or hedge trade in which a position is taken in soybeans and the opposite position is taken in its respective products.

Soybeans are often crushed to extract oil used in many food products known simply as *bean oil*. The substance left after extracting the oil from the beans is *soybean meal* and is often used as animal feed. Each of these products trades in the futures markets as a vehicle for hedgers to reduce price risk and for speculators to attempt to profit from price movements. Although they aren't as liquid as corn, wheat or soybeans, they are a good place for beginning traders to dip their toe in the water due to relatively low-margin requirements and generally less volatility than trading soybeans outright. As displayed in Table 3, *soybean meal* and *soybean oil* have unique contract sizes and multipliers; therefore, they require a bit more care when it comes to calculating profit, loss, and risk.

Table 3: Unlike the other grains, soybean meal and oil have unique contract sizes and pricing formats.

Contract	Multiplier	Contract Size	Min. Tick Value	Quote Terms
Soybean Meal	$100	100 tons	$10.00	Dollars and cents per ton
Soybean Oil	$600	60,000 lbs.	$6.00	Cents per pound

SOYBEAN MEAL FUTURES

Even though both bean oil and bean meal are derived from the same bean, when it comes to trading them in the futures markets, they have little in common. Soybean meal is quoted and traded in dollars and cents per ton, with a contract size of 100 tons. You might see meal futures trading at 330.2; this is referring to three hundred thirty dollars and twenty cents per ton, or $330.20. The minimum tick or incremental price movement is a dime. In other words, it could go from 330.20 to 330.30, but it can't trade at 330.25. Each dime in price movement represents a $10 profit or loss per contract for a futures or options trader. Likewise, each dollar in movement represents a $100 ($1.00 × 100 tons) swing in account equity to a trader with an open position. This makes sense because each dime of movement results in a $10 profit or loss, so a full dollar in price change would yield an amount 10 times the minimum tick. Thus, the multiplier for soybean meal futures is $100.

As shown in Figure 14, if a trader buys December soybean meal futures at 300.2, or $300.20 per ton, and later sells it back at 345.5, she would be profitable by $4,530 before considering transaction costs. The profit can easily be figured by subtracting the price at which the trader offsets the position from the price at which it was originally purchased and then multiplying the difference by $100 (([345.5 − 300.2]) × $100).

Figure 14: Trading certainly isn't this easy, but anything is possible. In any case, soybean meal futures are conveniently priced. The simplicity of calculation and mitigated leverage attracts many beginning trades to the market. (Chart courtesy of QST)

Calculating the results of a soybean meal option trade is identical to calculating the results for the futures. Had the same trader opted to buy a call instead of selling a futures contract, he might have purchased the December 300 call for 26.70 in premium, or $2,670, and later sold the option for 43.20 in premium, or $4,320. The net result would have been a realized profit of 16.5, or $1,650 before transaction costs. This is derived by subtracting the purchase price of the call option from the sales price and multiplying it by $100. Keep in mind that the same principles of buying low and selling high apply to option premium. We knew to subtract the purchase price from the sales price because the trader bought at a low premium and sold at a high premium, to create a profitable trade. Had the purchase price been higher than the sales price, we could have subtracted the sales price from the purchase price to determine the loss.

SOYBEAN OIL FUTURES

Traders often refer to soybean oil futures as *bean oil*. *Soybean oil* futures are traded in contracts of 60,000 pounds and are quoted in cents per pound. Looking at a quote board, you might see bean oil futures priced at 49.20. This is actually referring to $0.4920, or 49.20 cents per pound. The minimum tick for soybean oil futures is 0.01, which represents a price change in the amount of 1/100 of a cent. Each tick is valued at $6, making the multiplier $600 ($0.01 × 60,000 pounds) for a full penny of price movement. In other words, if the futures price went from 48.00 to 49.00, those holding short positions would have lost $600, whereas those with long futures positions would have been profitable by the same amount.

Case in point: If a trader went long December bean oil from 47.00 and was forced to sell a December bean oil to cover the position at 46.20, the total damage to the trading account would have been $480. This can be figured by subtracting the sales price from the purchase price and multiplying the difference by $600 ([47.00 – 46.20] × $600).

An option trader uses a similar calculation to determine the net results of a trade. The same trader might have chosen to buy a put option instead of selling a futures contract. If this is the case, it might have been possible to buy a December put with a strike price of 47.00 for 0.70 in premium, or $420 (0.70 × $600). After an adverse price move, the trader might have liquidated the option at 0.20, for a loss of $300 before commissions and fees. This can be figured by subtracting the premium collected from the sale of the put from the premium spent to purchase it and multiplying it by $600 ([0.70 – 0.20] × $600).

THE MEATS

Looking at Table 4, you can see that the CME has made an effort to keep the meat futures and options complex standardized in terms of contract size and point values. However, the feeder cattle contract has unique characteristics that can cause confusion for those unfamiliar with it.

Table 4: Feeder cattle is the odd man out in the meat complex but they are all priced in cents per pound.

Contract	Multiplier	Contract Size	Min. Tick Value	Quote Terms
Feeder Cattle	$500	50,000 lbs.	$12.50 (2.5 points)	Cents per pound
Live Cattle	$400	40,000 lbs.	$10.50 (2.5 points)	Cents per pound
Lean Hogs	$400	40,000 lbs.	$10.50 (2.5 points)	Cents per pound

Because there are two cattle contracts, live cattle, and feeder cattle, it is necessary to distinguish between them. Live cattle futures represent the going price for calves and young cattle weighing about 600 pounds up to 800 pounds. A calf typically needs about six months to reach this weight range, at which time it is transferred to a feedlot. When transferred, it is considered feeder cattle. Each meat is quoted in cents per pound, and there are 100 points to each cent. With the exception of feeder cattle, which have a contract size of 50,000 pounds and a point value of $5, the meats have a contract size of 40,000 pounds and a point value of $4. Therefore, a penny move (100 points) is equivalent to $400 in profit or loss in live cattle and lean hogs. This can also be figured by multiplying the contract size by a penny ($0.01 × 40,000). An equivalent move in feeder cattle would yield a profit or loss of $500 ($0.01 × 50,000). Thus, the penny value of each of these contracts is used as the multiplier in any calculations.

> The complex known simply as "the meats" is traded on the CME division of the CME Group. It consists of feeder cattle, live cattle, and lean hogs. The United States is the largest producer of high-quality grain-fed beef in the world.

Some confusion stems from the format of meat futures pricing. The meats are commonly quoted with decimals, causing some to infer that the price depicts dollars and cents. Conversely, the digits beyond the decimal point refer to the fraction of a penny in which the price is trading. Specifically, if January feeder cattle futures are trading at

131.25, this is equivalent to $1.31 and 25/100 of a cent. When this is understood, calculating the profit and loss is easy. Let's review an example using live cattle futures.

LIVE CATTLE AND LEAN HOGS

In Figure 15, a trader goes short live cattle futures on signs of an overheated market and a fresh annual high. However, the rally was just getting started. Going short the December cattle market from 112.50, or $1.12 and a half of a cent, would have quickly turned into a disaster. After a handful of consecutive limit-up trading days (meaning the maximum daily price change had been reached causing the exchange to lock up trading) the trader might have decided to end his misery by buying the contract back near 119.30 or $1.19 and 3/10ths of a cent. If so, the realized loss would be $2,720 before commissions and fees! Meat futures are notorious for having low margins, but they are also prone to violent and one-directional price moves that can catch countertrend traders off guard.

Figure 15: 2017 was uncharacteristically volatile in the cattle market. There were fortunes made and lost. Selling a fresh annual high near 112.50 would have proven to be an expensive mistake. (Chart courtesy of QST)

A hog trader wishing to buy breaks in a bull market might enter a *limit order* to buy an August futures contract at 78.20, a previous support level. Once filled on the entry order, if the same trader wishes to attempt to take a profit if the price of hogs returns to previous resistance, he might enter a limit order to sell the long futures contract at

84.90. As you should recall, with a *limit order*, the markets must "go through it to do it." To determine the profit potential of the trade, the entry *limit order* price must be subtracted from the exit *limit order* price, and the difference must be multiplied by $400. In this particular case, if the trader gets filled on his *limit order* to exit the position, the realized profit would be 6.70 cents, or $2,680 (6.70 × $400).

Figure 16: The profit and loss calculation in lean hog futures is identical to that of live cattle. Each full point is worth $400 to the trader. (Chart courtesy of QST)

The same trader might not be willing to face the theoretically unlimited risk presented by being long a futures contract. As a method of mitigating the risk of an adverse price move, the trader can place a *sell stop order*. Although *stop orders* are not guaranteed in terms of price, the use of *stops* can be effective in exiting a trade that has gone badly without the psychological turmoil of pulling the plug manually.

As you can see in Figure 16, a trader long an August lean hog futures contract wishing to mitigate risk might place a sell stop order at 77.00. As you should recall, a stop order becomes a market order when the price is hit. Therefore, the reported fill might be better or worse than your stated stop price. Any potential difference in actual prices relative to the named stop price is referred to as slippage and can be substantial in volatile market conditions. We already know the profit potential of the trade is 6.70 cents or $2,680. To determine the risk, ignoring potential slippage and transaction costs the trader simply subtracts the stop order price from the entry price and multiplying the difference by $400. In this example, the trader is risking 1.2 cents or $480 ((78.20 – 77.00) x $400).

Feeder cattle traders would utilize the same methodology of calculating profit, loss, and risk but instead of multiplying the price change in cents by $400, they would use $500 as the multiplier. Feeder cattle is a relatively thinly traded market, those wishing to participate in the meat complex are generally better off using live cattle and, occasionally lean hog, futures and options as the trading vehicles.

FOODS AND FIBER (THE SOFTS)

Unlike other commodity groups, the complex known as the softs doesn't consist of homogenous products. Coffee, orange juice, cocoa, sugar, and cotton all fall into this category and are all traded on the Intercontinental Exchange. There is an outlier in the complex, random length lumber, which trades on the CME. Although a majority of the contracts have food as an underlying product, cotton and lumber are primarily used as fibers. However, cotton oil is often listed as an ingredient in many of the foods that you eat. As discussed in "Chapter 4: Account Access, Trading Platforms, and Exchange Data Fees," the ICE charges a substantial fee for access to real-time market pricing within a trading platform or quoting and charting software.

> Soft complex price changes often catch unsuspecting traders off guard. Don't turn your back on these

It might seem as though these contracts were grouped together for a lack of anywhere else to put them, but they are categorized as such because a majority of production in the softs markets takes place outside the United States. Keep in mind that, just as production is done overseas, so is a compilation of statistics. Many of the softs are grown in third-world countries, and the data is far less reliable than that published by the United States Department of Agriculture (USDA) on domestically produced commodities.

The softs are among the most complicated commodity sectors to calculate in; each contract within the category has an exclusive contract size, tick value and, thus, multiplier (see Table 5). With the exception of cocoa and lumber, each of the softs are quoted in cents per pound. Consequently, although the multiplier is different, the methodology in figuring profit, loss, and risk is similar to that of the meats.

Table 5: Each of the soft contracts has unique specifications.

Contract	Multiplier	Contract Size	Min. Tick Value	Quote Terms
Coffee	$375	37,500 lbs.	$18.75 (5/100ths cent)	Cents per pound
Cocoa	$10	10 metric tonnes	$10.00 (1 points)	Dollars per ton
Orange Juice	$150	15,000 lbs.	$7.50 (5/100ths cent)	Cents per pound
Cotton	$500	50,000 lbs.	$5.00 (1 point)	Cents per pound
Sugar	$1,120	112,000 lbs.	$11.20 (1 point)	Cents per pound
Lumber	$110	110,000 bd. Ft.	$11 (1/10th dollar)	Dollars per 1,000 board feet

COCOA

Cocoa, unlike most other softs, is quoted in even dollar amounts per ton; therefore, prices are not broken down into cents. This concept is sometimes overwhelming for beginning traders who have grown accustomed to commodities quoted in cents. For example, if a quote source shows that the price of December cocoa is 2,100, this infers that the price is $2,100 per ton. Your broker would simply say "twenty-one hundred" to communicate the quote verbally.

Each cocoa contract represents 10 tons of product; therefore, the dollar amount of a market move is figured by merely adding a zero or multiplying by 10. To illustrate, if the daily price change is +22, a trader would have made or lost $220, depending on whether he was long or short the market. Likewise, a trader who goes short December cocoa at 2,175 and places a buy stop at 2,200 is risking a total of 25 points, or $250 plus commissions, fees, and potential slippage. This is figured by subtracting the entry price from the stop price and multiplying by 10 ((2,200 –

2,175) × 10). If the same trader places a limit order to take a profit on the trade at 2,140, it would be profitable by 35 points, or $350 ((2,175 – 2,140) × 10) if filled.

COFFEE

Coffee futures trade in contracts of 37,500 pounds; accordingly, each penny of movement in price is worth $375 to the trader ($0.01 × 37,000 pounds). For example, if March coffee rallies from 135.00 to 136.00, a trader long through the move would have benefited by $375 before accounting for transaction costs. The minimum tick in coffee is 0.05, or 5/100ths of a penny. Note that 135.00 represents a price of $1.35 per pound and would be verbally quoted as "one thirty-five." If the price were 135.55, the verbal quote would be "one-thirty-five-fifty-five."

> Coffee futures are prone to rallies during the spring months because of freeze threats in Brazil. However, a freeze occurs only about once every five years.

Similar to the meat complex, the decimal point in a coffee price isn't intended to separate dollars from cents. Instead, it's a way of breaking each penny into fractions of a penny. To clarify, if prices rise from 123.50 to 124.00, the market has appreciated by a half-cent.

ORANGE JUICE

Orange juice futures are written on 15,000 pounds of the underlying commodity, frozen concentrated orange juice, and has a multiplier of $150 ($0.01 × 15,000). As previously mentioned, orange juice futures are priced in cents per pound. The minimum tick value is 5/100ths of a cent, so you might see orange juice trading at 135.05, or 135 and [5/100] cents. The price could move to 135.10 or 135.00 but could never trade at 135.02. At 135.05, your broker would verbally quote the contract as "one-thirty-five-o-five." Don't forget that orange juice and coffee futures are similar to the meats, in that the decimal is intended to separate not dollars and cents, but cents and fractions of a cent. Consequently, 135.05 is actually $1.35 and 5/100ths.

As you have likely inferred from the multiplier, each penny movement in price is equivalent to a profit or loss of $150 for a futures trader. In other words, if the futures price moved from 135.00 to 136.00, a long trader would have made $150 and a short trader would have lost the same amount.

Imagine a trader who goes long orange juice futures at a dollar forty, or 140.00; with the current market price at 147.50, he has an unrealized profit of 7.5 cents, or $1,125. This is calculated by subtracting the purchase price from the current price and multiplying the difference by the multiplier ((147.50 – 140.00) × $150). Because the trader bought the contract at a lower price, we know that the trade is a winner in this amount.

SUGAR

Sugar #11 (not #14) futures are a worldwide benchmark based on a contract size of 112,000 pounds. With that said, each tick in sugar is worth $11.20 to the trader; each full handle of price movement (or penny) is equivalent to $1,120 and acts as the multiplier ($0.01 ×

> Brazil is the largest exporter and producer of sugar.

112,000). Don't make the potentially costly blunder of trading sugar #14 or its newer version, sugar #16—those contracts are based on domestically grown sugar and are extremely illiquid futures contracts.

Also similar to orange juice and coffee futures, don't mistake the decimal for separation of dollars and cents. Sugar is denoted in cents and hundredths of a cent per pound. If your quote vendor shows that March sugar is trading at 16.50, it is worth 16 1/2 cents per pound, and your broker might say that sugar is trading at "sixteen-and-one-half" or "sixteen—fifty."

Sugar used to be considered an ideal market for beginning traders. In the past, margins were relatively low, as were volatility and risk. However, in recent years, sugar futures have experienced large and violent price moves, making participation much more difficult—and perhaps more expensive—than it once was.

Figure 17: Selling the high and buying the low isn't as easy as it sounds, but if it were possible to sell the high and buy the low of this move, the trade would have netted nearly $9,000 before commission and fees. (Chart courtesy of QST)

For example, in Figure 17, October sugar futures dropped almost eight cents, from 20.50 to 12.75 in a handful of months. A trader lucky (yes, lucky) enough to have sold at 20.50 and bought the contract back at 12.75 would have realized a profit of 7.75 cents, or $8,680.00. This was calculated by subtracting the price at which the contract was purchased from the price it was originally sold and then multiplying the difference by $1,120 ((20.50 − 12.75) × 1,120). Such a move would be considered relatively mild for those accustomed to trading higher-leveraged contracts such as crude oil futures. However, for a market that was once considered a tame place for beginning traders to dip a toe in the water, this is a massive move. Unfortunately for countertrend traders, but fortunately for trend traders, such moves have become commonplace in sugar.

COTTON

Cotton isn't a food; it is a fiber. Nonetheless, it is most often grouped with the softs because it trades on the same exchange and, like the other contracts in this category, is primarily produced overseas. Cotton futures trade in 50,000-pound contracts and are quoted in cents per pound. Again, the decimal point isn't intended to separate dollars and cents; rather, it separates cents from fractions of a cent. In other words, if cotton is trading at 68.50, it is read as 68 1/2 cents.

> Seasonally, the highest prices for cotton futures normally occur between March and July. The lowest prices typically occur between September and November.

Due to the contract size, each minimum tick of price movement is worth $5 to a trader, and each penny in price movement is equivalent to $500 ($0.01 × 50,000). Therefore, if a speculator sells July cotton at 60.35 and is later stopped out of his position with a loss at 67.30, the total damage to his trading account would be 6.95 cents, or $3,475. This can be determined by subtracting the entrance price from the stop price and multiplying by $500 ((67.30 − 60.35) × $500).

With the exception of Treasury options, all commodity option calculations work the same as with the corresponding futures. The same trader might have purchased a July cotton 60 put for 1.25 and decided to sell it at a loss when the value had depreciated to 0.70. In this case, the trader would be out the difference, which is $275 ((1.25 − 0.70) × 500).

LUMBER

Lumber futures are not traded on ICE with the other softs, but they are often categorized with the group because lumber is a fiber. For reasons unknown to me, lumber futures attract beginning traders. Perhaps it is because it is the epitome of the definition of a commodity due to its widespread usage. Nonetheless, it is a sparsely traded contract by speculators, and until liquidity improves, I don't recommend trading it.

I have walked by the lumber trading pit only once (at the CME before merging floors with the CBOT), and there were three market makers passing the time by reading a newspaper. Of course, the lumber pit along with nearly all other CME Group trading pits has died, but you get the idea. As a speculator, it is never a good idea to trade in a market in which your order will be one of a handful of fills in the entire trading day.

If you insist on trading lumber, you must be willing to accept wide bid/ask spreads and a considerable amount of slippage getting in and out of your position. The contract size for lumber is 110,000 board feet, and it is quoted in dollars and cents. Therefore, each tick of price movement represents $11, and each dollar move equates to $110, which is what you use as the multiplier. In the case of lumber futures, the decimal is used in its usual context. If the market is trading at 316.80, it is interpreted as $316.80 per 1,000 board feet. Likewise, if a trader sells September lumber at 309.50 and is forced to buy back the contract at 318.60, the realized loss would be $9.10 in the futures market and would incur a drawdown of $1,001 to the trading account before commissions and fees ((318.60 − 309.50) × $110).

PRECIOUS METALS FUTURES

By definition, a precious metal is a rare metallic element of high value. To a futures trader, it is simply gold, silver, platinum, and palladium. Copper isn't typically described as a precious metal but is often lumped into this category. Nevertheless, we are going to discuss it in the "other" category later in the chapter.

Historically, precious metals are best known for their currency uses but are also utilized in art and jewelry. However, in a post–Bretton Woods world that took the US dollar off the gold standard, gold has lost most of its banking appeal. Despite this, droves of traders insist on speculating on gold prices, with the theory that it holds some monetary value. Accordingly, gold futures tend to trade at an inverse relationship to the dollar in the long run; as one increases, the other falls, and vice versa.

> Be aware of the dangers involved in trading what many call a safe haven, particularly in a leveraged futures account.

The precious metals futures complex attracts a lot of attention from beginning traders. Some of the appeal might be attributed to the fact that they are relatively easy to price, quote, and calculate.

Gold, platinum, and palladium are quoted just as they appear and the math for each is similar. The decimal included in the quotes is intended to separate dollars and cents. The numbers to the left of the decimal are dollars, and the numbers to the right are cents. In other words, a point in these metals contracts is synonymous with a cent. As shown in Table 6, we use even dollar increments as the multiplier for gold, platinum, and palladium futures.

Table 6: Precious metals futures are quoted in dollars and cents.

Contract	Multiplier	Contract Size	Min. Tick Value	Quote Terms
Gold	$100	100 troy ounces	$10.00 ($0.10)	Dollars and cents
E-mini Gold	$50	50 troy ounces	$12.50 ($0.25)	Dollars and cents
E-micro Gold	$10	10 troy ounces	$1.00 ($0.10)	Dollars and cents
Mini Gold (ICE)	$32.15	32.15 troy ounces	$32.15 ($0.10)	Dollars and cents
Platinum	$50	50 troy ounces	$5.00 ($0.10)	Dollars and cents
Palladium	$100	100 troy ounces	$5.00 ($0.05)	Dollars and cents

GOLD

A gold futures contract represents 100 ounces of the underlying commodity and is quoted in terms of price per ounce. Accordingly, each penny of price movement results in a profit or loss of $10 to the trader, and each full dollar movement in price represents $100 of profit or loss ($1.00 × 100 ounces). If gold is trading at $1,230.20 and rallies 60 cents, the price will be $1,230.80. One dollar in futures price movement represents a $100 profit or loss to a trader. Therefore, a 60-cent move would translate into a $60 gain for someone long gold futures and a $60 loss for anyone short before considering transaction costs.

You might have heard gold referred to as a safe haven or a hedge against inflation or systemic risk, but I encourage you to challenge this premise. The purchase or sale of gold futures is highly speculative and can result in large profits and losses, despite what you might have heard on television. Figure 18 displays just how volatile prices can be.

Figure 18: Despite being known as a safe haven, gold prices can be extremely volatile. Those on the wrong side of a price move might be unpleasantly surprised. (Chart courtesy of QST)

Had a trader bought into gold in response to end-of-the-world banter flooding airwaves following the election of President Trump in November 2016, the result would have been disastrous. In less than a month, a single contract traded might have lost approximately $21,000. Specifically, a futures trader who went long gold on election night near $1,345.00 and later liquidated the position by selling the contract at $1,135.00 would have lost $210 per contract, which equates to $21,000. Once again, this is figured by taking the difference between the entry and the exit price and multiplying it by $100 to account for the fact that a single contract represents 100 troy ounces. In early 2017, gold prices continued to trade in a volatile manner with peaks and troughs representing $60.00 to $100.000 in price changes, or $6,000 to $10,000 in profit or loss per contract on each selloff and subsequent rally.

When I think of a safe haven, Treasury bills and Eurodollars come to mind, not trading a highly leveraged futures contract that is capable of losing the value of a well-equipped economy car in a matter of days. Even if you remove the leverage component, the price exposure is substantial. On the other hand, a trader who sold at $1,345.00 and bought back the contract at $1,135.00 would have been nicely compensated for the risk taken.

E-MINI AND E-MICRO GOLD

The massive market moves in metals going into and following the financial crisis spawned the popularity of "mini" and "micro" gold futures contracts. These are lower-margined and lower-risk ways of gaining exposure to the gold market while still maintaining the simplicity and benefits of trading futures contracts outright. For instance, the COMEX division of the CME Group lists what it calls E-mini gold, which is half the size of the original 100-ounce contract.

My book *Higher Probability Commodity Trading* offers lower risk and lower margined scale trading strategies using e-micro gold futures.

Knowing that the E-mini version is half the full-size version, you've probably inferred that the contract size is 50 troy ounces and the multiplier is $50. In other words, for each dollar the price of gold moves, an E-mini gold trader makes or loses $50. The symbol for this 50-ounce contract is QO in most trading platforms. The COMEX division of the CME also lists an E-micro gold futures contract, which is one-tenth the size of the original (10 ounces). Therefore, each dollar movement in gold price equates to a $10 profit or loss to the trader. I am a big fan of the E-micro gold futures because it offers a low-risk and low-margin way for beginning traders to get their foot in the door. It also enables seasoned traders lacking in six-figure trading capital to partake in scale trading strategies in a relatively small account. If you would like to learn more about this strategy using the E-micro gold (and E-micro currency) futures, you will find an in-depth discussion in my book *Higher Probability Commodity Trading*.

Believe it or not, the commodity confusion continues. Along with the E-mini and E-micro gold futures traded through the CME Group, a viable mini gold contract is traded on the ICE. This contract represents 32.15 troy ounces or roughly one-third of the original contract size. Accordingly, traders face the risk of $32.15 per dollar movement in gold prices. This is the original mini gold contract and still retains a healthy amount of trading volume. The CME launched a Kilo gold futures contract, which is also 32.15 troy ounces, but speculators have mostly ignored it. Ironically, if liquidity picked up in this contract it would be a far better way to trade 32.15 ounces of gold than the ICE version (lower price data fees, longer hours, and more order types).

PLATINUM AND PALLADIUM

Platinum and palladium are the less-traded metals contracts and probably should be avoided by active swing traders. Long-term position traders might find it worthwhile to trade in these markets, but there are no viable options to use for hedging, which crosses them off of my list of tradable markets.

Platinum and palladium are treated the same as gold in terms of reading and interpreting quotes; there are no surprises here. However, their point values and multipliers do differ. Palladium has an equivalent point value as gold, $100 per dollar of price movement, but the point value and contract size of platinum is half of that of gold and palladium. Accordingly, a $1.00 price change in palladium is equivalent to a $100 profit or loss to a futures trader but a $1.00 move in platinum accounts for a $50 profit or loss.

THE OTHER METAL FUTURES

Silver and copper futures are quoted in cents per ounce instead of dollars and cents per troy ounce, as gold, palladium, and platinum are. Table 7 shows that silver calculations are conveniently similar to the grains; however, copper specifications are exclusive to that particular futures market.

Table 7: Silver futures are quoted similarly to grains due to the same contract size of 5,000.

Contract	Multiplier	Contract Size	Min. Tick Value	Quote Terms
Silver	$50	5,000 oz.	$25 (0.5 cents)	Cents per ounce
Mini Silver (ICE)	$10	1,000 oz.	$1	Cents per ounce
1,000 oz. Silver	$10	1,000 oz.	$1	Cents per ounce
E-mini Silver	$25	2,500 oz.	$31.25	Cents per ounce
Copper	$250	25,000 lbs.	$12.50	Cents per ounce

SILVER FUTURES

If you're comfortable working with grain quotes and values, silver shouldn't be a problem. Silver is quoted in an identical fashion to corn, wheat, and soybeans. The similarity in pricing and multipliers is directly related to the similarity in contract size. Although a grain futures contract represents 5,000 *bushels* of the underlying commodity, silver futures are written on 5,000 *ounces*. As a result, for every penny that the futures market moves, a trader makes or loses $50 ($0.01 × 5,000).

> Silver prices can be volatile; 20- to 30-cent moves from the previous day's close are common. At $50 a penny, profits and losses add up quickly.

Also similar to the grains, silver futures trade in fractions of a cent. In the case of the traditional 5,000 silver futures, the minimum tick is a half-cent. For example, if the price of silver is quoted at 16.305, it is valued at $16.30 1/2 per ounce and can tick up to 16.310 or down to 16.300. Keep in mind that the price always has five digits, even if the contract is trading at a whole cent value.

If a trader sells silver at 16.450 ($16.45) and places a buy stop order at 16.600, the risk is $750 plus transaction costs and possible slippage ((16.600 – 16.450) × 50). By the same token, if a limit order is placed at 16.330, to take a profit on the trade if the price of silver reaches the named price, the realized gain is 12 cents, or $600 ((16.450 – 32.330) × 50).

Both the COMEX division of the CME Group and ICE list a mini version of their silver futures contract with a contract size of 1,000 ounces. These contracts offer speculators a manageable $10 profit or loss per penny of price change in silver. However, at this time an E-micro version does not exist. The COMEX also offers an E-mini silver futures contract representing 2,500 ounces, which is half the full-size contract, which exposes traders to a risk of $25 per penny but liquidity is a real issue; speculators have yet to embrace this particular contract size.

COPPER FUTURES

Many people are surprised to learn that copper futures and options are thinly traded. This can sometimes create uncomfortable amounts of slippage in fills in the futures market—and insurmountable bid/ask spreads in copper options. The lack of liquidity leaves futures traders unable to turn to the options markets for hedging strategies. This combined with the excessive price volatility witnessed in the late 2000s has made copper a treacherous venue for speculation.

In contrast to gold and silver, copper is almost primarily used for industrial purposes. Also unlike the other metals that are referred to in terms of cents per ounce, copper is quoted in cents per pound.

The contract size is 25,000 pounds, making the multiplier $250 for a penny move ($0.01 × 25,000 pounds). Simply put, if copper rises or falls by one cent, a futures trader makes or loses $250. This makes sense because if the price of copper goes up by 1 penny, you make 25,000 pennies on a long futures position. Also unlike gold futures, copper prices trade in fractions of a cent. If you see copper quoted at 2.4825, it is trading at $2.48 1/4. Likewise, if copper rallies from this price to 2.850, it represents a gain of 36.75 cents or $9,187.50 ($250 × 36.25) per contract. This is great if you happened to be long, but a short trader during this move likely lost a lot of sleep. These types of moves are not uncommon in the volatile copper market. There is an E-mini futures contract listed by the COMEX division of the CME Group, which is half the size at 12,500 pounds and $125 per penny in profit and loss, but it too suffers from a lack of liquidity. There are market makers quoting bids and asks throughout the trading day, but you can expect to face a bid/ask spread of about four cents. Even on the E-mini version, that spread equates to hundreds of dollars in slippage while getting in and out of the market. Unless you are entering with a long-term speculative view, in my opinion, there are better markets to trade.

THE ENERGIES

Crude oil and its distillates are among the most talked-about commodities but are also among the most difficult markets to navigate successfully. Futures traders face relatively high margins and price risk, whereas retail option buyers must overcome extremely large premiums to turn a profit. This doesn't mean that these markets should be off-limits; the leverage they provide

> They don't call it "crude" for nothing. Energy futures are highly leveraged and price changes can be fierce.

makes them among the most exciting commodities to trade and as advocates of an option selling strategy, experienced traders might find crude oil to be an ideal marketplace for short option trading (if you are interested in option selling strategies, the topic is covered extensively in my book *Higher Probability Commodity Trading*). However, traders should be aware of market characteristics and, as in any market, should conduct due diligence in regard to their chosen strategy.

Petroleum futures have historically been a hotbed of speculation due to global political tension, OPEC policy, volatile demand from emerging markets, the US shale oil boom, and repetitive extreme price swings. If you plan to trade in these markets, you had better be willing to accept large amounts of risk because you are chasing potentially lucrative rewards. To put the stakes into perspective, after peaking at nearly $150.00 per barrel in 2008, crude oil quickly dropped below $35.00 per barrel. The move occurred in approximately five months and represents a ballpark value of $115,000 per contract. In other words, had someone been either long or short during the entire move, he would have made or lost $115,000 per contract. Feel free to revisit Figures 3 and 4 in the introduction of this book to get a visual sense of oil market volatility.

Looking at Table 8, you can see that WTI, West Texas Intermediate (not to be confused with Brent crude traded on ICE and representing European held oil), is quoted in dollars and cents per barrel. From a trading standpoint, calculating profit, loss, and risk is relatively simple because it is quoted in a format that we are accustomed to in everyday life. The contract size is 1,000 barrels, so each penny of price movement in crude represents $10 of risk to a commodity trader ($0.01 × 1,000 barrels), and each dollar in price movement is equivalent to $1,000 ($1.00 × 1,000 barrels). This number is used as the multiplier.

Table 8: The energy complex is quoted in a traditional dollars and cents format, making it easier for beginning traders to grasp the format.

Contract	Multiplier	Contract Size	Min. Tick Value	Quote Terms
WTI crude oil	$1,000	1,000 barrels	$10	Dollars and cents
E-mini crude oil	$500	500 barrels	$5	Dollars and cents
Brent crude oil (ICE)	$1,000	1,000 barrels	$10	Dollars and cents
Natural gas	$10,000	10,000 mmBtu	$10	Dollars and cents
E-mini natural gas	$2,500	3,500 mmBtu	$12.50	Dollars and cents
Unleaded gas (RBOB)	$420	42,000 gallons	$4.20	Dollars and cents
Heating oil	$420	42,000 gallons	$4.20	Dollars and cents

CRUDE OIL FUTURES

A price quote of 50.00 is just as it appears, $50.00 per barrel of crude. A drop in price from 50.00 to 48.00 is equivalent to a $2,000 profit or loss for a futures trader. Remember, each penny is worth $10 to a trader, and a $2 move in price is 200 cents. Knowing this, calculating option values is a cinch. If a July crude $60 call option is quoted at 1.20, it is valued at $1,200 (1.20 × 100).

Although the Brent crude oil futures contract is traded on ICE rather than the NYMEX division of COMEX as WTI crude oil is and represents a different grade and type of crude oil, the math is exactly the same. Brent crude oil is a relatively liquid market but it is far less liquid than WTI crude oil. Thus, unless a trader has a particular fundamental reason for trading the Brent contract, speculation should generally stay in the WTI version.

Heating oil and unleaded gasoline are much more complicated to figure. Both are quoted in cents per gallon, similar to how prices are displayed at a gas station pump. Consequently, in both cases, the decimal point separates the dollars from the cents and each trades in fractions of a cent. Both have a contract size of 42,000 gallons; each point in price movement is worth $4.20 to a futures trader, and each penny (100 points) is worth $420 ($0.01 × 42,000). To demonstrate, if heating oil is trading at 2.9120 ($2.91 [20/100]) and rallies to a price of 3.2140 ($3.21[40/100]), the futures contract has gained 30.2 cents, or $12,684 (30.2 × $420). By this example, you can see how easily money can be made or lost in the futures market. A price move of fewer than 31 cents could result in a profit or loss of several thousand dollars.

NATURAL GAS FUTURES

> Natural gas is one of the most volatile commodity markets. As a result, options have a tendency to explode exponentially. Short option traders should use additional caution here.

Natural gas is quoted in BTUs, or British Thermal Units, which is a measurement of heat. Nat gas, as insiders call it, has a contract size of 10,000 mmBtu, or million BTUs. Each tick of price movement in this contract is valued at $10, and there are 1,000 ticks in a dollar. Thus, for every dollar move in natural gas, the value of the contract appreciates or depreciates by $10,000 ($1 × 10,000 mmBtu). To illustrate, if the market rallies from 2.505, or $2.50 1/2, to 3.505, a trader would make or lose $10,000 (multiplier) on one futures contract. Yes, such moves happen frequently in natural gas futures. This might be enough to deter you from this market unless you have deep pockets and a high tolerance for risk, see Figure 19.

Energy option traders can expect the same computations. For example, if the March natural gas 3.00 call option is quoted at 0.492, it is worth 49 and 2/10 of a cent. Knowing that $1 is equivalent to $10,000, we can figure that this option has a value of $4,920. This is likely too pricey for the average retail trader; even those who can afford it would likely have a difficult time making money with such a purchase due to wide bid/ask spreads and the massive amount of premium that one must overcome to be profitable on a long option play. However, this is a popular market for hedge funds and some CTAs that have the proper amount of capital to trade in such an environment.

There is a viable E-mini version of this futures contract that is preferable to newer traders or those with limited risk tolerance or trading capital. The E-mini natural gas futures contract is one-fourth the size of the original at 2,500 mmBtu. Thus, E-mini nat gas traders are exposed to a far more manageable profit or loss of $2,500 per $1.00 in change of price.

Figure 19: In contrast to the equity markets, natural gas futures tend to go up faster than they go down. (Chart courtesy of QST)

CHAPTER 9: FIGURING IN STOCK INDEX FUTURES

When most people think of commodities, they imagine fields of grain or bars of gold; however, not all commodities are grown or mined. A futures contract might be written on any commodity in which the underlying asset can be considered interchangeable, often referred to by the term *fungible*. In essence, fungible

> A commodity is any interchangeable product.

products are those for which an end user would have no preference in choosing one over another. In other words, you wouldn't prefer one bushel of wheat over another. Assuming that the bushel meets the exchange's definition of a deliverable grade, wheat is wheat.

Most people don't realize that financial products can be looked at in much of the same way. One Treasury bond or unit of the S&P 500 is just as valuable, or invaluable, as the next. Consequently, financial products also can be considered commodities and trade accordingly in futures markets worldwide.

THE BORING BUT NECESSARY BASICS

If you are like most people, you work hard for your money; the last thing you want to do is see it evaporate in a trading account. Unfortunately, I have not yet found a foolproof way to guarantee profitable trading. What I am certain of is that you owe it to yourself to fully understand the products and markets that you intend to trade before risking a single dollar. This is true even of products that seem to be somewhat familiar, such as stock index futures. What you learn from this chapter is merely a stepping-stone. After reading it, you won't know when to buy or when to sell, but you will have the basic information you need to lay the foundation necessary to become a successful trader.

Stock index futures have become a popular vehicle for speculation because of the leverage involved, efficient 23-hour liquid trading, and perhaps the ability for people to relate to them. Unlike corn or soybeans, most people are aware of the basic fundamentals involved in the equity markets. Therefore, they view stock index futures trading as a venture that might not require as much homework as an unfamiliar commodity contract would. Whether this assumption is accurate is up for debate, but it undoubtedly has contributed to their popularity.

> Free leverage, lack of borrowing costs, tax preference, 23-hour liquid trading, and transparency make stock index futures popular among speculators, relative to their equity market counterparts such as the SPY and QQQ.

Four primarily traded futures markets exist, based on US stock indices: the S&P 500, NASDAQ 100, Russell 2000, and Dow Jones Industrial Average (see Table 9). With that said, you rarely see them referred to in this context. Instead, they are simply referred to as the S&P, NASDAQ, Russell, and the Dow. You might also hear the S&P called "the Big Board." Several other stock index futures are available, but as a speculator, you want to be where the liquidity is, and many of the other futures simply don't offer that.

Table 9: The "big" S&P 500 is the only remaining open outcry traded futures contract, and the only full-sized stock index futures market. Traders have migrated to the E-mini stock index futures.

Contract	Multiplier	Contract Size	Min. Tick Value	Quote Terms
S&P 500 (pit)	$250	$250 x Index value	$25 (0.10 points)	Dollars
E-mini S&P 500	$50	$50 x Index value	$12.50 (0.25 points)	Dollars
E-mini Dow	$5	$5 x Index value	$5 (1 point)	Dollars
E-mini NASDAQ	$20	$20 x Index value	$5(0.25 points)	Dollars
Russell 2000 mini (ICE)	$50	$50 x Index value	$5(0.10 points)	Dollars
E-mini Russell 2000 (CME)	$50	$50 x Index value	$5(0.10 points)	Dollars

Most of the stock index futures contracts trade on CME Group exchanges. Specifically, the S&P (both sizes), the E-mini Russell 2000, and NASDAQ trade on the CME division of the CME Group, whereas the E-mini Dow is a CBOT division product. The Russell 2000 is currently traded on both ICE *and* the CME, but before fall 2008, it was a contract cleared exclusively by the CME. Further, between 2008 and mid-2017 it was traded exclusively on ICE. The CME and the Russell index family opted to reintroduce the index to the CME in 2017. Because the CME has preferable hours and execution efficiency, I suspect the Russell 2000 will eventually be delisted from ICE and trade solely on the CME.

> In general, attempting to trade a financial futures contract in distant expiration months is a bad idea.

As is the case with all stock index futures contracts and other financial futures products, expiration occurs on a quarterly basis. In other words, each year, four stock index futures contract expirations take place in March, June, September, and December. Conversely, *options* that are written with financial futures as the underlying asset often have expirations in each of the 12 months of the year. The options with different expiration months as the futures contracts are commonly referred to as serial options. Serial options include January, February, April, and so on. Adding to the confusion, the CME has begun issuing weekly options in most of these products. In other words, there is now an options expiration on every Friday as opposed to every month. Also, the E-mini S&P 500 lists Monday and Wednesday options! Accordingly, in that particular market, there are options expiring on each Monday, Wednesday, and Friday of every week. In essence, the CME is moving toward offering traders the ability to hedge and speculate using options with extremely short time horizons. This is similar to trading binary options, which are traded outside of the futures markets but offer traders the ability to buy an option in the morning of a particular trading day that expires on the close. In short, binary options traders are wagering on where the market will close on that particular day. Similarly, those trading CME weekly options are betting on where the S&P will move in the next day or two.

In both the futures and options markets, contracts with expirations other than the front month have dramatically lower liquidity. This is especially true in the case of the futures contract. Therefore, in most circumstances, futures traders should avoid trading distant-month contracts because the lack of liquidity creates large bid/ask spreads and an unnecessary hurdle to overcome. I have found that beginning traders interested in holding a position for a considerable amount of time often want to trade in a back month to avoid the hassle and costs involved in rolling into the next contract month. In my opinion, this is destructive behavior because the hidden transaction costs faced in illiquid contracts can often far exceed the money saved in commission.

E-MINI DOW JONES INDUSTRIAL AVERAGE FUTURES

As mentioned, Dow futures are listed and traded on the Chicago Board of Trade (CBOT) division of the CME Group. The CBOT's version of the index closely follows the more commonly known Dow Jones Industrial Average, which consists of 30 blue-chip stocks.

Despite the fact that the Dow is the most commonly quoted index in mainstream media, it is not the most-traded futures index: Most traders opt for the liquidity and smoother nature of the E-mini S&P. Nevertheless, there is enough liquidity in the E-mini Dow to enable traders efficient futures speculation and somewhat reasonable option speculation.

At one time, the CME enabled traders to speculate on price changes in the Dow using three increments of risk and reward, but the original $10 Dow and the so-called big Dow have ceased trading. The only currently listed Dow futures contract is the E-mini, or $5 Dow. Industry insiders regularly refer to this contract simply as the *mini Dow* or even the *nickel Dow*. The nickel reference stems from the point value of the contract, which is $5 of profit or loss per tick. The larger Dow contracts were delisted by the exchange because most Dow traders flocked to the E-mini version due to lower margin requirements and lower risk and reward potential. Those unfamiliar with the realities of risk and reward might wonder why you would choose a contract that offers less leverage. Those privy to speculation realize that too much of a good thing can be disastrous. At $5 a point, there is plenty of excitement for most traders and those seeking more can simply trade multiple lots.

Unlike some of the true commodity futures contracts, the contract size of a stock index is not fixed. In fact, there is no contract size; instead, the contract value fluctuates with the market and is calculated by multiplying the index value by the point value.

For instance, if the E-mini Dow futures contract settled at 21,100, the value of the contract at that exact moment would be $105,500 ($5 × 21,100). Although $105,500 is the market value of the underlying asset, it is far more than the margin required to buy or sell a mini futures contract. Margins are subject to change at any time, but the average required deposit to trade the E-mini Dow seems to average between $3,000 and $5,000; in addition, day-trading margins are often as low as $500, making this a highly leveraged market. As you can imagine, being responsible for the gains and losses of roughly $105,500 worth of Dow stocks for a mere $4,000 in deposited margin could create large amounts of volatility when it comes to the value of your trading account. Nonetheless, the leverage has attracted many futures traders to the markets and keeps them coming back for more. Unfortunately, leverage has also been a major contributor in the experiences of many bitter ex-futures traders.

Calculating profit and loss in the E-mini Dow is relatively easy. Unlike many other commodities or even financial futures, the Dow doesn't trade in fractions or decimals; one tick is simply one point equal to $5. Consequently, if a trader goes long a March E-mini Dow futures contract at 21,272 and can liquidate the trade the next day at 21,345, the realized profit would have been 73 points, or $365 (73 × $5), before accounting for transaction costs. This is figured by subtracting the purchase price from the sale price and multiplying the point difference by $5 ([21,345 − 21,272] × $5).

Not bad for a day's work. Regrettably, it isn't always this easy. Had the trader taken the exact opposite position by selling a March E-mini Dow at 21,272 and buying it back at 21,345, the loss would have been $365 plus commissions and fees.

E-MINI NASDAQ 100 FUTURES

NASDAQ futures are a CME product that closely tracks the NASDAQ 100 equity index. If you are unfamiliar with the NASDAQ 100, this is an index of the 100 NASDAQ–listed stocks with the largest market capitalization. Similar to the Dow, NASDAQ futures come in only one size: an E-mini version. This is good news because the original NASDAQ was known as being a widow-maker to inexperienced traders. At $100 per point, it was capable of changing the lives of traders in the blink of an eye. The E-mini NASDAQ is a far more reasonable $20 per point.

> NASDAQ futures and the commonly quoted NASDAQ composite typically have drastically different values because the futures index only accounts for 100 NASDAQ stocks.

Of the major index futures, the NASDAQ complex seems to be more popular among speculators than the Dow but still falls behind the S&P and the Russell in terms of market participation as measured by open interest. However, daily volumes suggest that NASDAQ futures are a vehicle of choice for many day traders. This is likely due to attractive margins and low point values relative to other stock index futures; accordingly, E-mini NASDAQ traders are afforded more room for error.

With the futures market at 5,560.00, an E-mini NASDAQ contract is equivalent to $111,200 of the underlying index. To put this into perspective, had the full-sized NASDAQ futures contract still be in existence with the index at this level, the value of the contract would be a whopping $556,000 (5,560 x $100)! In my opinion, the CME make the right decision in eliminating the "big" NASDAQ futures contract. Profit, loss, and risk calculations on the E-mini version are much easier on the eye and the heart. Those traders wishing to trade with large size and massive leverage can simply trade multiple lots of the E-mini. Although I argue one or two is probably enough for most traders.

At $20 per point, it might seem as though trading the E-mini NASDAQ is relatively tame. However, as Figure 20 shows, profits and losses can add up quickly.

For example, in 2017 volatility in what traders were calling the FANG stocks (Facebook, Amazon, Netflix, and Google) cause the E-mini NASDAQ futures contract to trade in a wild switchback pattern. Traders could have made or lost a small fortune in a matter of days. The June rally from 5,560, which eventually peaked out near 5,900, equates to a $6,800 ((5,900 – 5,560) x $20) profit for anybody long the market for the duration of the move, and of course would result in an equivalent loss for any trader short the market. Within days, the E-mini NASDAQ fell 265 points in a little more than a 24-hour period; a $5,300 move (265 x $20). The biggest move came a few weeks later as the index rallied mercilessly from 5,560 to 5,995; an $8,700 ((5,995 – 5,560) x $20) profit or loss to traders!

> It is often said that the tech stocks lead the market in and out of bull and bear cycles. As a result, the NASDAQ can be extremely volatile. Therefore, traders must be nimble—and brave.

This is a rather extreme example, but it shows that even mini futures contracts shouldn't be taken for granted. The risks and rewards are high, so always respect the market. That said, during times when trade resembles its historical norms more, the E-mini NASDAQ is a relatively attractive arena for stock index speculation because it is generally a lower risk option relative to the E-mini S&P.

The E-mini NASDAQ doesn't come with mini-sized risk.

5,560 to 5,900 = 340 points ($6,800)

5,560 to 5,995 = 435 points ($8,700)

5,900 to 5,635 = 265 points ($5,300)

Figure 20: Even E-mini products deserve respect. Profits and losses can mount quickly. (Chart courtesy of QST)

S&P 500 FUTURES

The "big" S&P 500 futures are the only remaining futures contracts traded in an open outcry pit. The CME opted to keep it open to cater to hedge funds and institutional traders, but even they have abandoned the contract for the E-mini version.

The S&P 500 is by far the most popular speculation vehicle among stock index futures. Volume and open interest in both the options and futures markets dwarf that of the NASDAQ, Dow, and Russell. The attraction to the S&P futures and options products is likely the fact that it is a broad-based index that best represents the market as a whole and is, therefore, seen as a benchmark of large-capitalization stocks in the US.

The original full-size S&P 500 futures and options are used by institutions as a means of hedging portfolio risk and, in some cases, even speculation. However, this pit, in particular, experienced a dramatic drop in trading volume following the demise of MF Global simply because many of the S&P floor traders either were affiliated with MF Global or used the brokerage to clear the trades. Since then, traders have been consistently migrating into the E-mini futures and options despite the fact that they must execute a higher quantity of contracts, five to be exact, to achieve the same trading size as a single "big" S&P futures contract.

Although the "big" S&P futures still trade exclusively in a trading pit during the day session, I suspect it is on its last leg. Low volume and the resulting poor execution quality is driving liquidity into the E-mini and there is no reason to assume this will change. Due to slippage in the "big" contract at the hands of low volatility, it is more economical to pay the transaction costs on five E-minis than it is to trade a single full-sized contract. Thus, regardless of account size and desired trading size, I recommend executing all S&P 500 futures and options trades using the E-mini suite of products; it is best to avoid the dying S&P open outcry products. Nevertheless, we'll cover the contract specs and calculations for both sizes of S&P futures and options.

THE ORIGINAL S&P 500

The full-size S&P 500 futures contract trades in an open outcry environment during the day and electronically by night, making it available to traders nearly 24 hours per day. It is the *only* futures contract that has managed to avoid going electronic during the day and, up until late 2011 (the anniversary of the MF Global failure), had one of the more active trading pits on the exchange floor.

The full-size S&P futures contract has a multiplier of $250 with a minimum tick of 0.10 or $25 to a trader. Therefore, for every dollar, or point, of price movement in the S&P, the trader makes or loses $250. In other words, if the price moves from 2,400.00 to 2,401.00, the index has moved a dollar and would represent a $250 gain for those long the market and a $250 loss for those short the market.

> The S&P futures complex is the most widely traded stock index market on US exchanges and, arguably, the most traded in the world.

Knowing this, we can easily calculate the contract value of the index. Assuming that the futures price was 2,325.00, one full-size S&P 500 futures contract would be valued at $581,250. Although margins vary with market conditions, the average margin in the S&P tends to be between $20,000 and $25,000. As you can imagine, being responsible for the profit or loss for a contract valued at more than $500,000 with a deposit of less than $30,000 results in a highly leveraged endeavor. Both the rewards and the risks are magnified considerably, and traders must be willing to accept the consequences. That said, traders can essentially eliminate the leverage by depositing the full value of the contract being traded with leverage, profits, and losses adding up quickly; yet, I would venture to assume most traders aren't in the position to open a futures trading account with half a million dollars. Particularly, with the intent of trading a single "big" S&P futures contract.

For instance, a trader who goes long an S&P futures contract at 2,389.40 and is forced to sell it due to margin trouble at 2,253.20 would have sustained a loss in the amount of 136.2 points, or $34,050, plus the commissions paid to get into the trade ((2,389.40 – 1,253.20) × $250). Likewise, a trader short the market would have benefited in the same amount. Accordingly, many traders aren't willing to accept this type of volatility in their trading accounts and look to the E-mini version of the contract. Nonetheless, I doubt that even plentifully capitalized S&P traders would allow a loss to extend to such a degree, but it would be nice if a trader had the fortitude to let the winners run in this way.

OPEN OUTCRY S&P OPTIONS

Perhaps one of the most respected option trading pits left on the sparsely populated CME floor is that of the S&P. Institutions and large speculative traders are lured in by massive contract size. Because the options are written on such a large underlying contract, the premiums can be high. Accordingly, option sellers and option spread traders are attracted to what they believe might be favorable circumstances. However, the opportunities do not come without risks and hefty margin requirements for option sellers and diminishing liquidity works against fill quality.

As previously mentioned, the hidden cost of trading full-sized S&P products is price slippage and this can dwarf any commissions and fees traders believe they are saving by trading a single full-sized contract vs. five E-minis.

E-MINI S&P 500

Those trading the original full-size S&P 500 futures contract have a lot at stake; both the point value and the margin are high. As a result, most speculators, and even hedgers, have turned to the E-mini version of the contract, which is exactly one-fifth of the size. For the average retail trader, the reduced contract size supports more effective risk management and its electronic execution provides a more transparent and liquid trading venue relative to the full-sized S&P.

Trades in the E-mini S&P 500 futures market are executed exclusively electronically; an open outcry pit does not exist. As with the larger version of the contract, the E-mini S&P is open for trading nearly 24 hours per day. The minimum tick in the E-mini S&P 500 is a quarter of a point, or 0.25, which differs from its full-size counterpart's ticks valued at a dime, or 0.10. Because the point value of the E-mini S&P is $50, the minimum price movement is worth $12.50 (50 × 0.25) to a trader.

At $50 per handle, if the E-mini S&P 500 futures are valued at 2,325.00, the contract would represent $116,250 (2,325 x $50) of the underlying asset. Now that's more like it. An E-mini S&P futures trader is exposed to risk, but relative to the "Big Board" contract, the risk is much more manageable. When it comes to leverage and trading size, less is sometimes more. Let's take a look at an example.

If a trader opts to buy a March E-mini S&P at 2,401.50 but would like to protect himself from runaway losses by placing a sell stop order at 2,385.00, he would be risking 16.50 points, or $825 ((1,401.50 – 1,385.00) × $50).

E-mini S&P options are also popular among retail traders because of ample amounts of liquidity and the transparency of electronic execution. Unlike open outcry options, in which quotes are expensive and hard to come by without having a contact on the trading floor, electronic option quotes (bid/ask spreads) are readily available at a discounted price if you're with the right brokerage firm. In addition, the relatively low multiplier creates affordable options and attracts traders of all capitalization levels.

The financial crisis of the late 2000s ushered in a unique opportunity for option buyers in the E-mini S&P. In fact, most traders might not see that magnitude of volatility again in their lifetimes. For instance, it was possible to buy a December E-mini S&P 500 1,050 put for $10.50 in premium, or $525 (10.50 x $50), in mid-September 2008. Option buyers face a maximum risk in the amount paid for the option; therefore, the absolute worst-case scenario was a loss of $525 plus the commission and fees, and maybe a little bit of confidence. However, the profit potential of a long option is theoretically unlimited, as Figure 21 shows.

Figure 21: Long option traders are lured to the E-mini S&P due to relatively affordable premiums and perceived risk. Although option buying is a low-probability venture, it can occasionally produce magnificent profits. (Chart courtesy of QST)

As seen in Figure 21, by mid-October, it might have been possible to sell the same December E-mini S&P 1,050 put for as much as $181.00 in premium, or $9,050. Calculating the profit and loss of an E-mini S&P option trade works identically to calculating for futures; the purchase price is subtracted from the sales price and multiplied by $50. Assuming these fills, the trader would have realized a profit of $170.50, or $8,525 ((181.00 – 10.50) × $50).

This would have been an exciting and lucrative trade to be a part of; it is an extreme example of how a long option play can result in large returns to a trader. Nonetheless, this particular instance might be categorized as a once in a lifetime event: The market move that occurred during this period was one of the largest in history. In more normal market conditions, something like this generally isn't possible, nor is it likely. In my opinion, most long options can be thought of as a lottery ticket that has the potential to return abnormal rewards but isn't necessarily probable to do so.

ARBITRAGE

The price at which the large version of the S&P and the E-mini S&P are trading at any given time is nearly identical, aside from the differences in minimum tick values. This is made possible through the practice of arbitrage trading. As you should recall from Chapter 1, "A Crash Course in Commodities," the term *arbitrage* describes a risk-free opportunity. That said, we all know that truly risk-free trades are nonexistent.

Constant arbitration between the large and small contracts in each of the stock index futures ensures that all versions of a particular contract trade at or near identical prices.

Nonetheless, there's no shortage of traders who will try to beat the odds, and in some circumstances, the very quick stand to profit on the difference between valuations on two related contracts.

Some arbitrage traders attempt to profit on differences in price between the large S&P contract and the E-mini version. For instance, if the E-mini is trading at 2,350.50 and the full-size version is at 2,350.60, a trader might look to buy the cheaper version and sell the expensive version. Don't forget that it would be necessary to buy five E-minis against every original S&P contract.

Assuming fills at the noted prices, the trader is locking in a profit of 0.10, or $25 (0.10 × $250), before considering transaction costs. The constant search for such opportunities ensures that the spread between the prices of the two contracts remains narrow.

RUSSELL 2000 FUTURES

Russell futures have grown in popularity, perhaps because of the ease in calculating profit, loss, and risk. This index is considered to be a benchmark for small-cap stocks, a market sector that is notorious for experiencing volatility and leading markets in and out of secular bull and bear markets. Do not confuse the Russell 2000 futures with the Russell 1000 futures. Although the 1000 version is offered, it does not have enough market liquidity for efficient trading. Therefore, any time brokers or traders refer to the Russell, they are speaking in terms of the Russell 2000.

Russell futures only exist in one size, an E-mini version, and they currently trade on both the ICE and the CME. This causes a great deal of confusion for traders, but in my opinion, it will become less confusion as time goes on because liquidity will likely move from the ICE Russell to the CME Russell as traders seek a better trading environment (lower price data costs and more accepted order types and capabilities).

Regardless of which version of the index is traded (ICE or CME), the Russell is relatively easy to calculate. Each tick is worth $5 to the trader, and each full point is worth $50; this is what we use for the multiplier. Experienced traders might be confused by this because until 2017 the Russell futures were valued as twice the size ($10 per tick and $100 per point).

If the Russell drops from 1351.00 to 1350.00, a trader short the market gains $50. Had it dropped to 1349.90, the profit would have been $55 (1.10 x $50).

At this time, there are Russell options listed on both the CME and the ICE, but at the time this book was written, neither has enough liquidity to justify trying to trade them. I suspect this could be the case for years to come because traders enjoy trading E-mini S&P options and likely have little incentive to change their habits.

CHAPTER 10: CALCULATING INTEREST RATE FUTURES

> Interest rate futures do not earn interest; they are simply a speculative play on the direction of interest rates.

As discussed, the term *commodity* can describe a wide array of assets, including financial products. The formal definition of commodity is a physical substance or asset that is "interchangeable" in trade. From a general standpoint, a commodity is simply any product that trades on a futures exchange, and interest rate products fit the bill. Just as you wouldn't prefer one bar of gold over another, you likely wouldn't have a preference between one T-bill and another. The CBOT recognized this and created a complex of US Treasury futures products. Each of the standardized Treasury contracts represents government-issued fixed-income securities ranging from short-term two-year notes to the 30-year bond.

Not all interest rate futures are based on government-issued securities; the CME division of the CME Group is home to the Eurodollar futures contract. In its simplest definition, a Eurodollar represents US dollars deposited in commercial banks outside the United States. Due to liquidity and affordability, it is a popular tool for hedging interest rate risk, specifically the London Interbank Offered Rate (LIBOR).

The Eurodollar is the most heavily traded futures contract in the world. Much of the appeal comes from relatively affordable margin requirements and typically low levels of volatility. However, during times of economic turmoil or uncertainty, price moves can be uncharacteristically large.

The CME has even listed futures and options products using the Federal funds target interest rate and the underlying instrument. These products are a great way to speculate on the Fed's next interest rate policy change or to hedge such risks.

A COMPLEX "COMPLEX"

Several widely traded contracts are available in the realm of interest rate futures and options. Each of these contracts carries slightly differing market characteristics and, in some cases, different contract sizes, point values, and so on. For those unfamiliar with the futures markets, these discrepancies can be overwhelming. However, I hope to deliver the pertinent information clearly to make your journey into financial futures trading as pleasant as possible.

> Cash market bond securities are often quoted in yield, but futures are quoted in price.

Before I cover the basic specifications of each contract, it is important to be aware of a few facts regarding bond valuation and the characteristics of each underlying asset. Although thoroughly covering the details here is impractical, my intention is to give you the foundation needed to understand the mechanics of Treasuries.

FIXED INCOME SECURITIES

Treasury futures are similar to agricultural-based futures contracts, in that they represent the future delivery of the underlying asset. Therefore, a Treasury futures contract enables the buyer and the seller to agree upon a price today for delivery and payment of the asset at a specified date in the future. Confusion often stems from the fact that the underlying asset of Treasury futures is much more difficult to define than it is for a physical commodity such as corn or soybeans. This is because of the wide variation in expiration dates available in each Treasury category eligible for delivery and the various yields of similar securities.

The terms bond and note are commonly used in finance and even among the less-informed investment community, but the details of the instruments are often overlooked. I believe that it is worth the time to review some of the basic concepts behind the mechanics of bonds and notes to give you a better grasp of the instrument being traded in the futures market.

Treasury futures are futures contracts written with US government–issued coupon securities as the underlying asset, and thus it is important to understand the fundamentals. The US government issues three instruments based on the time to maturity: bonds, notes, and bills. The bond is often referred to as the *long bond* because it has the longest time to maturity, at 30 years; this contract also is referred to as the *T-bond* or the *30-year bond*. Notes can have maturities ranging from 10 to two years; the most commonly quoted note is the 10-year note, which is often referred to as the T-note or simply "the note," and is considered to be the benchmark interest rate. Treasury bonds and notes are collectively referred to as fixed-income securities or coupon bonds. This is because they are a claim on a specified periodic stream of interest income known as *coupons*.

The textbook definition of a bond or note is a debt security in which the authorized issuer is indebted to the holder. In essence, the bond issuer is obligated to repay the principal and interest (coupon) to the holder at a later date, termed *maturity*. In its simplest form, a bond or note is a loan with a fancy name. The issuer (seller) is equivalent to the borrower, and the buyer is the lender. The seller pays the buyer the coupon payment, or interest, to compensate the buyer for the funds borrowed. In essence, the seller collects money from the buyer and issues an IOU to be payable in the form of periodic coupon payments (interest) throughout the life of the bond and a lump sum paid at maturity equal to the principal paid to acquire the bond. This principal amount is also known as the *face value* or *par value*. In the case of Treasury bonds and notes, the issuer is always the US government. Therefore, Treasury buyers are believed to be virtually free of default risk because the US government has never defaulted on its obligations. Nevertheless, massive government borrowing in the late 2000s sparked questions on the ability of the US Treasury to continue to pay back its obligations.

To illustrate the point, a 30-year T-bond with a par value of $1,000 and a coupon rate of 5% ($50) might be issued to a buyer for $1,000. At this point, the buyer agrees to hand over $1,000 in exchange for an annual income stream equivalent to 5% of the par value ($50) for the life of the bond. At maturity of the bond, the holder is paid back the original $1,000 in principal in a lump sum.

DISCOUNT SECURITIES

The US government refers to its discount securities as Treasury bills, or simply bills. However, the CME no longer lists T-bill futures for trading. Instead, traders use Eurodollars and Fed fund futures. We discuss Eurodollars later in the chapter, but they trade like short-dated T-bills in regards to price and function but they are obviously not issued by the US Treasury. Instead, they are overseas securities issued by banks, not unlike a CD (Certificate of

Deposit) in the US. Fed fund futures, on the other hand, do not represent an actual security. Instead, they are simply futures contracts intended to provide speculators a method of directly speculating on the Federal Reserve's next move. This too will be discussed in further detail, but for now, you should be aware of the fact they are priced as if they were written with a discount bond as the underlying asset.

Discount securities are those that have no coupon or interest payment; instead, the bondholder can purchase the security at a discount to par, with the expectation of receiving the full par value back upon maturity. With this form of security, the interest isn't paid in coupon payments; it is paid at maturity as the difference between the face value and the purchase price. For instance, if an issuer sells a security with a face value of $1,000 for a price of $950, the holder will receive a 5% return upon maturity of the security because he will be receiving more at expiration than he paid to purchase the security. Unfortunately, 5% discount bonds seem to be a thing of the past; government-manipulated interest rates and the Great Recession drove discount yields to nearly zero and have only recovered slightly in the span of nearly a decade.

INVERSE RELATIONSHIP BETWEEN PRICE AND YIELD

The value of a bond, note, or discount security (the price in which it is trading) is inversely correlated with interest rates or yields. Accordingly, if interest rates go up, the price of interest rate securities drop, and vice versa. This can be explained by the value of the bond or note's stated interest rate. If market interest rates go up, any securities issued with lower interest rates are less valuable. Likewise, if market interest rates decline, the value of fixed income or discount securities issued with higher stated interest rates will increase. This is because the owner of that security will always earn the stated interest rate declared when the security was issued. Interest rates are constantly fluctuating; thus, the value of any particular previously issued security must also oscillate to accommodate the new market interest rate. This is true regardless of whether the stated interest rate is paid to the security holder periodically as coupon payments, or at the end of the security life in a lump sum.

Because a fixed-income security, such as a Treasury bond or note, is one in which the value is derived from the future cash flows (coupon and face value at maturity), its market price fluctuates along with current market interest rates. These future cash flows are coined *coupon payments* and are fixed based on the yield at the time of the bond or note issue. For instance, if the market rate at the time the Fed sells 10-year notes is 2%, the investor would receive periodic interest payments based on that rate and the size of the investment. This is true regardless of fluctuations in market interest rates.

The possibility of market interest rates changing after the issuer sells a bond or the buyer invests is referred to as *interest rate risk*. Naturally, if you purchase a bond at face value with a coupon at 2% and interest rates go up to 4%, you will feel a bit of buyer's remorse because while you are earning 2% on your investment, new investors are able to receive a 4% return. However, this is the risk (interest rate risk) that bond investors and sellers must accept and adapt to. On the contrary, if you bought a bond with a yield to maturity of 4% and the market interest rate drops to 2%, you will be ecstatic because you will continue receiving 4% coupon payments despite the fact that new investors are only seeing a 2% return.

> Bonds tend to be more volatile in nature than 10-year notes, and 10-year notes more so than five-year notes.

As mentioned, if current interest rates go up from the time of issuance, the value of the coupon payments on the existing bond goes down, as does the market price of the security itself. It is important to realize that bonds with longer maturities face increased levels of interest rate risk; accordingly, the prices of these securities react much more quickly and more violently to changes in market interest rates.

Keep these points in mind as you review the details of each contract because they can help you determine which avenue best suits your risk tolerance and personality when trading interest rate futures products.

WHAT DOES A TREASURY FUTURES CONTRACT REPRESENT?

The CBOT has declared that the underlying assets for its 30-year bond, 10-year note, and five-year note futures contracts are $100,000 worth of the respective US-issued Treasury securities. Unfortunately, this isn't as simple as it seems. Certainly, more than one maturity date exists for each of the fixed-income securities, with various coupon payments and so forth. The question you are probably asking is, which exact security is reflected by the price of the corresponding futures contract?

Instead of assuming that a Treasury futures contract represents a single bond or note (it doesn't), look at it as a proxy. Simply, it trades as an index for a variety of issues within a range that the exchange specifies. This noted range is commonly referred to as *deliverable securities*. The range of deliverable bonds or notes includes all those eligible for delivery based on CBOT standards. Here's where many people get lost: The CBOT has developed a conversion factor system to enable the futures contract price to reflect the full range of available fixed-income issues.

The exchange assigns a conversion factor to each bond or note eligible for delivery based on the CBOT specifications. Specifically, conversion factors are assigned to each cash market bond or note that meets time maturity specifications for the particular futures contract expiration.

The conversion factor allocated by the CBOT represents the price in terms of percentage, based on the price that the par value of the security would trade if it had a 6% yield to maturity. Specifically, a conversion factor is the approximate decimal price at which a $1 par of a security would trade if it had a 6% yield-to-maturity. As a result, government bonds or notes that have a coupon less than 6% are assigned a conversion factor that is less than 1. A conversion factor less than 1 signifies that the issues are returning a coupon that is at a discount to the 6% standard. Bonds and notes with a coupon greater than 6% have conversion factors greater than 1, to reflect that the security's coupon payment is priced at a premium.

Based on this brief discussion, it is probably obvious that the intricacies of the conversion factor can get somewhat complicated and are beyond the scope of this text. However, you should gain from this description of the process that the net effect of the conversion factor is to link the different prices of the bonds and notes eligible for delivery, to create a single price at which the corresponding standardized futures contract can trade. Simply put, the conversion factor enables Treasury bond and note futures to trade as if they were an index of the underlying securities eligible for delivery.

Knowing that the futures contract is based on conversion factors using a 6% yield, it is easy to see why the price of the futures contract typically doesn't correspond to the prices seen in the cash market. This is especially true in extreme cases such as the summer of 2016 when yields on the 30-year approached 2%. It is important to recognize that the current market yield will always be similar in reference to the futures market versus the cash market.

TREASURY FUTURES

Several years ago, the long bond, or the 30-year Treasury bond (a.k.a. the T-bond), was the primary interest rate product traded on the CBOT. During its prime, it was considered the *only* contract for experienced traders to be involved with. However, the Federal Reserve's failure to issue new 30-year bond contracts on a regular basis has worked against the popularity of the contract. In the meantime, shorter maturities, such as the 10-year note, have benefited in terms of volume and open interest.

Similar to the other financial futures contracts such as currencies and stock indices, all Treasury futures products are on a quarterly cycle. This means that there are four differing expiration months, based on a calendar year: March, June, September, and December. Unlike true commodities, traders typically avoid distant expiration months in financial futures and options. For example, if the official front-month 30-year bond contract were March, the volume and open interest in the June contract would generally be sparse, and there would be even less trading activity in the September contract.

As is the case in the stock indices, a mistake beginning bond traders often make is to try to enter the market using a distant contract month, with the intention of holding the position for a considerable period of time. Their reasoning in doing so is to avoid the additional transaction cost associated with entering the front month contract and being forced to roll into the next contract month upon expiration of the current month. This thought process is flawed. As I have mentioned, the lack of liquidity in the distant expiration months results in wide bid/ask spreads; therefore, the hidden transaction cost paid by the trader is often far greater than the commission saved. Accordingly, this practice might be much more harmful than helpful.

We've noted that the 30-year bond is often referred to as the long bond because of its lengthy maturity, but you might also know it simply as "the bond" because other Treasury issues are known as notes.

Table 10: Most Treasury futures contracts are based on $100,000 in par value of the underlying asset.

Contract	Multiplier	Contract Size	Min. Tick Value	Quote Terms
Thirty-year bond	$1,000	$100,000	$31.25 (1 point)	Fractions of par
Ten-year note	$1,000	$100,000	$15.625 (0.5 points)	Fractions of par
Five-year note	$1,000	$100,000	$15.625 (0.5 points)	Fractions of par
Two-year note	$1,000	$200,000	$15.625 (0.25 pts)	Fractions of par

T-BOND FUTURES

Because the 30-year bond has the longest maturity of the Treasury complex, it is situated at the end of the yield curve and typically carries the highest yield. The yield curve is simply a plot of the relationship between interest rates and their time to maturity. As for the rest of the yield curve, under normal circumstances, the notes carry less of a yield relative to the bond, and Eurodollars and CDs pay less than the notes. This scenario has been dubbed a normal curve and makes sense because an investor who locked into a security for 30 years would demand more compensation than one who invested for 10 years. In general, the securities at the long end of the yield curve will be more volatile than those on the short end of the curve.

As Table 10 shows, the face value of a single T-bond futures contract written with the bond as an underlier is $100,000. Knowing this, it is

Bond and note futures and options values are quoted in fractions.

easy to see that a contract can be looked at as 1,000 points, or trading handles, worth $1,000 apiece. What isn't very obvious is that each full point or handle can then be looked at as a fraction.

The term *handle* often describes the stem of a quote. This usage began in reference to currency futures to describe a penny move but is now commonly used as slang in nearly all futures contracts. For example, if the Euro rallies from 121.00 to 122.00, some might say that it has moved a handle. Likewise, if the T-bond drops from 151'00 to 150'00, it is said to have moved a full handle. You might have already started wondering how the T-bond futures contract could possibly be trading at such a premium over par. In addition to dramatically lower interest rates in the 2010s, there are other factors at play that has led to this.

Treasury bond futures trade in ticks equivalent to 1/32 of a full point, or $31.25, figured by dividing $1,000 by 32. Remember, each 30-year bond future is based on a $100,000 par value, or 100 $1,000 increments that trade in 32nds. Adding to the confusion, in early 2008, the CBOT decided to alter the contract by allowing traders to buy or sell bond futures in half-ticks, or $15.625. In other words, this change made a minimum price movement in the T-bond futures 0.5/32. Ironically, in fall 2009, the exchange opted to return to the original format, which no longer permitted trading in half-tick increments. At the time this book was going to print, the 30-year bond trading in 32nds, not a half of a 32nd. We suspect the exchange will avoid tampering with the format going forward; traders are creatures of habit who don't always welcome change. The futures and options trading arena can be frustrating because it seems as though the rules are constantly changing. Nonetheless, it isn't the trader's job to analyze why or how the exchange determines contract specifications; traders must simply be aware and accept them.

Bonds are quoted in terms of their $1,000 handles. Thus, a typical bond quote can be 142-24. This is read as "142 handles and 24/32nds" and is equivalent to a contract value of $142,750. It is calculated by multiplying 142 × $1,000 and then multiplying 24 by the point value of $31.25. You could also come to the same conclusion by multiplying the fraction 24/32 by $1,000. In my opinion, this method causes the least amount of confusion, so we use $1,000 as the multiplier. On a quote board, you might see something that looks like this: 147'24. It is read simply as "one-forty-seven-twenty-four."

Those comfortable with the process of adding and subtracting fractions can easily derive profit, loss, and risk; those who are fractionally challenged might find trading Treasuries frustrating. Yet, I am confident that anyone can quickly become proficient in bond futures calculations after looking at the following examples.

I don't expect you to understand or even remember bond futures prices by simply looking at a quote and the multiplier, but the following examples should add some clarity. If a trader buys a December T-bond futures contract at 147'22 and can later offset the position by selling the contract at 148'24, the trader realizes a profit of 1'02, or 1-2/32. We know that the trade was a positive one because the purchase price is below the sales price. Therefore, subtracting the entrance price from the exit and multiplying the result by $1,000 results in a gain of $1,062.50 ((1-2/32) × $1,000). If dealing with both full numbers and fractions is confusing, it is possible to split them up before multiplying and add the results of each. For example, we know that the profit was at least $1,000 (1 × $1,000) because of the full handle of gain. To calculate the remaining portion, we simply multiply the fraction by $1,000 (2/32 × $1,000) to arrive at $62.50; together, we get $1,062.50.

The multiplication involved in bond futures calculations is relatively standard, but people tend to be unjustifiably intimidated by fractions. If you recall the concept of borrowing, you will be fine. In the preceding example, it wasn't necessary to borrow. The numbers were convenient enough to simply subtract the numerator (the top number in the fraction) of the buy price from the numerator of the selling price and multiply the result by $1,000. Likewise, you would have subtracted the handle of the buy price from the handle of the selling price and multiplied the result by $1,000.

The math isn't always this opportune. Sometimes you need to borrow from the handle to bring the fraction to a level at which you can properly figure the profit or loss; this is where many opt to trade another market. For example, a trader who sells a June bond at 148'12 and buys back the contract at 146'27 might have a challenge when it comes to calculating the exact profit. In this case, it is easy to see that the trade was profitable because the trader bought low and sold high, in the opposite order. However, unless you have been doing this for a while, determining the net profit takes a little work.

In this example, the numerator of the selling price, 12, is much smaller than the numerator of the buy price, 27. Therefore, we know that we must borrow from the handle to properly net the fractions; otherwise, we would end up with a negative number and, likely, mass confusion. The least complicated way of coming to a fraction that is easily workable is to reduce the selling price handle to 147 from 148 and increase the fraction by 32/32. In other words, after reducing the selling price by a handle, we add 32/32nds to the existing fraction of 12/32nds, to arrive at 44/32nds.

Then we can easily subtract 27/32 from 44/32 to determine a profit of 1'17 ((147 − 146) + (44/32 − 17/32)). From here, we can convert the fraction to dollar value by multiplying by $1,000. Assuming these fills, this trade would have been profitable by $1,531.25 before commissions and fees ((1'27/32) × $1,000)).

T-BOND OPTIONS

As if trading and calculating bond futures weren't difficult enough, the CBOT created options written on Treasury futures with a slight twist to the valuation. Instead of quoting bond options in 32nds as the futures contracts are, the exchange opted to value them in 64ths. The multiplier remains $1,000, so each handle still carries the same value; the only difference in figuring the options as opposed to the futures is the fraction it is multiplied by. Let's look at some examples.

One of the most memorable and dramatic bond rallies of all time occurred late in 2008 and caught a majority of traders by surprise. The example that we visit is strictly for the sake of understanding how bond option values are calculated and in no way represents a trading strategy that I recommend employing. However, as you will see, doing so would have worked out very well in this instance. Dramatic market conditions make this a fun trade to imagine happening to you, but based on my experience and conversations with others, most traders were speculating in the wrong direction. Instead of the windfall of profits you are about to witness, some had the opposite experience.

> The Treasury bond and note futures complex is the only one in which options are quoted in different terms than futures.

Let's revisit the events of late 2008 in which many of the financial markets experienced volatility that might never be matched. In mid-November of that year, T-bond futures successfully broke out of a trading channel that began in September. However, with yields at historically low levels, many traders doubted the ability of the market to make considerable gains; remember, when bond prices are high, interest rates are low. Many were treating the breakout as a potential bull trap in which prices would quickly reverse and trade lower into the trading range. Those who were keen enough to see what was coming next might have opted to purchase a March bond 125 call option for 1'58, or $1,906.25 (1-58/64 x $1,000), as shown in Figure 22. Normally, I wouldn't recommend spending such a dollar amount on an option that could very well expire worthless. After all, most options are worthless at expiration. Once again, this is simply being used as a mathematical example.

Figure 22: Strictly long option strategies don't necessarily provide traders with optimal odds of success, but for those in the right place at the right time, the payoff can be large. (Chart courtesy of QST)

What happened next could have never been predicted. The March 30-year bond futures swiftly rallied above 135 to crush previous standards of what was then an all-time high in price and low in yields. This particular rally was the icebreaker for what the market eventually came to know as the "new normal." By the early 2010s, 30-year bond futures frequently traded in the 150s. Back to the example at hand, a trader willing to risk nearly $2,000 on an option with a strike price well above and beyond levels normally seen in the T-bond would have been compensated handsomely for what seemed like a long shot.

Looking at Figure 22, you can see that, by mid-December 2008, approximately a month later, the option once purchased for 1'58 was valued at 11'51. Assuming that the option could have been sold for such a premium, the dollar value of the sale would be $11,796.88 ($1,000 × 11-51/64). Accordingly, this trade would have resulted in a net profit of $9,890.63, figured by subtracting the purchase price from the sales price and multiplying the difference by $1,000. To make the fractions "workable," it is necessary to borrow a handle from the entry price and add 64/64 to the exit price. When this is done, the following equation can be easily figured to arrive at $9,890.63.

((10-115/64 − 1-58/64)) × $1,000) = $9,890.63

The purpose of these examples is to give you an idea of how T-bond traders can calculate their trading results. Obviously, not all bond trades or traders make money, but I hope that giving you the proper background in the basics of futures trading allows you to focus on your speculative skills and increase your odds of success as a result.

10-YEAR NOTE

The 10-year note, or simply "the note," has many similarities to the long bond. The contract size, the point value, and the manner in which options are quoted are all common characteristics. Similarly, if you can come to peace with the 30-year bond calculations, the 10-year note won't pose any hurdles.

To reiterate, the contract size of the note is $100,000, which is split into 1,000 handles equivalent to $1,000 and a tick value of 1/32, or $31.25; however, the T-note futures and options *do* trade in half-ticks (0.5/32), valued at $15.625. Therefore, if you see notes priced on a quote board as 122'295, they are trading at 122'29-1/2, not 122-295/32.

Calculating profit, loss, and risk for the 10-year note is identical to calculating for the 30-year bond. To demonstrate, if a trader goes short the 10-year from 128'29.5 and places a buy stop to defend himself from an adverse move at 130'15.0, the risk on the trade would be 1'17.5, or $1,546.87. This is calculated by subtracting the entrance price of the short position from the potential fill price of the buy stop, at 130'15.0. Once again, the math requires borrowing from the handle to properly subtract the fractions. This is done by adjusting the stop price from 130'15.0 to 129'47 ((130 − 1) + (15/32 + 32/32)) before doing the math. After this, you can easily subtract 128'29.5 from 129'47.0 to arrive at 1'17.5 of risk, equivalent to $1,546.87.

As with bond options, note options are quoted and calculated in 64ths rather than 32nds. Thus, if a trader sells a June 133 10-year note put for 35/64, she is collecting $546.88 (35/64 × $1,000). If she is later forced to cover the position by buying it back for 52/64, the net loss would be 17/64, or $265.63 (17/64 × $1,000).

FIVE-YEAR NOTE

In many aspects, the five-year note is identical to the bond and the 10-year note. As with the others, each futures contract represents a face value of $100,000 of the underlying security. The five-year note is also broken into handles valued at $1,000 each, and each of these is divided into 32nds. Unlike the bond and the 10-year note, each point (32nd) in the 5-year note is traded in quarter-ticks. In other words, each 32nd moves in increments of 0.25/32. As you should recall, the T-bond and T-note have a minimum price fluctuation of 1/32 and 0.5/32, respectively. If 1/32 is equal to $31.25 and 0.5/32 is worth $15.625, then we know that 0.25/32 must be $7.8125. Nobody said this would be easy. The futures markets can be potentially lucrative, but there is no such thing as easy money.

Other than the fact that they trade in quarter-ticks, there aren't any surprises when it comes to five-year note calculations. Although the process remains the same, the tick increment requires an additional digit to be typed into your calculator.

A trader who goes short a December 5-year note from 122'24.25 and subsequently places a limit order to take profits at 121'21.50 will be profitable in the amount of 1'02.75, or $1,085.94. This is figured by subtracting the limit order price from the original sales price and multiplying the difference by $1,000 ((122'24.25 − 121'21.50) × $1,000).

TWO-YEAR NOTE

The two-year note is the "oddball" of the Treasury complex. Likely in part due to the CBOT's anticipation of commercial hedgers and speculators using the two-year note as a trading vehicle, they adjusted the contract size in a way to cater to larger transactions. Unlike the others, this contract has a face value at maturity of $200,000. Thus, the value of a point (handle) is $2,000, and 1/32 is equivalent to $62.50. As with the five-year note, the minimum tick is a quarter of a 32nd, or simply 0.25/32. In dollar terms, this is $15.625.

> The two-year note is the only contract in the Treasury futures complex with a differing contract size and point value.

Another reason for the difference in contract size of the two-year note relative to the other Treasury futures products is that the US government issues significantly more debt in the two-year maturity. Accordingly, more two-year Treasury notes are traded in the underlying cash market. In other words, the CBOT opted to list the contract with a $200,000 maturity face value to provide "economies of scale" for market participants. This translates into saving the hassle of paying an additional commission, which is interesting and noble logic for an organization that thrives on trading volume in the form of exchange fees charged on a per-contract basis.

With the diversity in contract size and point value relative to the other Treasuries, calculating profit and loss in the two-year note must be slightly adjusted. A trader who is long a September two-year note futures at 108'10.75 and is later stopped out of the trade at 106'02.25 would have realized a loss of 2'08.50, or $4,531.25 (remember, one handle = $2,000).

SHORT-DATED DISCOUNT BOND FUTURES

There are two popular interest rate products that are not part of the Treasury complex: the Eurodollars and the 30-Day Federal funds futures. Each of these futures contracts are quoted in traded as discount bonds. This means that their value is 100 basis points minus the current yield, or at least expectations of the future yield based on the expiration date of the futures contract. For instance, if the market expects the Fed fund futures rate to be 1.25% upon expiration of the June futures contract, the June contract will be priced at 98.7500 (100 basis points − 1.25).

Table 11: Although each of these futures products comes with a large contract size, they are relatively low margin and moderate risk markets.

Contract	Multiplier	Contract Size	Min. Tick Value	Quote Terms
Eurodollars	$25	$1,000,000	$6.25 (0.25 points)	100 - Yield
Fed Fund Futures	$41.67	$5,000,000	$10.4175 (0.25 points)	100 - Yield

Don't let the massive contract sizes fool you. These futures contracts are relatively slow moving when it comes to trader profit and loss because they are at the lowest end of the yield curve. The lack of volatility in these markets is precisely why the CME opted to list them with contract sizes in the millions rather than $100,000 as most currency futures are. Even with seven-digit contract sizes, these two

> Eurodollar and Fed funds futures are a great place to start for beginning traders or for those who are simply risk averse.

futures products are relatively low margined and are considered to be low-risk speculative vehicles. As a result, beginning traders and those with limited trading capital tend to flock to the Eurodollar and the Fed fund futures contracts.

EURODOLLAR FUTURES

Many traders confuse Eurodollars with the forex currency pair Euro/dollar. They might *sound* the same, but that is where the similarities end. A Eurodollar futures contract is written on a three-month interest rate vehicle denominated in US dollars but is deposited in offshore banks (see Table 11). At its simplest, it is an interest-bearing deposit of US funds in a foreign bank and is based on the London Interbank Offered Rate, or LIBOR. It can be thought of as a type of certificate of deposit (CD) with perhaps slightly more risk premium. Consequently, the interest rates offered to Eurodollar holders (in the cash market) are relatively low due to the minimal perceived risk of default.

It is important to note that Eurodollars have nothing to do with Europe; dollar-denominated deposits in Asia are also deemed to be Eurodollar deposits. The *Euro* prefix merely indicates any currency held in a country in which it is not the official currency. An example is the commonly discussed Euroyen, which are Japanese yen-denominated deposits held in banks outside Japan.

Eurodollar futures have become wildly popular among speculators and commercial hedgers. Their appeal stems from the fact that they are extremely liquid and, although highly leveraged, typically see less trading volatility relative to other futures contracts. Unlike the other financial futures markets, the liquidity in Eurodollars ranges well into distant expiration months. It is possible to actively trade Eurodollar with maturity dates spanning from several months to years. This seems like an opportune time to warn you that distant-month Eurodollar futures move much more quickly than do the closer months. Therefore, the benefit of reduced volatility diminishes as you choose contracts with longer expiration dates.

> Eurodollar futures involve a considerable amount of leverage due to low margin requirements and large contract size. However, the short-term natures of the underlying interest rate product works to keep prices relatively slow moving.

Together the CME Eurodollar futures and options lead the worldwide industry in open interest. The daily volume averages over two million, making this the most liquid futures market in the world. All of Eurodollar futures and the majority of Eurodollar options volume is executed electronically through the CME Globex platform. However, at one time, the CME's Eurodollar open outcry pit was just as enormous in square footage as it was in trading and audio volume. Yet, the advent of electronic trading has been detrimental to the world of open outcry, and the Eurodollar pit was no exception.

A Eurodollar futures contract represents $1,000,000 of the underlying asset. To put the amount of leverage into perspective, the margin on a Eurodollar futures contract is typically near $1,000. Thus, a trader can enjoy, or suffer from, the profits and losses based on a million dollars deposited overseas with a mere $1,000.

Similar to the other interest rate products, Eurodollar contract expirations are quarterly: March, June, September, and December. Fortunately, the point values and minimum increments are quoted in decimals rather than fractions, as is the case with other interest rate products.

The Eurodollar is typically quoted in five digits, with the last representing a fraction of a point. Eurodollar prices are verbally communicated just as they look. For instance, if the December Eurodollar is trading at 98.450, it is said that it is "ninety-eight forty-five." However, 98.455 would be spoken as "ninety-eight forty-five and a half." Each trading handle of a Eurodollar futures contracts represents $2,500 to a trader. Accordingly, each individual point in price movement results in a $25 gain or loss in a trading account. Therefore, the full handle value of a Eurodollar is $2,500, and the tick value is $25. This contract has a minimum price movement of a half-tick, or $12.50 for most months, but it is a quarter-tick, or $6.25 for the nearest expiring month. Simply put, if the price of a June Eurodollar futures rallies from 98.550 to 98.560, a profit or loss of $25 would have occurred. For a plunge from 98.550 to 97.550, the move would represent a profit or loss of $2,500.

The difference in minimum tick increments between contract months is likely because the near-month Eurodollar futures contract doesn't typically see much in the way of price change. The daily price change in the front month is typically less than five ticks, making it a great place for beginning speculators to get their feet wet. However, as previously mentioned, the deferred Eurodollar contracts react more violently to changes in interest rates or climate. If your risk tolerance is low to moderate, stay with the near months.

Eurodollars are quoted in handles and decimals and are simply an inverse of the corresponding yield that is tied to the LIBOR. For example, a Eurodollar price of 98.500 implies a yield of 1.5%. This is figured by subtracting the contract price from 100 (100 − 98.5000). Rates this low are somewhat rare but can and do happen. For example, the infamous credit crisis of the late 2000s sparked a massive flight to quality in which the Eurodollar was a beneficiary. Naturally, Eurodollar futures rallied to compensate for increased demand in the spot market. The result was incredibly high valuations and low yields.

Before the financial meltdown of 2008, I was convinced that yields couldn't go to zero. However, massive buying of Treasury bills in fall 2008 and well beyond did create a scenario in which investors were essentially paying to park their funds in a security guaranteed by the federal government because T-bills were trading at a negative yield (their market price was higher than the par value received at expiration). On the other hand, Eurodollars are not backed by the US government—or any government, for that matter—so there is some perceived risk of default. Conceivably, we can infer that the Eurodollar will probably never trade at 100.00, which would imply a yield of zero. Thus, in general, as the futures price approaches 100.00, you should consider the technical setup of the market and fundamental forces to construct a bearish strategy.

Calculating in Eurodollars is much less cumbersome than that of the Treasury complex because it lacks fractions. A trick simplifies the process. Before you begin your calculation, merely move the decimal point two places to the right and multiply each (full) tick by $25.

As always, the process involves determining whether the trade is a profit or loss, subtracting the lesser number from the greater, and multiplying it by the appropriate figure, but don't forget to move the decimal point. Consider an example: If a trader buys a December Eurodollar futures contract at 98.0350 (98.0 3 1/2) and later sells it at 98.220, the realized profit on the trade is 18.5 ticks (98.220 − 98.035), or $462.25 (18.5 × $25).

In my opinion, beginning traders and those who simply prefer a slower-paced market should strongly consider trading Eurodollar futures and options. With that said, even Eurodollars experience periods of excessive volatility, making it important that traders in this market consciously avoid complacency.

In addition, Eurodollar traders often make the mistake of letting losers run simply because of the slow-paced nature of the market. For instance, if an open position is consistently losing $25 to $50 per day, it isn't going to break the bank in the beginning. However, if this is persistently the case, losses can mount, and pulling the plug on such a trade might be psychologically difficult.

FED FUND FUTURES

Most interest rate speculators are trading futures and options using the 30-year bond, 10-year note, and the five-year note futures contracts. However, there is a suite of futures contracts that can be used to speculate on the Federal fund interest rate, which is a function of monetary policy set forth by the Federal Reserve. Specifically, Fed fund futures are derivative contracts written with the FOMC's target overnight bank lending rate as the underlying asset.

Fed fund futures aren't necessarily optimal speculation vehicles for the average retail trader. However, I figured I should mention it in this section because there are a lot of media outlets and fundamental traders who use the Fed fund futures markets as a source of fundamental guidance. That said, Fed fund futures offer a low-margin and low-risk speculative vehicle. But I am not a fan of assuming the Fed fund futures market offers any amount of predictive guidance.

In a bare-bones example of how the Fed fund futures work, a trader who believes the FOMC will be increasing interest rates would sell a Fed fund futures contract; a trader who believes the Fed will lower rates would buy a Fed fund futures contract. This might sound counterintuitive, but the price of an interest rate product moves inversely to rates. Thus, if interest rates rise, bonds, notes, and even Fed fund futures contracts fall, and vice versa.

For example, if the March Fed fund futures contract was trading at 98.250. The implication is the market believes, in that moment, the Fed fund interest rate will be 1.75% at the time this futures contract expires. This is figured by subtracting 98.250 from 100.00. Fed fund futures trade like a discount bond in which the price of the contract is equal to 100 minus the interest rate. This is true unless we are in a negative interest rate environment. If the cash market Fed fund rate, not necessarily the futures rate, is negative, banks in general and even the central bank would be paid to accept deposits! Such a policy is aimed at luring banks to proactively lend funds to the general public because sitting on cash deposits represents an expense.

The point value of the Fed fund futures contract is odd, making calculations messy. Nevertheless, the process is the same. Each point is worth $41.67 to a trader. Thus, if the price moves from 98.250 to 98.260, the trader has made or lost a little over $40. On most days, the market doesn't move more than a tick or two but there are times in which it can see double-digit moves.

Many speculators look to the Fed fund futures market for answers for when the Fed might be taking action next. While most traders in Fed fund futures are highly sophisticated and are likely buying and selling these futures contracts after extensive research, they might still be wrong. Simply put, the Fed fund futures market gives us a glimpse into the expectations of other traders but does not tell us with certainty what the future will bring.

The CME Group provides a highly valuable resource to traders interested in dissecting the Fed fund futures markets known as *FedWatch*. By navigating to the CMEGroup.com website and searching for FedWatch, you would be able to unearth a wealth of knowledge, including the prices of several Fed fund futures contracts with various expiration months—more important, what contract values imply in regards to the probability of a rate hike at a particular point in the future.

To reiterate, the Fed fund futures contracts tell us what market participants believe the overnight bank lending rate will be at a particular time in the future. Between now and expiration, it is possible to see shrill changes in outlook. The rate may be a snapshot of today's thoughts, but two weeks from now, we might see completely different expectations blooming from the Fed fund futures market. Ultimately, nobody can predict the Fed. Not even Fed members know what the committee will be thinking or doing several months from now.

CHAPTER 11: COUNTING PENNIES WITH CURRENCY FUTURES

Most have heard of the foreign exchange market (also known as forex or FX) in which cash market currency transactions take place. Fewer are aware that currency futures are traded every day at the CME via its electronic Globex trading platform. In stark contrast to the forex market, which is, arguably, an under-unregulated marketplace, currency futures have always fallen under the jurisdiction of the NFA and the CFTC and all transactions are guaranteed by the CME. Accordingly, some of the regulatory and counterparty risks (risk of the other side of the trade not paying up on winning trades) that exist for FX traders are irrelevant to currency futures traders. Nevertheless, US regulators have made significant strides in enforcing compliance rules in the forex markets.

Currency futures are mostly traded in "American terms." This simply means that the prices listed in the futures market represent the dollar price of each foreign currency, or how much in US dollars it would cost to purchase one unit of the foreign currency. To understand the point of view of the futures price, ask yourself, "How much of our currency does it take to buy one of theirs?"

EURO, FRANC, AND YEN

Euro, Swiss franc, and yen futures have little in common except that they have identical profit-and-loss calculations. Each of these currencies has a tick value of $12.50 and a multiplier of the same value. However, the CME has recently changed the minimum tick in the Euro and the yen to 0.5 ticks. Thus, these contracts don't always trade in full points. Nevertheless, every tick of either the Euro, the franc, or the yen creates a profit or loss to the trader of $12.50, but a half tick move in the Euro and yen is possible and yields a profit or loss of $6.25. Despite the similarities in the multiplier, the contract size of yen is vastly different from that of the Euro or franc. The size of a single Euro futures contract is 125,000, whereas a yen futures represents 12,500,000 yen (see Table 12). When using $12.50 as the multiplier, however, it is necessary to remove the decimal point in the currency price before calculating to mitigate confusion and the odds of a miscalculation.

Table 12: With the exception of the Japanese yen and the British pound, most currency futures have a contract size of either 100,000 or 125,000 units.

Contract	Multiplier	Contract Size	Min. Tick Value	Quote Terms
Euro	$12.50	125,000 Euro	$6.25 (0.5 ticks)	Cost of 1 unit in dollars
Swiss Franc	$12.50	125,000 Franc	$12.50 (1 tick)	Cost of 1 unit in dollars
Yen	$12.50	12,500,000 Yen	$12.50 (0.5 ticks)	Cost of 1 unit in dollars
British Pound	$6.25	62,500 British Pounds	$6.25 (1 tick)	Cost of 1 unit in dollars
Canadian Dollar	$10	100,000 Canadian Dollars	$10.00 (1 tick)	Cost of 1 unit in dollars
Australian Dollar	$10	100,000 Australian Dollars	$10.00 (1 tick)	Cost of 1 unit in dollars

To clarify, if the Euro has a value of $1.25395, it is equivalent to saying that a single Euro could be purchased for $1.2539 and a half US dollars. In other words, the digit in the fifth place on the right of the decimal will display any fractions of a tick. Nonetheless, you can always use $12.50 multiplied by each tick (the fourth digit to the right of the decimal) to determine the value of any position then account for the partial tick separately. Also, don't forget to remove the decimal completely before calculating profits and losses.

The Euro is a relatively new phenomenon; it was introduced to the world financial markets in January 1999 and replaced the former independent European currency units. The Euro is the official currency of 16 of the 27 member states of the European Union, known collectively as the *Eurozone*.

Another currency with a tick value of $12.50: the Swiss franc. Unlike the Euro, the franc does not trade in half ticks. Many traders refer to this contract simply as the "franc," and it is identical to the Euro in terms of size and point value. Before the Euro, the franc was a widely traded futures contract. However, in the current environment, the volume traded in the Swiss franc is a fraction of that seen in the Euro.

Figure 23: Don't be fooled by seemingly quiet currency markets; they have the potential for explosions. Traders should utilize proper risk management to avoid devastation in extreme scenario. (Chart courtesy of QST)

When figuring profit and loss for the Euro, the franc, and the yen, the tick value is best used as the multiplier. As mentioned, for each tick higher or lower than the futures price moves, a long trader would have made $12.50, and a trader short the market would have lost $12.50. Although $12.50 might not seem like much, it adds up quick.

Thus, if the Euro moves higher from $1.25395 to $1.25490 it has increased by 9.5 ticks or $118.75 ((125490 - 125395) x $12.50). However, in Figure 23 we opted to use the value of a full point (one penny in the change of the price of a Euro in terms of the US dollar), which is $1,250 (100 x $12.50) rather than the $12.50 tick value because of the magnitude of the move. In this example, the Euro dropped 35 cents against the dollar, which represented a move of $43,750 per contract (($12.50 x 100) x 35 cents)!

AUSSIE AND CANADIAN DOLLARS

Known as the commodity currencies simply because their valuations tend to be correlated with commodity prices, the Australian dollar and the Canadian dollar future contracts are similar in nature. Both have a stated contract size of $100,000 of the corresponding currency (not the US dollar) and a tick value of $10. Similar to our calculations with the Euro, the franc, and the yen, the multiplier is the tick value. Accordingly, for every tick that a trader gains or losses, he experiences a profit or loss of $10. Thus, if a trader buys a September Aussie dollar futures contract at 0.8300 and places a limit order to sell it back at 0.9310, the realized profit would be $100 (before commissions and fees) after the profit target is executed. This is figured by subtracting the purchase price from the selling price and multiplying the difference by $10 ((8310 – 8300) × $10).

BRITISH POUND

The British pound is in a league of its own, in that its specified contract size and tick value are vastly different from any of the other currencies. The British pound, sometimes referred to as the "cable," when paired against the US dollar, trades in contracts of 62,500 British pounds. Accordingly, each tick in price movement results in a profit or loss of $6.25 for any trader with exposure in this market. You might have noticed that the contract size and the tick value are exactly half that of the Euro, the franc, and the yen. Despite much different contract specifications, calculations of profit and loss are similar to the other currencies. Therefore, if a trader is short a December British pound futures from 1.2950, meaning that it would take $1.2950 in US dollars to purchase a single pound, and is later stopped out at 1.2975, the loss on the trade would be $156.25. This is figured by subtracting the original sales price from the fill of the stop loss order and multiplying the difference by $6.25 ((12975 – 12950) × $6.25).

Don't let the lower tick value fool you into thinking that there is a relatively lower risk in trading the British pound; this is far from the truth. In fact, the pound is capable of unbelievably volatile moves. I have personally witnessed a single trading session in which the British pound futures market traded in an approximate range of 1,000 points, or $6,250 per contract. This type of move is extremely rare—it has happened only twice—but anything is possible at any time. As shown in Figure 24, the British pound experienced unusual volatility following the Brexit vote of 2016.

Figure 24: Traders should respect the potential for sizable moves in the British pound—and any other market—despite the relatively small tick value. It isn't uncommon to see moves that equate to several thousand dollars of profit or loss to a trader. (Chart courtesy of QST)

CONCLUSION ON FIGURING PROFIT, LOSS, AND RISK IN FUTURES AND OPTIONS

The information covered in Chapters 8 through 11 certainly won't carve your fate as a trader. However, without familiarity of the basic contract specifications and corresponding risk and reward, you aren't giving yourself a fair shake. The odds of successful trading are characteristically unfavorable, making it imperative that you do everything in your power to shift them in your direction. I believe that awareness and experience will do just that. After all, being properly educated about the "boring" details might prevent emotional trading decisions that could endanger your hard-earned money.

CHAPTER 12: COPING WITH MARGIN CALLS

Unlike equity accounts, in which margin is granted only to a few, all futures accounts are margin accounts. Further, this margin is granted without any cost or strings attached. Accordingly, it is up to traders themselves to keep their risk and leverage at reasonable levels. Unfortunately, not all market participants are capable of doing so.

Thanks to movies and other media outlets, many beginning traders have become overly frightened by the idea of a margin call. Truth be told, if you trade responsibly, you shouldn't receive many, but it can—and eventually will—happen. When it does, there's no need to panic; most margin calls can be alleviated via position adjustment instead of adding funds to the account or outright liquidating trades. A good brokerage will be able to help traders to do just that. However, for those trading with an inexperienced broker, or brokerage, your positions might be liquidated at the first sign of trouble without any opportunity to alleviate the margin shortage. This can be a painfully expensive lesson to learn. In short, being aware of the mechanics of margin and choosing a brokerage with a flexible and accommodating policy when it comes to alleviating margin calls might be the most important steps a trader takes to improve the overall outcome of trading ventures.

> Futures traders are not charged interest on money borrowed, as equity traders are.

WHAT IS MARGIN?

The margin is simply a specified amount of funds stipulated by the exchange and required to be held in a brokerage account to enter and keep open positions in a futures market. In its simplest form, it is a good-faith deposit or financial collateral used to cover credit risk. By demanding margin required to trade in any given contract, the exchange mitigates the possibility of traders defaulting on their trading; in other words, margins reduce the odds of traders losing more money than they have on deposit, which causes them to fail to meet their obligations to those on the other side of the trade. This is how futures exchanges guarantee all transactions. While that seems like a given, it isn't. Forex traders run the risk of making a winning trade but not being able to withdraw their profits from the account if the other side of the trade wasn't able to cover the trading loss.

Although the futures exchange sets margin requirements, brokerage firms have the authority to increase margin rates. That said, brokerage firms are forbidden from decreasing margin or allowing undercapitalized traders to hold positions in the long term. We will soon discuss that this rule does not apply to day traders.

Additionally, keep in mind that margin requirements are dynamic. The exchange and brokerage firm can change them at any time and without notice.

INITIAL MARGIN

You can use the terms *initial margin* and *margin* synonymously. Specifically, *initial margin* is the amount of capital the exchange expects a trader has on deposit in a corresponding trading account to hold a given futures contract, or short option position, beyond the close of trade of the session in which the order was executed. Simply put, if the *initial margin* on a T-note futures contract is $1,400, a trader should have at least this much in his trading account to buy or sell, and hold, a single contract.

Initial margin should be looked at as the minimum funding for holding a particular position beyond the close of any trading session. However, the appropriate funding is much higher in my opinion. In summary, the initial margin is the bare minimum a trader should have in a trading account but those wishing to trade profitably, as opposed to thrill seek, should consider holding considerably more than the initial margin requirement.

MAINTENANCE MARGIN

Maintenance margin, on the other hand, is the minimum account balance that must be maintained at the close of trade to avoid a margin call. The *maintenance margin* is typically 90% of the initial margin. When the account equity dips below the maintenance margin measured on the close of trade on any particular day, a margin call is triggered, and the trader is required to bring the account equity above the initial margin requirement by either liquidating positions, adding funds, or mitigating the margin through position adjustment. Bringing the equity above the maintenance margin level is no longer enough; once a margin call is triggered the account must be above the initial margin requirement at the close of the trading session to alleviate the margin call.

It is important to note that margin calls are not relieved until the account is within the required initial margin at the close. Beginning traders often assume that if they get the account under control on the morning of the margin call, what happens the rest of the day is irrelevant. However, this is not the case. If a trader liquidates or adjusts positions or wires funds to meet the margin call in the morning but the positions in the account move adversely to the point in which the account is under margined at the close of trade, the margin call will age to the next trading session. In short, margin calls can only be met by ensuring the account is within the requirements at the close of the trading session.

DAY TRADING MARGIN VERSUS OVERNIGHT MARGIN

A big misconception looms concerning how margin is levied by the exchange. Most people assume that traders must have the proper exchange-required margin to enter a position. This isn't necessarily the case; instead, the brokerage firm, or your individual broker, determines whether you have the adequate margin to initiate a trade. Exchange-stipulated initial margin requirements don't come into play until the end of the trading session. At this time, the exchange margins any open positions accordingly. Many traders are surprised to discover that the exchanges have little say on the margin charged for day trading activity, which is any buying or selling of futures and options that takes place during a trading session prior to the close of trade. To further specify, most futures and options markets trade 23 hours per day; a day trade is considered any position entered and offset within that time frame. Thus, it is possible for a trader to purchase an E-mini S&P 500 futures on the open of trade at 5:00 p.m. Central on a Tuesday, and offset it just before 4:00 p.m. Central on Wednesday without being subjected to the exchanges initial margin requirement. Although the position was held overnight, it is considered a day trade because the entry and exit occurred in a single trading session. With that said, not all brokerages grant day trading margin rates for orders

> When it comes to margin, just because you can doesn't mean that you should. Remember, a fool and his money are soon parted.

placed in the overnight session, so the ability to hold a 23-hour trade based on highly discounted day trading margin rates will depend on the brokerage being used.

Depending on a trader's established relationship with a brokerage firm—or, more important, an individual broker—the margin charged on any intraday positions is generally anywhere from 10% to 50% of the exchange's stipulated overnight rate. Naturally, only clients who are believed to be responsible enough to have access to excessively low margin requirements are granted the privilege because irresponsible traders are a credit risk to the brokerage. This is similar to the threats posed to credit card companies by consumers with low credit scores. With that said, some platforms can now automatically liquidate the account if it is in danger of going negative or losing more than what is currently deposited.

If auto liquidation (the process of offsetting positions once a particular loss threshold is reached) is a capability of the platform, more lenient margin policies might be offered to day traders. After all, similar to the way a trader analyzes the market in terms of risk and reward, a brokerage firm assesses clients on a risk/reward basis and proceeds accordingly. Brokerage revenue is commission based; they want you to trade, but not if it isn't worth the potential consequences of losses exceeding available trading capital.

Therefore, traders with little money in an account can trade with a margin well below the exchange's stated margin level without ever receiving a margin call, assuming that they always exit their positions before the close. For instance, a broker might permit a trader with an account balance of $2,500 to day-trade one E-mini S&P futures contract even though the overnight margin requirement is upward of $4,500. In extreme cases, brokerage firms have been known to extend discounted margins to traders to the tune of 5% to 10% of the overnight rate. Thus, assuming an exchange stipulated margin of $5,000, a trader might buy or sell the futures with as little as $500—or maybe less. Keep in mind that although it is not a good idea, aggressive traders have been known to abuse leverage because they have the freedom to do so.

Again, once a trader holds a position beyond the closing time of the day session, overnight margin rates are imposed and, if appropriate, margin calls are issued.

WHAT ARE MARGIN CALLS?

The term *margin call* seems to infer that a trader is contacted by phone about a margin deficiency, but margin calls are typically communicated by email, thanks to modern technology. Brokerage firms provide clients with daily activity statements in which a margin call is noted, if applicable. A separate margin call notice might also be emailed to stipulate the amount of the margin deficiency and a countdown of the days.

An official margin call can only be triggered based on the value of the account at the close of trade relative to the exchange's maintenance margin level. If the account balance is below the maintenance margin at the close of any particular trading session, a margin call is triggered. Please note, a margin deficit during the trading day that corrects itself by the close of trade will not trigger a margin call. Nevertheless, a trader should take note that the risk exposure is excessive and action should probably be taken to bring the account to a healthier level of risk and margin excess.

HOW TO HANDLE A MARGIN CALL

Beginning traders are prone to panic when a margin call is received; however, this is an unnecessary emotion that can cause poor trading decisions. Margin calls can be eliminated in one way or a combination of three ways:

ⓢ **Partial or total account liquidation.** In many cases, traders who have received a margin call notice are holding several positions. They might be spread across a handful of markets or all in the same contract.

Nonetheless, a margin call doesn't require that all the positions be offset; the trader must liquidate enough of them to bring the account into good standing.

With partial liquidations, it is important to monitor the positions throughout the day and pay special attention to the closing prices of the contracts in your account. This is because the exchange levies margin requirements based on your positions *at the close of the day session* in conjunction with the closing prices of all the positions in your account. If values of the remaining positions change from the time the original margin deficit was calculated, the time the partial liquidation took place, and the close of trade, it is possible that the actions taken were not enough to eliminate the margin call.

For instance, consider a trader who is long two E-mini NASDAQ futures in which the initial margin requirement is $4,300 per contract and an account equity balance is $5,000 at the time one of the two contracts was offset. All else being equal, the trader faces an initial margin requirement of $4,300 and has approximately $700 in excess of the required funds. However, if the market drops sharply from the time the first contract was liquidated into the close, the margin call might remain an issue. In this example, this would occur if the E-mini NASDAQ drops approximately 35 points (35 x $20 = $700) from the price the position was reduced to one contract from two because the drop in the NASDAQ would cause the account balance to drop below $4,300.

ⓢ **Margin adjustment through trade and risk alteration.** Although the exchange-required margins for any given futures contract are relatively fixed, it is possible to adjust the margin of your overall portfolio of positions using options or even futures. For example, a trader who is long a futures contract can purchase a put option in the same market as a method to reduce the risk—and, therefore, reduce the margin requirement—on the futures contract. The same trader can also look to sell a call option for a similar but less effective impact on margin. If you are unfamiliar with options or these types of margin reduction strategies, you might be interested in reading my book *Higher Probability Commodity Trading*. Unfortunately, the scope of this book does not permit paying proper attention to these somewhat complicated strategies. Nonetheless, you need to realize that there are ways to alleviate margin issues, aside from throwing in the towel and liquidating the account or depositing additional funds. If the opportunity arises to utilize such strategies and your broker, or brokerage, is unable to help you, then it is time to look for another broker.

Similarly, futures traders might look to reduce their risk and, more important, margin requirement by taking the opposite position in a highly correlated contract. For instance, a trader long March corn can sell a July corn contract to mitigate margin and hopefully alleviate a margin call. This is effective because the July contract tends to move in the same direction as March. However, after such an adjustment is made, a trader faces tough decisions on how to move out of the spread. At some point, completely exiting the trade or lifting one leg at a time will be necessary. This type of strategy can be compared to putting a Band-Aid on a wound. It conceals the injury but doesn't necessarily heal it. Moreover, the Band-Aid eventually needs to be removed—and this could be painful.

$ **Wired funds.** This is the most straightforward method of bringing an account within the stipulated margin requirement. Still, it is not without its complications due to the timing in which the margin is measured and levied. For example, the exchange charges margin on any positions being held at the close of trade, but margin calls are expedited late in the evening or early in the morning on the subsequent day of the issued account statement in which the margin call was triggered. The trader then has the entire trading session to act before margin is calculated again.

Market conditions frequently are drastically different from the time the initial margin deficit is calculated to the time the margin call is received—even more so by the close of trade the following day, at which point the account is reassessed. Therefore, it is possible for traders to wire funds to meet the stated margin call, only to find out that, due to adverse price changes in the remaining positions, the wired amount was not sufficient to meet the call. For this reason, it is a good idea to wire more than the stated margin deficit. If the margin call is for $2,000, it is a good idea to wire at least $3,000 and preferably well over $4,000 to reduce the risk of chronic margin trouble.

THE MARGIN CALL COUNTDOWN

Similar to the manner in which margin is imposed, margin calls are measured in terms of days. As we have mentioned, measurement of whether a margin call has been met takes place at the close of day session trade. Any accounts that have failed to meet the initial margin requirement go into the next day with an aging margin call.

> "The safe way to double your money is to fold it over once and put it in your pocket."
> – Frank Hubbard

The amount of time a firm gives for eliminating the margin call varies but is most often within one to three days. Yet, it is always preferable to take care of margin deficits immediately. If you find yourself in the midst of a margin call, it might be a good idea to follow a timeline, as outlined next; carrying a margin call too long or putting the account in danger of going negative could result in forced liquidation by the margin department. Simply put, if the margin department of a brokerage firm must step in to bring an account in line with required margin, it pays no attention to the prices or circumstances of liquidation. Its goal is to get the account under control in the quickest manner possible. As a trader, you never want to put your account in a situation in which third parties have a say in when and where you exit a trade. Additionally, most brokerages charge clients fees for liquidating over-leveraged trading accounts. For instance, it is not uncommon for a brokerage to charge $50 per contract if a client lets losses run to dangerously low account balances or aging margin calls. I've witnessed this happen to over-leveraged and traders with hundreds of contracts open. You can do the math; it adds up quickly.

Note that many deep discount brokerage firms are much stricter when it comes to margin calls. Due to their ultra low commissions, they can't afford to accept the risk of account debits as much as a balanced firm might. As a result, they might practice tight controls that could have a negative impact on overall trading results. Once again, sometimes saving money on transaction costs is actually more expensive when looking at the big picture.

DAY ONE

A first-day margin call, issued the trading session following the margin deficit as measured on the close of trade, is a friendly warning that you have gotten in a little over your head and should reevaluate your positions. Unless the account is in danger of losing more than what is on deposit, known as *going negative* (you might also hear this referred to as *going debit*), a brokerage firm generally allows you to treat the first day as a freebie. In other words, even in the absence of any action taken by the trader, a good brokerage will avoid liquidation of the positions.

Although action might not be immediately required, during the course of the first-day margin call, a trader should determine a plan of action that includes either wiring money, liquidating some or all the positions or, preferably, adjusting current positions to meet the pending margin call. With that said, if the trader intends to adjust the margin by using hedges with futures and options, he should begin the adjustment process on day one of the margin call.

Some brokerage firms charge margin call fees to accounts that allow the margin deficiency to go beyond the close of trade on the first day of the margin call. Fees typically range from $25 to $50 per day, starting on day two. In addition, some firms put the account on liquidation-only status.

I highly recommend that traders attempt to alleviate a margin call on the first day. It is human nature to put our heads in the sand and see what the next day brings, but more often than not the situation gets worse as the margin call ages. It is better to nip things in the bud by reducing risk and margin as soon as possible.

DAY TWO

Hopefully, traders take care of the problem on the first day; if not, on the second day of a margin call, traders are expected to take some action to alleviate the margin call. Additionally, adding positions to the account is considered irresponsible, so traders should refrain from trading unless the broker handling the account has granted consent. Excessive abuse of trading privileges can lead to tighter controls on the trading account, thus creating an undesirable situation for both trader and broker. Clearly, brokers and brokerage firms prefer that you trade more, not less, but they are also second-party risk bearers to their client's trading accounts. Not only do brokerages answer to the exchange and pay fees in relation to client margin deficits, but they also are responsible for seeing that any debit (negative) account balances are covered. This often entails withholding broker commissions until the client refunds the account to bring it to a positive balance, or at least zero the account out.

If a trader fails to eliminate the margin deficit but has made an effort through position adjustments and/or partial liquidation, the brokerage firm generally sees it as cooperation and might grant the trader some freedom going into the third day of the margin call. Nonetheless, it is recommended that traders take care of their margin responsibilities within the first day or two of the margin call.

DAY THREE

If at all possible, a trader should avoid taking a margin call into the third day. However, it is understandable that, in certain circumstances, it can happen. In this situation, the trader used the first and second day wisely and reduced the margin deficit. Doing so makes it much easier to assess the actions necessary to get the margin under control. Therefore, on the third day of a margin call, traders should be seriously focused on eliminating the margin deficit, regardless of the consequences. Most brokerage firms begin to take action on an account when a margin call is carried into the third day. This means that they have the authority to liquidate the account as they see fit to bring the account within the margin requirement. Trust me, this is not something that you want to experience. To reiterate, margin clerks aren't traders. Their sole purpose is to get the account compliant, which means they are not necessarily concerned with getting you the best fill price. Additionally, they tend to be heavy-handed, in that they sometimes liquidate above and beyond what is necessary to compensate for possible market movements in other positions. Even worse, they often charge traders an arm and a leg for the hassle of being forced to step in and regain risk control.

ACCEPTING MARGIN CALLS

I thoroughly believe that psychology plays the largest part in determining whether a trader is successful, and margin calls are an important part of the equation. It is imperative that traders recognize that margin calls can, and do, happen; thus, traders should be properly prepared to cope with them. Margin call management for clients is an area in which a good broker will earn his money.

Traders who understand the process and have reviewed contingency plans for margin issues stand a much better chance of defeating the overwhelming sense of panic that occurs when time and capital limits are applied to a position. Also, just as consumers are better off living within their means, traders should make every attempt to speculate within the confines of the capital available. Too often, beginning traders assume that more leverage will result in quicker profits; in reality, this couldn't be further from the truth. In reality, it is a good idea to get into the habit of utilizing 50% or less of the available trading margin. I've noticed that the higher the margin excess in a trading account, the higher the odds of long-term trading success. Some of the better traders I've seen use a mere 20% to 30% of their trading account toward margin at any given time. The remaining capital works as a rainy day fund enabling traders to withstand temporary shocks in market volatility. Unfortunately, the over-leveraged and undercapitalized traders have as strong tendency to run out of money at the worst possible time. Yet, those utilizing a small percentage of their trading capital are generally in a position to recover from large drawdowns rather than being forced to shut the game console down and walk away. This is what separates the winners from the losers.

CHAPTER 13: THE ONLY MAGIC IN TRADING— EMOTIONAL STABILITY

As an industry insider, I am repeatedly confronted by those looking for a magic indicator, trading system, or newsletter. They want somebody, often me, to tell them where to buy and where to sell, and do it with impeccable accuracy. Regrettably, I am forced to bring them into reality.

> "If all the economists in the world were laid end to end, they still wouldn't reach a conclusion."
> – George Bernard Shaw

In my years as a broker, I have come across droves of retail and institutional traders and just as many trading strategies and methodologies. I have yet to discover any individual system or style that is capable of making money in all market conditions all of the time. Those who find a way to make money more often than not require excessive dedication to research and adjustment. In other words, there is no Holy Grail or easy money. Simply reading a few books on trading or subscribing to a signal service isn't going to ensure that you will trade profitably, but doing so could point you in the right direction. If you are looking for magic, go to Disneyland; you will not find it in a trading seminar, a book, or a newsletter—at least, not without putting your blood, sweat, and tears into it.

The only "magical" tool I have found in trading is the ability to keep emotions under control; without that, the best indicators or trading recommendations in the world won't be helpful. For instance, if in March 2009 I told you to buy the E-mini S&P futures at 688 and continue to roll over the position to avoid delivery until you have the opportunity to sell it back at 2,450 in mid-2017, do you really think that you would have had the emotional stability to hold the position through all the peaks and valleys—or, better yet, the faith in my recommendation to do so?

Clearly, very few people, if any, would have the fortitude to execute a trade of this magnitude. Even if psychic powers were involved, in 2009, it would have been difficult to imagine that the value of the S&P would nearly quadruple in value. After all, to reap the entire reward of 1,762 points in the S&P ($88,100 in the E-mini or $440,500 in the full-sized contract), the trader would have had to resist liquidating the trade prematurely at any point in the roughly eight-year time period that it took to complete the recommendation. All the while, surviving massive corrections such as those seen in mid-2011 and mid-2015 in which many TV pundits were calling for the S&P to revisit the 700 level, or worse. Further, most rational thinkers would have looked at the March 2009 S&P and thought the upside potential was massive relative to the downside risk. Yet, at the time few were in such a frame of mind. In fact, many individual investors were converting what little was left of their retirement accounts into cash.

> "Nothing gives one person so much advantage over another as to remain always cool and unruffled under all circumstances." – Thomas Jefferson

This is obviously an extreme example, but the same difficulties and emotions are involved in following a trading signal, recommendation, or idea of your own. The argument I am trying to make is that perhaps trading success is equally, or more so, reliant on psychology because it has a large influence on the implementation of the actual trading technique, philosophy, and indicators used or systems purchased.

The majority of trading literature emphasizes the impact that fear and greed can have on trading decisions and, ultimately, the bottom line. However, I believe that another emotion has the potential to wreak havoc on traders and their account balances: frustration. Each of these emotions is necessary but, in excess, can be catastrophic.

Warren Buffett's take on the subject is incredibly insightful. According to the "Oracle of Omaha," traders should "Be fearful when others are greedy and greedy when others are fearful." This is simply saying that traders should buy low and sell high in terms of market sentiment rather than price.

Traders who flock to the latest craze or newsworthy buzz are likely to get burned. This is because after a market has attracted attention, there is a good chance that the move has run its course. On the contrary, the best opportunities can often be found in markets that have fallen out of interest with the general public.

> "When everybody starts looking really smart, and not realizing a lot of it was luck, I got scared."– Raphael Yavneh

The study of emotion and trading is ongoing, and an unlimited number of theories focus on managing the sensations that one feels before, during, and after any given trade. Believe it or not, as a broker I have seen many futures and options traders get more satisfaction out of the rush of being exposed to the markets than they do making money. I have to admit, part of what sparks me to get up in the morning is seeing what the markets have in store for our clients and me. Whether it is good or bad, it keeps us all coming back for more. Nonetheless, my motivation will always be money rather than thrill.

More to the point, studies have shown that traders with the ability to stabilize their emotions, in both winning and losing situations, see more positive trading results than traders who are less capable of managing their feelings. Unfortunately, unless you are born with a natural ability to effectively cope with the excitements of trading, the ability to do so will come only with experience.

THE THREE EMOTIONS IN TRADING: FEAR, GREED, FRUSTRATION

In this chapter, I briefly discuss a few of the most influential emotions that traders experience. Expecting that you will walk away from this book with all the insight that you need to control your emotions while trading is impractical. Yet, I do believe that by getting a broad-based overview of what you can expect and some of the common traps that traders fall into, you will at least be able to identify such emotions; this is the first step toward managing them.

FEAR

If you have ever participated in the financial or commodity markets, you are well aware of the fears associated with them, such as the fear of losing money, being wrong, or leaving money on the table. Fear is a natural and necessary emotion, especially when money is involved. After all, if you are completely fearless when it comes to your trading, the odds are in favor of taking excessive risks and eventually losing your trading capital. Despite the financial theory that suggests additional risk is equivalent to additional profit potential, the correlation diminishes when a certain threshold is met. The line in the sand is difficult to draw, but when you cross it, you will know—and at that point, it might be too late.

In my experience, fearless traders might have intermittent success simply because they are swinging for the fence and will achieve their goals from time to time. However, long-term success for such traders is unlikely because unnecessary risks will eventually haunt irresponsible traders.

> "A market is the combined behavior of thousands of people responding to information, misinformation, and whim."
> – Kenneth Change (*The New York Times*)

Instead, traders should give the markets an appropriate amount of respect and approach them with a modestly fearful attitude. I believe that some fear of loss can work to keep traders humble and emphasize that, regardless of the countless hours of research performed and even an Ivy League education, traders can lose money trading commodities. In theory, a controlled fear of the markets and the devastation they are capable of can encourage more objective and sound trading decisions.

Although I speak of having a moderate amount of fear as though it is as simple as hitting a switch, managing that fear is far from being this easy. The general public and even seasoned traders often have difficulties managing their emotions. Thus, keeping feelings of fear at a controlled level is much more difficult than it sounds. In reality, many traders need years of practice before they can avoid the feeling of panic in an adversely moving market or even a profitable trade in which they are wrestling with the fear of giving back some of the gains or missing out on potential earnings.

Now that I have established that fear of the markets can be positive, if kept at a reasonable level, and addressed the difficulty in managing such emotions, I point out the influence of being too fearful. Traders who aren't capable of properly managing feelings of trepidation are prone to making irrational trading decisions, such as panic liquidation or failure to act. Either scenario has the ability to cause considerable financial harm.

As a broker, I have had the unfortunate experience of having a front-row seat to the carnage that ill-timed panic can cause and of course, I've experienced it in my own trading endeavors. Many traders have a strong tendency to exit a trade "gone bad" at the exact worst possible time. For example, they often ignore the well-known reality that prices are inclined to overshoot their equilibrium level before coming back to a more sustainable price. In the heat of the moment, fearful traders might exit their trade prematurely only to find the market traded favorably without them.

UNDERCAPITALIZATION BREEDS FEAR

Traders who are underfunded are typically more prone to fearful trading and, thus, poor results. This is because the less excess margin in a trading account, the less room for error there is. Whether the lack of breathing room is the result of too many positions, not enough money on deposit, or a combination of the two, one big mistake could take the trader out of the game, and he knows this.

As a result, the trader is more likely to liquidate positions prematurely, causing unnecessary losses and, in many cases, avoidable transaction costs. Inexperienced traders have been known to rack up a large commission bill trying to trade in and out of a market while being dominated by the fear of loss or even fear of missing an anticipated price move.

This is not to say that it is necessary to deposit hundreds or even tens of thousands of dollars in an account. Regardless of the funding, traders should trade within their means. Thanks to products such as mini and micro futures and options on futures, this is possible even for the smallest of accounts. I remind you that this is not unlike the concept of living within one's means when it comes to budgeting personal finances. There is no shame in trading small!

GREED

As Gordon Gecko would say, "Greed is good." Without greed, you wouldn't be reading this book, and in all likelihood, the futures markets wouldn't exist. Greed is the emotion that inspires speculators to enter the markets in hopes of abnormal profits as opposed to investing in Treasury bills. However, with all the opportunity that greed creates in the world of trading, it also breeds misery.

Greed is a word that is used frequently to describe the personal desire for monetary wealth. In fact, the formal definition of greed is the excessive desire to acquire or possess more material wealth than one needs or deserves.

"It is an unfortunate human failing that a full pocketbook often groans more loudly than an empty stomach." – Franklin Delano Roosevelt

Anyone who has ever had money at risk in the market understands that greed works in two ways. On any given trade, the goal before entering the position is to bring profits to the trading account. Nevertheless, when the trade becomes a losing proposition, the yearning for profits quickly turns into the need to be right, or at least not wrong, by avoiding locking in a loss. At this point in time, greed turns from being solely monetary based to also involving ego. The combination of these two types of greed can be extremely powerful and often leads to financial ruin—or at least a depleted trading account.

Those who cannot accept humility have the odds of productive trading stacked against them. There is little room for ego in the markets because it can be the biggest enemy to a trader; it can prevent a trader from cutting losses when wrong and taking profits when right. A trader driven by greed and ego tries to justify losses as being too early as opposed to being wrong and, therefore, is susceptible to an account-draining defeat on a single trade. Similarly, traders might also believe that the winners will obtain infinite gains, deterring them from taking profits while they are available. This outlook often leads to a scenario in which winning trades turn into losers.

A perfect example of greed in the marketplace is the internet boom of the late 1990s. Investors with a get-rich-quick mentality were flocking to any stock that had a .com at the end of it. Greed and speculation drove share prices to unrealistic and unsustainable levels. As we all know, those who allowed greed to suck them into the euphoria paid dearly when the tech party ended.

Commodities are not immune to the same irresponsible price swings. The commodity rally that began in 2007 and consumed much of 2008 before coming to a screeching halt was arguably the result, at least in part, of greedy speculation as stock investors who were bored of flat-lining returns looked to the commodity markets for alternatives. A similar occurrence took place in 2011 in the gold and silver markets. Although strong commodity fundamentals lured money into the metals, irrational greed and ego kept the money flowing to a point at which unsustainable prices were reached. Similar to the dot-com craze, the commodity bubble eventually popped, leaving many market participants wishing that they hadn't taken part in the latest investment trend. Unfortunately, this is a long-term recurring phenomenon, and few markets have been spared its wrath.

FRUSTRATION

The influence of frustration on trading decisions is often overlooked, but having the ability to avoid letting disappointment take over is priceless. This is perhaps the single most important difference between a profitable trader and the masses.

Frustration can be a part of any trading scenario but primarily stems from one of two events: exiting a position with a loss or exiting a position with a profit but leaving potential gains on the table. An irrational trader repeatedly allows the emotions experienced in these scenarios to trigger an attempt to recoup what he believes the market "wrongfully" took from him. Such conduct is often the beginning of the end of a trading career.

THE ANGST OF TAKING PROFITS "EARLY"

For those who have never executed a trade, it might seem odd that aggravation could arise from a profitable speculation. However, imagine being a trader with the insight and gumption to sell crude oil short in mid-2014 at $105 per barrel, and subsequently taking a profit on the trade at $95 per barrel to lock in a gain of $10,000 minus commissions and fees. This was clearly a great trade. Conversely, the personal anguish felt by the same trader who later watched crude prices plummet to less than $30 per barrel by early 2016 is indescribable.

From the outside, a $10,000 winner is a triumphant victory, but from the inside, a trader who hasn't developed the ability to control her emotions might see it as a loss. After all, had the trader continued to hold the position, she might have walked away with a six-figure winner. I have personally witnessed many traders who simply could not deal with the reality of cutting a winning trade too early and, as a result, began making unfounded trading decisions in their quest to get back what was lost—or, at least, not won.

A trader in this frame of mind isn't considering what it would have taken to hold the position to the end. She might react similarly to a contestant on the TV game show *Deal or No Deal* who just realized the million-dollar prize was in her briefcase after settling for a deal of $235,000 by putting herself through the mental agony of questioning the decisions that led to the winnings earned.

The reality is, there is no way to predict how far a market will go, just as there is no way to know which case you are holding on *Deal or No Deal*. In addition, it is unfair for a trader to agonize over what could have been, simply because it is impossible to predict what decisions would have been made as the market moves from point A to point B.

Going back to our *Deal or No Deal* analogy, few contestants can take the game all the way to the end because there are a lot of tough decisions to make in the meantime. Those who do take it to the final two cases often come up empty-handed. The same is true in trading. From my experience, the successful traders are those who can live with the fact that they will almost never pick the top or bottom of a market but are happy to take a piece out of the middle.

THE PAIN OF TAKING A LOSS

One of the most difficult things to do as a trader is to exit a losing trade. This is because doing so confirms incorrect speculation, timing, or both. Accordingly, locking in a loss not only does damage to a trading account but also takes its toll on the psyche of the untrained trader.

While a position is still open, regardless of the size of the paper loss, the trader is consumed with hope that the market will turn around and the losses will be erased. There is a sense that if there is no harm in the end, there is no foul. However, large losses often don't correct themselves; instead, they get even larger. Although taking a small loss is financially and mentally painful, don't forget that large losses can be nearly unbearable from both a mental and a monetary standpoint.

The biggest fear that traders have in taking a loss is the possible subsequent market reversal that might have eventually allowed the position to be profitable. In a situation such as this, the frustration can be multiplied to a point at which an out-of-control trader can cause a lot of harm via poor trading decisions and maybe even poor personal decisions.

As a broker, I often communicate with other traders and brokers, some of whom are located on the floor of the exchanges. Over the years I have heard some heartbreaking stories of traders who couldn't deal with their losses and chose to take their own lives. One in particular that sticks out took place in October 2008, during the infamous equity market crash. A CME local trading his personal account took his life after sustaining losses to the tune of several millions of dollars on a short S&P play. The trader's account was force-liquidated by the clearing firm due to a margin deficiency. As it turns out, he was correct in being short the market but unwisely had too many positions on and was unable to ride out the volatility simply because he ran out of money. Subsequent to the premature liquidation of his positions, the market moved in the anticipated direction without him in one of the most treacherous bear markets in history.

Clearly, this is an extreme and unfortunate case. However, all traders who have taken a substantial loss can relate to the emotions involved. The most common reaction is an irrational attempt to get back losses from the very market that took them. This mindset can wreak havoc on a trader and, although we will never know for sure, might have been the catalyst causing this trader to over-leverage his account.

After a devastating loss has occurred, the trader might have difficulty analyzing the market objectively and sticking to the original trading strategy or theory. Too often the story ends in out-of-control and mindless trading that benefits the brokerage firm, thanks to excessive commissions, but does, even more, damage to the trading account and the trader's ability to behave rationally.

Another instance in which I have noticed that traders allow their emotions to get the best of them is subsequent to being stopped out of a trade. Describing a filled stop order as premature is appropriate if, after the order is filled, the market moves in the intended direction. Unfortunately, this is a common occurrence and is one of the biggest arguments against using stop orders.

For example, a trader who is long a March crude oil from $45.60 per barrel with a stop loss placed at $44.60 in an attempt to limit the potential losses on the trade to $1,000 plus slippage is anticipating higher prices but is also allowing the market some amount of freedom. The emotional turmoil caused by a situation in which March crude futures drop to exactly $44.60 to trigger the working stop order, forcing the trader out of the market, and then stage a large rally can destroy the emotional stability of an untrained trader. Although the total loss on such a venture would be $1,000 plus transaction costs, assuming that the stop order was filled at exactly $44.60, in the mind of an undisciplined trader, the loss is considered to be that which was realized plus any potential profits that would have occurred by being long during the successive rally.

This type of market approach creates the dismal odds that retail traders face. An unseasoned speculator, and even a well-experienced and successful trader, can easily fall into the trap of vengeful trading. However, doing so generally leads to unreasonable trading decisions and even more losses. In my opinion, traders can take a step toward bettering their odds of a particular trade and eliminating the potential emotional turmoil caused by premature liquidation through the use of long and short options for managing the risk of a futures position rather than a stop loss order. Once again, I cover this topic extensively in *Higher Probability Commodity Trading*.

VENGEFUL TRADING IS COUNTERPRODUCTIVE

The act of revenge is described as inflicting punishment in return for injury or insult and is typically sparked by an event that leaves a person feeling as though he was wronged. It isn't hard to imagine why or how a trader would feel victimized by the market, causing vengeance to emerge.

Traders who have experienced one of the preceding scenarios or have been part of similar incidents in suffering losses, or potential gains foregone, often seek revenge. Feelings of revenge typically begin as losses are mounting, well before the damage is realized by exiting the trade. However, in many cases, the yearning for retribution never subsides. Even those "lucky" enough to recoup what was lost from the very market that took it have a hard time satisfying their craving to settle the score. As you can imagine, traders who allow emotions to dictate the market they trade and influence the way they trade it will have a difficult time achieving financial success.

A symptom of the vengeful trader is a phenomenon known as *marrying* a trade. Traders often fall into this trap when they have done a great deal of research in a given market and feel overly confident in their speculation. As the market begins to move against the open position, the trader is susceptible to becoming attached to his opinion and dedicated to recovering lost capital, based on the premise that he is right and the market as a whole is clearly wrong. I have found that egotistical traders with the opinion that they are somehow smarter or are armed with more knowledge than all other market participants tend to be destined for failure.

In turn, I believe that the most effective means of combating feelings of ego and revenge in trading is humility. In my experience, successful traders are those who allow themselves to be humbled by the markets. We are all working with the same resources; unless you have a much faster internet connection than everyone else on the planet or you have somehow figured out how to fast-forward your television, you and all market participants are equipped with the same fundamental news.

> As stated by Max Amsterdam, "Business is the art of extracting money from another man's pocket without resorting to violence." I believe that the same can be said of trading.

Additionally, it is unrealistic to assume that you are capable of interpreting the news more accurately than everyone else. Although there is, without doubt, a pool of unsophisticated traders lurking in the futures markets, to achieve profits, you must compete with the well-informed and even better trained. After all, each trader is in competition with the next. You might recall Gordon Gecko's view of market completion in the movie *Wall Street*: "It's a zero sum game. Somebody wins, somebody loses. Money itself isn't lost or made; it's simply transferred from one perception to another."

CAPITAL PRESERVATION, A.K.A. RISK MANAGEMENT

A majority of trading books and courses refer to the idea of capital preservation as risk management. The concepts are essentially the same, but my perception of the practice is slightly different. In my view, risk management is the practice of actively identifying and managing risk of loss in trading, whereas capital preservation takes it a step further.

In its simplest form, capital preservation is the acknowledgment that one bad day can end a trading career. Making money in the markets is impossible if you risk all your trading capital on one speculation. If you don't live to trade another day, you might as well hang up your trading hat; all speculative decisions should be made with this premise in mind. The bottom line is that markets can stay irrational, or what you believe to be irrational, far longer than most people can stay solvent. Therefore, trading them requires a certain amount of humility.

> "You can't grow long term if you can't eat short term."
> – Jack Welch

Accordingly, my belief is that traders are best off entering a market with the assumption that the position will likely lose money. Doing so could entice them to take profits and avoid running losses.

In Chapter 14, "Trading Is a Business—Have a Plan," I discuss the use of trading plans in capital preservation.

CHAPTER 14: TRADING IS A BUSINESS—HAVE A PLAN

Trading is not a passive investment; trading is a business. Any activity engaged with the purpose of profits should be treated as such. Confirmation of this comparison can be seen in the odds of success. It has been said that approximately 80% of all traders fail to trade profitably, and some studies have suggested that the odds are even worse. For example, I have seen estimates that as many as 90% of all traders fail within the first six months. We can argue over the percentages, but it is clear that most traders are destined for an undesired outcome. Nevertheless, those who achieve success can be rewarded handsomely.

> "The average man desires to be told specifically which particular stock to buy or sell. He wants to get something for nothing. He does not wish to work."
> – William LeFevre

The probabilities of profitable operations are similarly stacked against small business owners; a large majority of new business ventures fail within the first year. Accordingly, whether your ambition is trading or starting your own business, you owe it to yourself to become familiar with the marketplace and organize a plan of attack. After all, those who can find a way to make money in business or trading often enjoy a considerable amount of success. The journey can be long, but if reached, the destination can be highly rewarding from both a financial and a psychological standpoint.

THE TRADING GAME PLAN

Contrary to what your perceptions might be, there are no right or wrong ways to trade in terms of strategy. However, I do believe that there is a right outlook and a wrong outlook on the risks and opportunities the markets present, and this is ultimately judged by profits and losses.

> Trading isn't black and white, but making money is.

Despite your strategy, risk tolerance, or trading capital, having a plan is one of the most important components of achieving success in these treacherous markets. Without a plan, traders are left to rely on their emotions and instincts. Let's face it—the average person isn't born with a knack for trading or for controlling feelings of fear and greed.

With that said, based on my observations, I have concluded that, along with the ability to keep emotions in check, one of the most important characteristics of a profitable trader is the ability to adapt to ever-changing market conditions. Being nimble is key; being stubborn is detrimental. Keeping this in mind, it seems logical to establish a game plan with the premise that rules are meant to be broken in some, but not all, circumstances. Thus, a trading plan should not be considered concrete, and in many circumstances, deviating from the original intentions of the trade is prudent.

Much of what you read about a trading plan involves specific entry and exit rules and risk management tactics. Nevertheless, in my opinion, a trading plan must be flexible to accommodate altering environments and unforeseen events. For instance, I have witnessed too many traders fail to take a profit on a successful trade because a target price had not been reached. This type of mindset can often turn winning trades into losing trades and make constructive emotions into feelings of revenge that can be detrimental to trading decisions.

Simply put, I believe that a trading plan should, on occasion, have some human discretion for market entry, exit, and assumed risk. This is not to say that traders should make it a habit to completely disregard their trading rules or strategy, but they should have an open mind about making small adjustments. For instance, it is against the law to speed, but if you are rushing a loved one to the hospital, being heavy-footed might be justified.

AUTOMATED TRADING SYSTEMS

Throughout this chapter, I play devil's advocate when it comes to system trading. I'm not trying to brainwash you into believing that you should avoid system trading at all costs; this simply isn't the case. In fact, my brokerage (DeCarley Trading) offers clients access to several hundred developed and tested algorithmic trading systems that can be implemented with the click of a mouse. Nevertheless, I want to open your eyes to the advantages and disadvantages of various approaches. In addition, it is important to realize that even a proven system on autopilot should be monitored, and you might want to consider adjusting parameters or even actively trading the system itself by turning it off and on as it produces drawdowns and profits.

> "What technology does is make people more productive. It doesn't replace them." – Michael Bloomberg

Without involving some cognitive decision making, a trading plan becomes known as a trading system, which is the use of stringent and automated trading rules with little or no outside intervention. Assuming that the shorter the time frame of the system, the less vulnerable it is to changing market conditions might make sense. For instance, subtle price distortions might create arbitrage opportunities that the naked eye wouldn't identify, nor would a human be quick enough to react to them. If a programmer was capable of accurately creating something that could exploit such opportunities, a profitable system might have little intervention necessary, or even possible. On the other hand, system creation (or, at least, profitable system creation) takes a lot of time and dedication.

Although trading systems, as opposed to trading plans that can be modified on the fly, have grown in popularity due to technological advances and the availability of such system software to the general public, the odds of success facing retail traders haven't seemed to improve. This leads me to believe that, even in the absence of human emotion, significant challenges stand in the way of creating a profitable trading model. I am not implying that profitable trading systems don't exist, but I believe that, as is the case with any other type of market approach, developing such a system takes extensive time and trial and error. Further, chasing performance tends to be a poor approach to system trading. Perhaps the best systems to implement are those with a strong long-term track record but are in the midst of a drawdown.

A TRADING SYSTEM ALONE ISN'T A "BUSINESS PLAN"

Opposing the views of many, I don't believe that a trading system is necessarily synonymous with a trading plan. Again, a futures trading system is a defined set of technical rules and parameters that ultimately determine entry and exit points for a given contract. If all the stipulated technical events occur, a buy or sell signal is created and a trade is automatically executed *without* human intervention. In essence, system traders are putting their trading profession on autopilot. I have yet to find a business owner willing to hand over operations to hired staff and, therefore, can't imagine a trader doing the same. That said, there is an undeniable amount of interest in system trading and there are some glaring advantages to partaking in such a strategy. After all, some large hedge funds and proprietary trading desks rely solely on system trading, and I am sure they wouldn't allocate resources to such strategies if they didn't see the potential for profit.

System developers spend an incredible amount of time optimizing the system to manage risk and increase the odds of profitable results in any environment. Each system consists of specific ingredients and circumstances, but they most commonly involve moving averages, stochastics, and other computer-generated oscillators. As you can imagine, the results are highly dependent on how well the rules perform in various market conditions; consequently, changing market conditions could prove to be a disaster. What worked for a purely technical system in one time frame might not work in the future due to changing market characteristics. With little human intervention or discretion, the losses could be staggering. However, as we know, large profits and losses are the reality of any trading strategy or market approach.

Systems aren't all bad. They offer some distinct advantages, such as the elimination of emotion, time saved by the freedom to leave the computer and the markets during the trading day, and the convenience of letting the system do all the work.

For some, system trading is the best fit for their personality, risk tolerance, and strategy; for others, the thought of being out of control can lead to high levels of anxiety and the tendency to detrimentally interfere with the system parameters. Going back to the small-business analogy, you probably wouldn't trust your employees to handle and account for all the money, so why would you behave this way in your trading? Instead, I believe system traders should take a more proactive role; I discuss this idea in further detail later in the chapter.

WHERE SYSTEM TRADING CAN FAIL

Systems don't have common sense and, in the long run, might not have the capability to be profitable without some type of intervention. This is because technical systems are driven by specific parameters that were determined well in advance of trade execution. As a result, mechanical trading systems often generate signals that might be considered low-probability trades. For instance, a technically driven system might trigger a sell signal at or near the all-time low of a contract. Likewise, a system might look to buy a market at an exuberantly high price.

> Purchased trading systems should be viewed as a trading tool, not the "be all, end all" solution to making money in the markets.

Although system trading is intended to eliminate the emotions involved in deciding whether to enter or exit a market, there might be unintended psychological consequences. For instance, enduring a trade that contradicts your opinion can be challenging. This could mean a system going long a market in which you are highly bearish or short one in which your opinion is bullish. Either way, the turmoil that system trading is meant to avoid can easily be rekindled. Such emotions have been known to cause traders to interfere with the system and, in many cases, greatly affect the performance—often in a negative way.

Another disadvantage to trading systems (as opposed to discretionary trading, which relies on some combination of technical, fundamental, and seasonal analyses paired with common sense) is that system traders rely on historical market activity to dictate their current and future trading.

Futures trading systems are often developed through a process referred to as back testing. In other words, they filter through historical price changes in search of system parameters that would have provided profitable results.

However, doing so gives the system developer information on what the mechanical strategy would have done if the trader had implemented it in the past.

It isn't reasonable to assume that similar results would be obtained in real-time trading or, even more so, at any point in the future. After all, market conditions are dynamic, whereas the parameters of a trading system are constant. Even system developers dedicated to tweaking the elements of the trading system can sustain considerable losses before recognizing the need to adjust parameters. Also, temporary events or market behaviors can lead to an unnecessary alteration of the system. In such a case, proactive adjustments to the system ingredients can result in needless losses.

Despite what software and system vendors want you to believe, if making money in the markets were as easy as buying or leasing a trading system, there would be no need for you to be reading this book. In fact, I would have no incentive to write it. Instead, we would all quit our day jobs and let our money and our newly acquired trading system lead us to a life of luxury.

I am sorry to report that being a profitable market participant is much more complicated than purchasing a trading system. Although an unlimited number of sales representatives will do whatever it takes to convince you that their product can provide consistent returns, I have yet to find the Holy Grail of trading that many claim to be selling. That said, those willing to fund an account with a considerable amount of excess margin and approach a well-research system with realistic expectations in regards to painful drawdowns might be pleased with the results.

Two important factors are at play when it comes to system vendors. First, if their systems were magical and successful in all types of market conditions and throughout all time frames, they likely wouldn't be selling them. There is much more money to be made in the markets than there is in selling products (although the hefty price tags of many suggest that it is possible for some to make a great living doing it). On that note, the higher the price of the system, the more you should be wary of claims.

Second, the Commodity Futures Trading Commission (CFTC) and the National Futures Association (NFA) regulate the futures industry. For the most part, the jurisdiction of these two agencies does not extend beyond those registered or required to register with the agencies. Those required to register are brokers, commodity trading advisors, and futures commission merchants. Many authors, software vendors, and system developers are not registered with the NFA and CFTC, nor are they required to be. Accordingly, they are not necessarily held to the same regulatory standards that those registered with the regulators must be. In some cases, no third party has verified the performance history disclosed by system vendors, and because they have not registered with industry regulators, they enjoy freedoms of speech that pave the way for possible deception.

I can't caution you enough about trading systems that promise spectacular returns. Just as anything else in investing and trading, if it sounds too good to be true, it probably is. You owe it to yourself to get the facts before putting your money on the line. As a consumer, it is imperative that you know who you are dealing with and what is realistic in terms of performance.

> "If there is something that you really want to do, make your plan and do it. Otherwise, you'll just regret it forever." – Richard Rocco

Despite my cautions, there are legitimate systems in existence that have proven to be productive over time and in the right circumstances. Additionally, some software and system vendors are honest and forthright with their products and what to expect from them. In all fairness to those who are not required to be registered with the regulatory bodies, certainly, some registered members don't conduct business with the integrity that is expected of them, just as some who aren't registered with the NFA and CFTC *do* follow ethical practices. In short, when seeking out automated trading systems, keep your mind and eyes open but always keep a healthy amount of skepticism.

THINK OUTSIDE OF THE BOX: TRADING A TRADING SYSTEM

In my opinion, the success of any individual trading system cycles along with the market. Therefore, it seems as though trading systems might be best used as a trading vehicle rather than a long-term strategy.

Speculators can actively trade a futures system performance by implementing and ceasing trading of the system based on the peaks and valleys of returns. In essence, this is similar to buying or selling any financial instrument. As always, the goal is to buy low and sell high. For example, it might be an opportune time to begin trading a system that is experiencing a drawdown and call it quits after a good run. This is because market conditions often fluctuate in cycles in which the performance of technical futures trading systems also oscillates. In other words, when it comes to technical trading systems, traders might be better off avoiding a buy-and-hold mentality.

Also, automated trading systems are probably best used as a small component of a trading portfolio. Rather than relying on the success of a single trading system, it is a better idea to have a handful of trading systems running simultaneously as well as some other type of discretionary (non-system) trading approach. Not unlike the need to diversify stocks between market sectors, it is a good idea for futures and options traders to diversify among trading strategies; if one trading approach is underperforming, hopefully, another is outperforming.

CONSTRUCTING A BUSINESS PLAN IN TRADING

The process of creating a trading plan should be based on the same premise as constructing a business plan. Just as a business develops a blueprint of its intended operations and the possibility of success, traders seek to make predictions on the likelihood of a particular event occurring and they use risk-management techniques to improve the odds of success and limit the chances of a devastating blunder.

The preparation of each individual trade should include a relatively detailed outline of the structure of the trading strategy and a contingency plan in case the market deviates from the original speculation. As I have previously mentioned, I don't believe that trading plans should necessarily be set in stone because of the evolving nature of the markets. From my perception, trading with overly strict trading rules could lead to financial peril. Nobody is perfect, and neither is any trading plan; therefore, being nimble but wise is ideal. Conversely, this is my viewpoint, and other books or courses might give you a completely opposite impression. The truth is that trading is an art, not a science; what is right for one might not be right for the next. I hope that the various opinions in this book give you the background you need to determine what types of trading styles work best for you.

A trading plan has two primary components: price prediction and risk management. Price prediction is simply the method used to signal the direction and timing of trade execution. This can involve fundamental or technical analyses or both. Risk management, on the other hand, specifies when to cut losses, when and how to adjust a position, or, better yet, when to take profits.

PRICE SPECULATION (IDEALLY, PREDICTION)

Regardless of the market or the instrument traded, the only possible way to make profitable trades is to buy low and sell high. Although this is a simple theory to grasp, implementing it can be challenging. For this to happen, whether trading futures, options, or baseball cards, the trader needs accurate speculation and timing. It isn't always enough to be right in the overall direction of the market; I can't emphasize enough that being right and making money are two completely separate events. Many factors come into

> Be honest with yourself about your risk tolerance. Failure to do so will result in incompatible indicators and a flawed business plan.

play to determine whether a trader can buy at a low price and sell at a higher price. Unfortunately, determining an opinion on where the market prices could or should go is only half the battle. In fact, I argue that timing and a properly capitalized account are more relevant than market direction, in some cases. After a trader has done his homework in fundamental and technical analyses (or a combination of both), he must construct a trade that will profit if the market moves as anticipated but will bring relatively little pain if it doesn't. Even better, the use of options as spreads or in conjunction with futures positions can enable traders to utilize strategies that stand to make money, even if the original speculation was incorrect! In my opinion, employing these types of strategies offering significant room for error are ideal. For specific details on these types of strategies, refer to my book *Higher Probability Commodity Trading*.

TIMING IS EVERYTHING

In trading, timing is everything. Again, through my newsletters and conversations with clients and prospects, I constantly remind them that there is a big difference between being right in the direction of the market and actually making money. I have witnessed traders who were absolutely correct in their speculation of price movement but missed getting into the trade because they had unfilled limit orders (sometimes within ticks) or were too early, causing them to run out of money or patience before the anticipated price move actually occurred.

For example, as the stock market rallied in 2008 to reach a high in the Dow Jones Industrial Average near 14,000, an old friend of mine predicted that the Dow would soon be trading under 7,000. As many others did, I scoffed at the idea—and was later proven wrong by a vicious bear market. However, the man who had predicted the slide lost a substantial amount of money trying to sell into the rally too early; to my knowledge, he didn't reap much of the reward as the market fell precipitously. This is simply because, once the bear market finally became a reality, his trading capital had dwindled to the point at which he was largely unable to participate in a meaningful way.

> The difference between genius and stupidity is finding the balance between risk and reward.

Without a crystal ball, the timing of a trade can be uncertain. Unfortunately, knowing whether a trade was well timed is impossible until the results are known. That said, an unlimited number of tools and indicators is available to help traders find a timing methodology that works with their trading style and personality.

For instance, timing can be based on computer-generated oscillators such as stochastics, Williams's %R, RSI, and so on. Some traders also use psychological barometers such as the amount of television coverage a particular market might be getting or market sentiment polls. Those trading the S&P 500 futures and options often look at the Chicago Board of Options Exchange's (CBOE) volatility index, known simply as the VIX. The VIX is often referred to as the fear index because it is said to be a representation of the market's expectation of volatility in the 30-day period. Some fundamental traders even look to supply-and-demand stats as a means of timing their entry and exit of a given trade.

I am a firm believer that there aren't right or wrong trading tools. The tool that works for one trader might not work for the next because of differences in personality and trading style. Therefore, traders must determine what they believe will help them achieve success, based on their needs and desires.

The indicator used to time entry and exit might not necessarily be important, but the tool chosen must be one that the trader is comfortable with and confident using. Clearly, indicators won't be accurate all the time. Therefore, it is necessary to use those that optimize the odds of any particular trading approach. In essence, a scalp trader likely wouldn't be wise to use a timing indicator that is relatively slow, such as the MACD. Similarly, a position trader wouldn't want a fast-paced indicator that might create many false and/or early signals, such as fast stochastics.

Based on my observation and experience, I have found that blindly taking all the buy-and-sell signals triggered by each of the computer-generated oscillators independently would yield similar results in terms of profit and loss before considering transaction costs. Of course, transaction costs would weigh down the performance of quickly triggered indicators. Simply put, a trader executing positions solely based on one oscillator would likely see similar results as a trader relying solely on another.

What does determine the success of a trader is the emotional constraint that prevents panic liquidation and the ability to properly place stop orders or exit adversely moving trades. In other words, good instincts and experience are likely more valuable than any technical indicator or supply-and-demand graph you will run across.

You might have heard this motto: Guns don't kill people, people kill people. Trading indicators can be compared to guns, in this sense: The indicators themselves don't determine the outcome, the traders using them do. In trading, oscillators or charting tools don't siphon trading accounts; unfortunately, traders sometimes do it to themselves.

After you determine your speculative tool of choice and determine your conclusion on the direction (or lack thereof), it is time to construct a strategy that will benefit if your assessments are accurate and mitigate risk if you are wrong. This might include using options, futures, or a combination of both as the trading vehicle. The method you choose should be based on your risk tolerance, personality, and risk capital.

CHOOSING A TRADING VEHICLE

Futures and options exchanges list several products, and speculators bring enough liquidity to many of these instruments to create an abundance of options in terms of trading vehicles. Not only are there several contracts to choose from, but traders also have the ability to combine instruments to construct a strategy with a specific goal and risk/reward profile.

As with indicators, a strategy that works for one trader might not work for the next. The goal for every trader, aside from being profitable, should be to find a strategy that provides a manageable risk profile while still offering a profit potential that makes the risk worthwhile. In the world of finance, it is well known that increased risk is equivalent to increased potential reward. Conversely, excessive risk usually ends in a largely negative reward scenario. The appropriate balance between risk and reward is a fine line; the side of the line chosen determines the probability of a gain rather than an unfounded

"Money often costs too much."
– Ralph Waldo Emerson

hope of one. Aside from a lucky few, traders who accept reckless amounts of risk will be prone to dismal trading results.

To illustrate the seemingly infinite possibilities of risk and reward, a Treasury bond bear might sell a futures contract, purchase a put option with various strike prices, sell a call option with various strike prices, or even use a combination of all of these. Each of these strategies can be constructed with various levels of possible risk and reward to conform to the personality of the trader.

The possible combination of instruments is extensive and, in some cases, complex. Therefore, covering the topic in detail isn't feasible in this particular text; however, you should be aware of the alternatives available to you and know which fits your personal trading profile before you ever put money on the line. Again, I'll refer you to my book *Higher Probability Commodity Trading* for a detailed explanation of using options and futures together to manage risk.

RISK MANAGEMENT

All business plans must account for potential hardships and achievable recoveries. Similarly, a solid trading plan should include proper coverage of risk management and appropriate contingency plans in case the plan goes awry.

Because of the leveraged volatility and the inherent danger of being on the wrong side of a runaway market, the *meat* (no pun intended) of a proper trading plan is risk management. As elementary as it sounds, the most important component to trading success is making sure your account lives to trade another day. As with any business, without sufficient capital, the outcome looks bleak. Traders must be ready and willing to pull the plug on any trade that endangers the ability of the "business" to continue, regardless of how much research they applied and how certain they are about their speculation.

To keep emotions at bay, it is critical that you establish thresholds of loss that you are willing to accept before you enter a market. Honesty is the best policy. If you are focused on the potential reward rather than the potential risk, the odds favor a dramatically unfavorable conclusion.

Establishing and following a risk threshold might simply mean placing an appropriate stop-loss order, along with determining a profit objective and placing a limit order accordingly. Although I personally prefer the use of options as a hedge or, in some cases, ensure limited risk, but the overall idea is the same.

I can't emphasize enough that the trading plans are for guidance and shouldn't be followed blindly. Don't be the trader who misses taking a healthy profit because the price came within ticks of the limit order, yet he held out for the extra $20. On the other hand, even if your trading strategy or plan doesn't involve a trailing stop, don't be a fool. Markets don't go up or down forever; if you have a large open profit, tighten your stop or place protective options or option spreads. Even better, lock in the profit and walk away.

THE ART OF RISK MANAGEMENT

Thanks to the plethora of tradable futures and options products made available by the various exchanges, traders have unlimited ways to adjust the risk and reward of a futures position. The idea of a trading plan is to aid your decision-making process, not bog you down and prevent you from ever entering the market. Therefore, a trading plan can't possibly cover all market scenarios—but writing down a few potential ideas can keep you from freezing in the heat of the moment.

For instance, imagine a trader who goes long a futures contract and finds himself with a nice profit yet believes there is room for the market to continue to move favorably. He might hedge his position by selling a call option. The premium collected acts as a form of income, but it also provides the trader with a risk buffer to hedge against a market reversal. Likewise, in line with this strategy, the trader might want to use the proceeds of the recently sold call option to purchase a put and protect himself from the risk of an adverse price movement. I strongly recommend that traders take the time to learn about options and entertain the idea of employing them for risk management. Being prepared and creative can pay dividends!

RISK AND REWARD: GIVE YOURSELF A CHANCE!

Contrary to your likely perceptions of trading, some of the best traders struggle to keep their win/loss ratios above 50%. Therefore, when assessing your risk tolerance on any given trade and your profit target, you must be realistic.

Knowing the average probability of success on each trade, even for the pros, it isn't practical to consistently risk more on a position than you plan to make if you are right; this is simply because you likely will have more (or just as many) losers as you will have winners. For instance, if your average risk on a trade is $600, you should have an average profit target of at least $600. Anything less than this is putting the odds greatly in favor of your competition and works against your long-term prospects of success.

Keep in mind, the win/loss percentage will be largely dependent on the strategy you choose. Therefore, the profit and loss targets will need to be adjusted accordingly. For instance, a futures trend trader generally wins 20% to 30% of his trades; thus, the average winner must be much larger than the average loser to account for the probabilities.

OPTION SELLING PROVIDES FAVORABLE ODDS BUT DOESN'T GUARANTEE SUCCESS

Although favorable odds are key to sustainable trading success, there are no guarantees. In this game, winning far more trades than you lose is only the beginning.

This concept is especially important for option sellers who face optimal odds of success on a per-trade basis but are subject to limited profit potential and possibly unlimited risk if selling naked options. It has been said that as many as 80% of options expire worthless. Assuming these odds, a trader would win on nearly eight out of 10 trades. However, the danger lies in the vulnerability of the two losing trades. An option seller must be savvy enough to prevent the small percentage of losing trades from wiping out months of profit and part (or all) of the original trading capital. In general, an option seller will likely experience larger average losses than average gains, but in a lower frequency. This is the opposite prognosis than the aforementioned futures trend trading strategy that stands to lose roughly 80% of its trades but experiences occasional out-sized winners to make up for the dismal win/loss ratio.

> Most options expire worthless, but odds alone are not enough to ensure success. Option selling requires ample skill and instinct to be profitable in the long run.

The perils of option selling shouldn't deter you from the strategy altogether. In fact, I prefer and recommend this approach to the markets. However, those who participate in this practice must be willing to face the consequences during drawdowns. They must also be humble enough to exit a poor trade before the consequences are too much for the trading account to bear.

A rule of thumb many option sellers adhere to is to risk the amount of premium collected for the option. Therefore, if a trader can collect $500, or 10 points, for a short E-mini S&P option, and the value of the option doubles to $1,000, or 20 points, it is likely a good time to admit that the speculation was incorrect and accept the loss of $500.

In my opinion, option sellers are generally better off using a triple-out rule. This is because options often double in value temporarily only to quickly retreat in value. Those liquidating each time an option doubles in value would likely experience a high probability of small losses. In short, small losses will slowly eat away at the trading account rather than the trader allowing the strategy to work as it should.

Using the same example, a trader who sells an E-mini S&P option for 10 points ($500) should look to exit or adjust the trade if the option triples in value to 15 points ($1,500). This equates to a loss of $1,000 on the trade, double the maximum profit potential. At this point, it is fair to say that you were either wrong or really early, and liquidation should be strongly considered to move on to the next opportunity. Or if the required margin isn't an issue it is often a good idea to adjust the trade to move risk away from the market but gives the trade a chance to recover should volatility decline. I talk about this concept in great detail in my book *Higher Probability Commodity Trading*. As difficult as it is to admit fault and lock in a loss, it will be even more painful if the $1,000 loser doubles or triples in size. After all, assuming option sellers will make money 80% of the time, losing double the profit potential on two out of 10 ventures is still an overall profitable trading plan. Of course, anybody that has participated in a short options trading strategy knows that option values can move quickly and without warning. Further, traditional stop loss orders used in futures trading aren't necessarily feasible in options trading, nor accepted by the exchange (although stop/limit orders are). Accordingly, keeping losses to the planned levels isn't always possible. If you would like a refresher on the difficulty of placing stop loss orders on options, revisit "Chapter 7: Order Types and How to Use Them." Rather than placing stop/limit orders on short options, I believe in monitoring short options closely and having a mental stop loss in mind.

As mentioned, the triple-out policy (or double-out if that is your preference) is simply a rule of thumb, and sometimes breaking it is prudent. Despite what you might have read elsewhere, it shouldn't be looked at in black-and-white terms. In my opinion, trading is an art, not a science, and should be treated accordingly. For instance, if you are short a call in a rallying market and the option has reached the triple-out point but you see significant resistance approaching, it might not be the best time to throw in the towel. Even if you decide that you are no longer comfortable with the trade, in many cases, the market will, at a minimum, stall at the resistance area, allowing for a better exit price. Similarly, if you strongly believe that the futures price will hold resistance, exiting your position in panic and at top dollar doesn't make sense. However, those using the triple-out method should recognize that in nearly all circumstances some sort of trade adjustment is prudent once the predetermined risk level is hit. In other words, a short call position that is sharply underwater (has reached the triple-out point) could be rolled into a distant strike price using an options expiration with a distant date. Rolling an option in this manner simply entails buying back the current position, and then selling a new position in the next expiration month and at a strike price further out-of-the-money. This keeps the integrity of the position intact, as well as retaining the ability to recoup losses if the market normalizes, but it also reduces margin and risk. It is the best of both worlds.

On the contrary, traders who refuse to adjust their risk or exit the position altogether begin to rely on hope instead of logic and research. Once the losses start to mount, they cross the line between being a player and being a prayer. Unfortunately, seeing the line can be difficult until it has already been crossed; at that point, you will feel it.

Challenging decisions such as this make or break a trader. The difference between success and failure often comes down to a few decisions in crucial circumstances. The ability to properly manage such scenarios can be derived only from instinct and experience. Although reading books and attending trading seminars might be helpful, there is no substitution for hands-on trading experience.

THE 10% RULE

Unless this truly is "the first book on commodities" you have read, you've likely run across the 10% rule of risk management. The argument suggests that traders shouldn't risk more than 10% of their trading account on any individual trade. This premise stipulates what the maximum risk should be, but it implicitly implies that the minimum risk should be similar. Although I can't argue with the logic of having a risk threshold, risking 10% of the trading account might not be feasible for everyone. After all, what if you were trading a $1,000,000 account? Risking $100,000 on a single speculation seems a bit excessive.

Additionally, a risk-averse or inexperienced trader might not be psychologically equipped to handle such a loss, and this can repeatedly lead to irrational trading behavior. It is easy to underestimate the consequences of trader psychology; nonetheless, after a trader loses his logical bearing, recovering can be difficult, leading to large losses.

Imagine the emotions felt by a trader who opens her first futures account with $10,000 and immediately loses 10%, or $1,000, on the first trade. Someone not in complete control of her psyche—and, therefore, her actions—might dedicate subsequent trades to recovering losses on the original. This type of destructive behavior often leads to overly aggressive trading, such as premature entry and a greedy refusal to exit profitable trades. It is feasible to imagine a trader reacting in this manner, and it supports my premise that some traders might not be capable of accepting a 10% loss without detrimentally impacting the trading plan.

It is also important to realize that restrictions come with the 10% rule that can work against the odds of success. In some markets and during volatile conditions, constructing a trade with realistic probabilities of success might not be possible without surpassing the 10% threshold. Whether this is the case depends greatly on the size of the account and whether options or futures are used, but it can be a drawback of the theory. Clearly, if you cannot derive a strategy in which the potential risk does not exceed 10% of available trading capital, the trade is better left untouched. Nonetheless, as humans, we are naturally drawn to that which we shouldn't be.

DON'T BE ASHAMED OF ONE-LOT ORDERS

The thrill of calling a broker and placing an order for 10, 50, or 100 futures or options contracts at a time is unmatched. Or, in today's electronic world, a better example of this ego booster might be placing the order via a trading platform and posting a screenshot of the trade to social media. In any case, there is no room for showboating in the commodity markets. For those who don't have the experience and the trading capital to back trading large quantities at a time, it is highly counterproductive and potentially devastating.

One of the most destructive behaviors I have witnessed is the execution of multiple contracts in a moderately funded account. Brokerage firms often extend lower-margin requirements to day traders, and this can lure traders into taking excessive risks. That said, just because higher leverage is granted doesn't mean traders should use it.

> Take care of your money, and some day it might take care of you.

Raw traders assume that trading several contracts at a time will maximize their "return," but they are actually maximizing risk and minimizing the probability of a successful trade. If you are truly looking at trading as a business and as a means of making money as opposed to feeding an inner ego, you will be content with trading one contract at a time until you are comfortable enough to properly capitalize and manage multiple trading lots. In my view, unless the account has six figures, traders should be trading one lot per venture. This isn't to say a trader should only trade one contract and one market at a time. Instead, having one contract in a handful of positions is ideal.

MANAGING RISK WITH STOPS

Using stop loss orders is probably the most common form of risk management. As you have learned, a stop order is habitually used as a means of exiting an existing trade if the market moves against the position to a predetermined price. Depending on whether the stop order is trailed as the market moves favorably, the stated price might result in a loss or might lock in a profit. Nonetheless, it is filled only after adverse price movement. As you should recall, a stop order essentially becomes a market order when the named price is reached. Therefore, slippage from the intended price is possible. Yet, as we learned in Chapter 7 in the section "A Disclaimer to Stop Loss and Market Orders in an Electronic Trading World," the exchange does offer prices protections against excessive slippage, but that might mean the stop order is skipped over, leaving the trader without any means of risk management.

Keep in mind that a stop order can also be used to enter a market. Such a stop order is often placed above areas of significant technical resistance or below support, in an attempt to capitalize on a potential price breakout. When used in this manner, stop orders don't fall into the category of risk management.

Stop orders are useful only if they are properly placed, and this is a task that is much easier said than done. Stop orders that are placed too close to the market regularly lead to the premature liquidation of a trade that would have eventually gone in an anticipated direction. If stop orders are placed in a manner in which a fill is probable during the normal ebb and flow of the market, this is no longer a risk-management technique—it is a near guarantee that you will lose money. On the other hand, stop orders that are placed too far from the market might create a scenario in which too much risk is accepted. This too is highly counterproductive.

Although stop orders might be popular in the trading community, they are not necessarily the most effective. Remember, most retail traders lose money. As with many aspects of trading, placing stop orders is an art, not a science. In truth, many seasoned traders prefer to be without stops by trading "naked," or by using alternative risk-management tools such as options. I happen to share this view. If you are interested in learning the strategy of using long and short options as a hedge instead of stop loss orders for risk management, I go into great detail of this concept in my book *Higher Probability Commodity Trading*.

Deciding whether to use stop orders and where and when to use them isn't a black-and-white process. Many areas of gray are involved including market conditions and characteristics, as well as the personality, account funding, and risk tolerance of the trader. Understanding each of these aspects is critical; stop placement is a skill that comes only with experience and is shaped by individual needs, desires, and temperament.

Guidance on stop placement might be a good argument in favor of beginning traders using a full-service broker. Nonetheless, even an experienced broker cannot see into the future and faces the same challenges that you do. Still, you can't put a price tag on experience; in theory, using a seasoned and savvy broker might have a positive impact on performance, despite slightly higher transaction costs involved in doing so.

As you should already realize, stop orders aren't a guarantee of risk because of the potential slippage involved and the unlikely, but possible, scenario of the market bypassing your stop because it could not fill the order within the exchange's stipulated reasonable price zone. Nonetheless, such an event is rare. In most cases, stop orders are not overrun and the difference between the intended stop price and the actual fill price is moderate. Yet, in some circumstances, the slippage can be substantial, such as in low-liquidity and high-volatility environments. Further, on the off chance the exchange is not able to fill the stop order within its price band limits, a runaway market could leave a trade with massive losses amounting to hundreds or thousands of dollars.

In some cases, avoiding placing stops by using unconventional risk-management techniques might be possible— and wise. An experienced broker might help construct option spreads and buy or sell outright calls and puts as an alternative in risk aversion. For example, a short option or futures position might be hedged with a one-by-two ratio write if the volatility and premium allow. Likewise, futures traders can buy options that benefit from an adverse move in their futures position to limit the risk of loss and avoid being subject to the risk of being stopped out prematurely. Doing so can be considered buying insurance against being wrong; it might be pricey, but sometimes it can be useful. That said, this type of protection is feasible only in markets and instances in which option premium is affordable.

I believe that using options in risk management instead of stop orders eliminates some of the stress and emotion involved in trading. Traders often have sleepless nights over concerns of being stopped out of a position, only to watch it recover without them. Traders who use options as a hedge or for absolute insurance can relax, knowing that the homework is done, the risk is mitigated, and the position isn't in danger of being prematurely offset.

IT IS YOUR MONEY

In theory, we all participate in the markets with the same goal: to make money. (Believe it or not, though, some traders seem to be trading for the thrill as opposed to potential profits.) Despite our common goals, the road to success is much different for one trader relative to another. In fact, a strategy that one trader lucratively employs might not yield the same results when executed by another. The difference in performance from one trader to the next is typically not about the fundamental information available or the technical tools used; it involves the methodology and mentality in which the information is put to work. More important, it depends on the manner in which we react to stressful and timely situations. As I have attempted to make clear, trading is an ambiguous game; most aspects of speculation have no right or wrong answer.

We don't all wear the same shoe size or have the same hobbies, so why should we all use the same trading strategy and risk-management techniques? We shouldn't. By nature, we each have different boiling points and must be familiar enough with ourselves and the risks we take to avoid irrational and destructive trading behavior.

My personal perception of a reasonable trading strategy or approach and how much money should be risked on a particular trade is far different than that of many of my clients. I can honestly say that one mindset isn't necessarily better or worse than the other—they're all just different. To specify, I tend to be a risk-averse trader (if there is such a thing in trading futures and options). Accordingly, I prefer some of the lower-margined and slower-moving markets and strategies, such as the 10-year note, corn, meats, and spreads between options and futures. Some of my clients, on the other hand, are much more aggressive and prefer to trade markets and strategies that are capable of providing a magnified risk/reward profile. And that is okay, too.

Only you can determine what fits, and that requires patience, discipline, and an open mind. The most important feedback on your progress will be your account statements. That's not to say that you should hang up your trading jacket if you experience a drawdown or even a complete account blowup, but you must be realistic. Some people tend to remember only the good trades; others remember only the bad. Each of these distorted perceptions of reality can have an adverse effect on your trading. Successful traders remember the good trades and the bad trades, but most important, they learn from all of them.

CHAPTER 15: WHY YOU SHOULD SPECULATE IN FUTURES AND OPTIONS

My aim has always been to provide readers with a candid account of the realities of trading rather than fill them with unrealistic expectations. I believe that doing so can better prepare traders for what lies ahead and, accordingly, might improve their odds of becoming a victorious trader. Throughout this book, I have outlined the difficulties of trading, but hopefully, I haven't discouraged you from involving yourself in the commodity markets. After all, the futures and options markets can be potentially lucrative for those willing to accept and properly manage the corresponding risks. Furthermore, I am a broker who makes a living through the commission earned as my clients trade commodities. The last thing that I want to do is deter qualified parties from the futures markets. However, it is important that I encourage traders to come to futures and options for the right reasons and certify they know what to expect when they get there.

Regardless of what your impression has been up to this point, let it be known that, along with the significant risk of loss involved in futures trading, there is potential for momentous profits. Substantial profit potential is why speculators flock to the markets and it is what keeps them coming back—even if they didn't achieve what they were looking for the first time around.

There is a lot of money to be made, or lost, in all markets, but for those with the willingness and the capital to speculate, the futures and options on futures markets offer some glaring advantages over other vehicles.

SPECULATING IN FUTURES VERSUS SPECULATING IN STOCKS

Unfortunately, at times to their peril, humans tend to gravitate to what they are more familiar with. As we all know, in many cases, convenience and ease might not necessarily be the optimal choice. I believe that the same can be said of the option that speculators have in participating in either the equity markets or the commodity markets.

Horror stories circulating about large losses suffered by commodity traders and the forced delivery of 5,000 bushels of corn have kept the futures market a dark mystery for many retail traders. However, losses are possible in any trading environment, and well-organized traders utilizing proficient commodity brokers don't have to worry about the hassles of the delivery process. I don't think it is fair to blame the trading venue for life-ruining outcomes; more accurately, it is often the fault of market participants themselves. As discussed in Chapter 1, "A Crash Course in Commodities," traders choose how much leverage to employ in their strategy and which markets to participate in. Sharp losses at the hands of undercapitalized trading accounts, over-active trading, or a sheer gambling can only be attributed to one party—the trader. That said, participating in the futures and options markets requires an additional amount of self-control due to easily accessible leverage and 23-hour trading sessions. If you can't control yourself while surrounded by the temptations of flashing lights and promises of big payouts in a casino, you probably won't be successful in the commodity markets either.

In this discussion, we focus on the most popular stock index futures contract, the E-mini S&P 500, in comparison to trading stock index ETFs (exchange traded funds), but similar principles apply to all commodities. For instance, for those speculating on the price of gold, ignoring cash market options such as bullion, they have the choice to use a gold ETF, the stock of a gold mining company, or they can trade gold futures contracts. Similar stock and ETF opportunities exist for corn, soybeans, and most other commodities. Each choice can potentially enable traders to profit from correct predictions in the price of the underlying commodity—and lose if they are incorrect—but there are inherent advantages to trading futures over stocks that shouldn't be ignored. In addition, ETFs or stocks that are correlated to a commodity such as GLD, CORN, WEET, and USO are likely not perfectly correlated, and this creates a less efficient means of speculating on the price of a given commodity. In fact, due to ETF rebalancing and the costs involved in rolling over futures contracts within the fund, it is possible for ETF buyers to miss out on profits despite correct speculation in the underlying asset itself. Even worse, those with incorrect predictions of a commodity price playing their hunch with ETFs will likely suffer larger losses in the ETF than they would have by speculating directly on the commodity price in the futures market (ignoring leverage, of course). In other words, the ETF price doesn't always track the asset price it is intended to.

LEVERAGE AND MARGIN

Some people might say leverage is a reason you should *not* trade futures because it can work for you as well as against you. As you must realize by now, the use of leverage supercharges profits in accurate trades but has the potential to create dramatic losses for those on the wrong side of a market move. Naturally, the amount of leverage—and, thus, position volatility—is highly dependent on the market being traded and the strategy used. Moreover, traders can reduce leverage altogether by depositing the full value of the futures contract rather than the minimum margin required by the exchange or the broker. Specifically, although the exchange sets a minimum overnight margin requirement, the trader decides how much leverage to use through account funding and position size.

Throughout this book, I have noted that most futures brokers and brokerage firms offer relatively lenient day-trading margins, in addition to stringent yet generous overnight margins. At some firms, you can day trade a single E-mini futures contract with as little as a $500 margin requirement. That said, just because it is possible to buy 20 E-mini S&P futures in a $10,000 account doesn't mean that it should be done. In fact, doing so would equate to the trader making or losing $1,000 per point of price movement in the futures market, or 10% of the trading account, on a small price move. On the other hand, futures margins are flexible; with the S&P valued at 2,300, an E-mini trader can eliminate the leverage provided in the futures markets by depositing $115,000 (2,300 × $50) and trading a single contract. Obviously, there's a big difference between day trading on a $500 margin and fully funding an account with $115,000 in deposited margin per contract traded. This is a great depiction of how much control the trader has over leverage, and how the temptation of leverage has the power to control traders.

To put the leverage of trading commodities into perspective, consider an example. I have seen a long-option-only account go from a net liquidation value of $10,000 up to an intraday value of nearly $500,000 in a matter of weeks. Unfortunately, I witnessed the same account eventually give back all the profits, plus a lot more. The circumstances surrounding this incredible rise and fall are unique: It occurred during one of the biggest stock-market plummets of all time. I am sure the 2008 crash will be etched forever in the minds of those who let riches slip through their hands. However, the point is that aggressive traders can potentially make or lose life-changing amounts of money. Of course, not everybody is willing to lay so much on the line—nor should they be. Still, the potential is there for those who want to spin the roulette wheel.

On the other hand, I have worked with clients who, after years of familiarizing themselves with the markets, found a way to make a comfortable living trading futures and options on futures. It didn't happen overnight, and I can guarantee that they weren't quick to quit their day jobs. But after putting in adequate time and paying their dues in the form of expensive market experience, they are now living the dream. I can assure you that these types of traders are approaching the markets in a more conservative way than those looking for a get-rich-quick solution to their problems; nonetheless, easy access to leverage might have played a part in their triumph.

Conversely, stock traders are not allowed to use margin—well, at least not without paying for it. For a stock market speculator to buy a greater number of shares than she has money for (trade using leverage), she must first apply for a leverage account and then pay her brokerage firm a fee for the funds borrowed. The costs associated with using leverage can be substantial and simply make it more difficult for a speculator to trade profitably. Similarly, most stock brokerage firms require a rather large trading account balances to qualify for margined (leveraged) trading. Many approve margin accounts only for clients with more than $100,000 on deposit. Others approve the use of leverage but charge higher rates of interest or margin for accounts of less than six figures. Conversely, *all* futures accounts are granted *cost-free* leverage, regardless of account balance. To give you an idea of how favorable trading on leverage in the futures markets relative to equities can be, a commodity trader with $1,000 is treated the same in regard to the margin as a stock trader required to deposit $100,000 would be in the equity arena.

LIQUIDITY AND EFFICIENT EXECUTION

As I have pointed out throughout this text, it is important to speculate in liquid commodity markets. There are a handful of futures contracts that simply don't have enough market activity to enable seamless entry and exit; these contracts should generally be avoided. However, the major commodities such as oil, natural gas, gold, silver, corn, soybeans, wheat, Treasuries, and stock index futures trade electronically in high volumes and with narrow bid/ask spreads nearly around the clock. On the contrary, many commodity ETFs and equity stock index products, particularly leveraged securities, are illiquid. Further, they do not trade overnight; speculation can only take place during traditional stock market hours.

To summarize, futures traders can easily enter and exit the market with minimal transaction costs and acceptable amounts of slippage in fill price nearly 24 hours per day. The price paid for executing a lightly traded ETF can be substantial and can only be done for about seven hours per day.

As a trader, it is imperative that you fully understand the consequences of trading in markets that have few participants and, even more important, that you do your homework on each product that you are interested in trading. This is true regardless of the trading arena chosen.

BUY OR SELL IN ANY ORDER

One of the most compelling arguments for futures trading relative to stocks or ETFs is the ability to quickly and efficiently sell a contract in anticipation of the market going lower. In the world of commodity trading, this is the case regardless of market circumstances or account size. The idea is to buy back the contract at a better (lower) price at some point in the future. Of course, things don't always work out as planned, and a short trader may be forced to buy back the contract at a loss (higher price). Nevertheless, the convenience of speculating in both directions with the click of a mouse and the absence of interest charges is unique to the futures markets.

An equity trader can also sell shares short, with the intention of buying them back at some point in the future. Nevertheless, to do this, he must first borrow the shares from his brokerage firm and pay interest charges accordingly. In addition, the stock broker must have shares on inventory to loan to traders who want to short them. This is much less expedient and more costly. Once again, stock brokers typically require an account with tens of thousands or hundreds of thousands of dollars to grant traders the same leverage privileges that futures traders receive without stipulations. Futures traders enjoy the simplicity of buying or selling without hassles; their only concern is accurate speculation.

LOW ACCOUNT MINIMUMS

Before equity traders can sell shares with the intention of buying them back at a lower price or trade with leverage by spending more money on shares than they have on deposit, they must qualify for a margin account. The process of opening a margin account involves slightly more paperwork and a quick background and credit check by the brokerage firm. In futures, all accounts are opened on margin; additional paperwork and aggravations are not necessary. Nonetheless, a background and credit check are standard among futures brokerages, to prevent money laundering and ensure that futures traders are financially equipped to accept the risk of participating in such markets. After all, when trading on leverage in a margin account, traders are essentially being granted credit. Thus, the process of opening a commodity trading account is similar to applying for a credit card or small loan.

In addition to the supplementary barriers to entry for a margined stock account, most stock brokerage firms will not approve a margin account application for clients with less than $50,000—and they may require far more. On the other hand, some futures brokers allow clients to day trade the E-mini S&P with initial funding balances as little as $2,000. In addition, long commodity option traders face limited risk and are often free to open accounts with even smaller balances. Of course, an ultra-small trading account might not provide an ample number of opportunities, but it is nice to know it is possible.

NO INTEREST CHARGES OR BORROWING FEES

As if the time delay and restrictions of borrowing shares in addition to the obstacle of large account minimums weren't enough of an argument for futures market speculation relative to stocks, equity brokerage firms typically charge interest on margined positions. Such a trade might also incur additional transaction fees. Conversely, futures and options on futures traders are not expected to pay interest on leveraged trading activity. The exchanges and the corresponding brokerage firms provide the leverage free of charge. Simply put, for a stock trader to turn a profit on a short position, he must first be right enough in the direction to overcome the interest charges paid to the brokerage firm in return for borrowing shares. Yet, a futures trader's breakeven point is dependent merely on the transaction cost of a few dollars.

I argue that all else being equal, similarly skilled traders utilizing an identical strategy in similar products yet two alternative arenas—stocks and futures—might see superior results in the futures trading account due to a lack of interest payments.

With that in mind, it is also important to point out that futures contracts do not pay dividends as some stocks and ETFs might. These dividends work in favor of speculators long shares, but those who have borrowed shares from their brokerage to short a stock must pay the dividend to the buyer of that stock!

LEVEL PLAYING FIELD

Futures contracts are generally filled on a first-come, first-served basis, with little or no human intervention. This wasn't necessarily the case when open outcry was the primary method of execution. The idea behind the creation of the futures exchange's electronic platforms is to provide an arena in which a trader executing 1,000 contracts at a time and one that is trading a single lot will be treated the same in terms of execution. On the other hand, this might not be true in venues that involve market makers, such as equities, ETFs, and open outcry executed commodity options.

FAVORABLE TAX TREATMENT

In general, profitable equity traders face a much larger tax burden than commodity traders do. In addition, the process of claiming trading profits and losses at the end of the year is much simpler for a futures trader than one who is actively trading equities.

The IRS requires equity traders to list each transaction and the net result of each trade. You can imagine the frustration involved for day traders. However, on a brighter note, it encourages a daily trading log and can make it easier for equity traders to look at their results realistically.

Futures traders, on the other hand, report a lump-sum profit or loss figure on a 1099 at the end of the year. The 1099 displays the performance of the trading account net of commissions and fees, accounting for deposits and withdrawals. In essence, your futures broker takes on the burden of figuring out the math; all you and your accountant need to do is input the final number on Form 6781 in your tax return.

However, the tax benefits of speculating in a futures account, compared to a stock account, don't end in convenience; there are substantial monetary advantages as well. All futures, and options on futures, market gains are taxed at a 40%/60% blend between long- and short-term capital gains, regardless of the time span of the trade. Because long-term capital gains are taxed at a more favorable rate than short-term gains, assuming that they are profitable, futures market speculators enjoy a considerable tax break relative to stock traders.

EXCITEMENT

Let's face it, commodity trading is exciting and unpredictable. Not only is it somewhat mysterious to the common investor, but at times it also can change the lives of market participants. I have seen call options in sugar bought for $200 grow to values in the several thousands. I have also witnessed a trader take an account from approximately $250,000 to more than $4 million and then back down to eventually produce a negative balance! Of course, these examples are the exception rather than the rule, but the point is that nearly anything is possible.

I have come in contact with futures traders who have yet to find a way to consistently make the amount of money in their trading ventures needed to justify the time spent, but simply yearn for the adrenaline rush; that is enough to keep them coming back for more.

I could never recommend that traders come to commodities solely for entertainment because that type of attitude will likely lead to substantial losses resulting from unnecessary risks taken. Nonetheless, I cannot deny that this is one of the most compelling reasons that traders venture into futures and options. In fact, from more than one avid commodity trader, I have heard stock trading compared to watching paint dry. Keep in mind, however, that I am referring specifically to speculation, not investing—there is a big difference between the two forms of market participation.

COMMODITIES WON'T BE DELISTED AND REFLECT TRUE POSITION

Most of the contracts of interest to speculators and listed by the futures and options markets have been traded for decades and have an ample amount of liquidity. On the other hand, many of the commodity ETFs that speculators use to wager on the direction of crude oil, soybeans, Treasuries, the VIX, or other commodities were brought to existence in recent years as a result of the commodity boom and attempts at Wall Street to retain the business of commodity speculation. Unfortunately, with the financial collapse of the late 2000s, many of the newly listed ETFs were forced to cease operations due to a lack of interest. Although ETFs are growing in popularity in regards to money flow, there are a substantial number of ETFs in existence with dismal trading volume and perhaps a limited life. Although investors in delisted ETFs do get their money back, this can be a significant speed bump in the progress of their speculative plays.

Another strike against trading ETFs is the so-called "short" or "ultrashort" products that are designed to mimic the return of being short an asset or index. In many cases, due to the way the fund tracks the daily fluctuation of the asset it is intended to mock, the performance of the ETF will match underlying assets on a short-term basis, such as one day or two. Traders hoping to buy and hold the ETF might find themselves in a situation in which they were right about the market direction but incurred a loss because of the way the ETF rebalanced. Most agree that short or ultra short (leveraged) ETFs are designed to be a day trading vehicle and should not be considered an effective way of speculating in time frames beyond of a few days.

In my opinion, ETF versions of long or short commodity markets are extremely inefficient. Those who are truly interested in playing in the commodity markets should do so in the futures markets, where it is the real deal.

YOU *CAN* TRADE FUTURES AND OPTIONS IN AN IRA

I would never advocate allocating a major portion of any retirement account to commodity trading. However, so few traders even realize that this is an option that I felt obligated to mention it. As you can imagine, there are definite tax benefits to trading funds earmarked for futures speculation in a retirement account. Specifically, tax-deferred or tax-free growth is possible depending on the type of qualified IRA (individual retirement account); rollover 401(k)s are also candidates for futures trading. In theory, trading accounts within the shelter of a tax-friendly IRA have the potential to grow at much more rapid speeds compared to those in a nonqualified account (outside the IRA umbrella).

Of course, only profitable traders enjoy the advantages of an IRA. For those less fortunate in the markets, trading within an IRA can become a burden: Losses are not tax-deductible as they would be in a nonqualified account. Similarly, trading futures within an IRA typically involves incremental fees paid to an account custodian, which can slightly exaggerate trading losses or reduce gains.

There are diversification arguments in favor of allotting 10% to 20% of retirement account savings to managed futures programs, algorithmic trading systems, or even discretionary trading for those with ample experience. I personally trade a small IRA account as a mix to a traditional stock and bond portfolio.

RISK CAPITAL ONLY

As this chapter has outlined, there are many reasons to trade futures, but there are also reasons not to. In a few cases, the same arguments for speculating in commodities are the reasons that attract speculators—and capital—to the futures markets that shouldn't be there.

Regardless of your intentions or vehicle in speculation, one common rule persists: Never trade money that you can't afford to lose. If you are like me, it seems that there's no such thing as money that can be lost without some type of anguish. Nonetheless, risk capital is defined as an amount of money that, if lost, would not alter your current lifestyle. Even those who trade for a living will have bad days; it is important that they don't let a bad day, week, or month turn into ruin. A good way to ensure this is by limiting trading accounts to expendable funds.

Each trading account opened by a brokerage firm undergoes some scrutiny in terms of an applicant's net worth, income, and bankruptcy history, if any. Most commodity firms require that applicants have a net worth of at least $20,000 and a minimum annual income of $20,000 but there aren't any black-and-white limits. Each application is taken on a case-by-case basis. The reasoning behind the policy is twofold: First, sufficient income and net worth confirms that a trader could, or should, have some risk capital to allocate to the treacherous game of speculation. Also, as you should realize by now, futures traders can lose more money than they have on deposit in their trading accounts. Accordingly, brokerage firms must determine whether the risk posed by clients who might lose more money than they can pay back is worth the reward of accepting them as clients of the firm.

Yet despite attempts of brokerage firms to prevent traders from trading with money that, if lost, might cause significant changes in their financial well-being, such capital manages to find its way into the marketplace anyway. Unfortunately, those doing so are opening the door to financial hardships, ruined marriages, or worse. Again, the commodity markets are often blamed for negative outcomes, but it is the participants who generally bring it upon themselves. Whether you are actively trading equities, futures, or options on futures, it is important that you realize that speculation is a risk, not an investment; only risk capital should be used.

CONCLUSION

The commodity markets provide speculative opportunities that other markets simply can't offer. In my opinion, the convenience of gaining leverage and the ability to quickly buy and sell trading instruments in any order creates an extremely efficient, and unbeatable, means of betting on anticipated price changes. Also, the tax benefits of profitable speculation in commodities, as compared to equities, are dramatic and can potentially have a profound impact on the overall results. For these reasons, those who fully understand speculation and are willing to accept the risks associated with it should strongly consider doing so in the futures and options markets.

As I have noted, speculation itself is a difficult task to master. In fact, some of the most successful traders report account-draining losses on numerous occasions before gaining the experience needed to be among the estimated 20% of profitable traders. However, despite the challenge, achievement is possible, and under the right circumstances, life-changing profits can happen.

CHAPTER 16: FUTURES SLANG AND TERMINOLOGY

Outsiders might think that the futures industry has created its own language. Many of the terms brokers and traders use take a new meaning from their origin, and becoming familiar with the slang can prevent costly miscommunications, or at a minimum save some face on social media or online forums. After all, even self-directed online traders will need to communicate with their brokerage firm from time to time regarding their account. Some of the terminology covered in this chapter has been covered already, but when it comes to building a foundation of trading knowledge, it is important to seal any cracks. I believe that these are worth a second look.

BULL VERSUS BEAR

The terms *bull market* and *bear market* certainly aren't isolated to the world of commodities, and within the current decade, we have seen record-breaking cases of each. Although you are most likely aware of the concept of *bull* and *bear* markets, and this might seem elementary, you might not be familiar with all the related terms and variations that you will likely be exposed to when speaking about the futures and options markets.

The origin of the bull and bear market comparison is bleak at best, but one thing is for sure: It stuck. Theory suggests that the use of the *bull* to express a runaway market has to do with the herding action often seen in market moves that occur as the masses look to jump on the bandwagon. On the other hand, a *bear* depicts a dangerous and vicious beast that shares characteristics similar to a declining market. Moreover, it starts with a *B* and seems to ring well with *bull*.

Here's a recap of the seemingly obvious: A *bull market* is described as one in which prices are consistently moving upward or one that is forging higher highs and higher lows. You might hear the terms *bull* and *bear* attached to talk about the commodity or stock markets in general, but the terms also can refer to individual contracts. Industry insiders have dubbed a rallying market as a *bull* run. Conversely, the consistent downward pressure is often described as a *bear* market.

In addition, the expressions *bullish* and *bearish* are synonymous with *optimistic* and *pessimistic*, respectively. For example, a trader who believes that the price of gold will go higher is said to be *bullish*. If the same trader believes that the inverse relationship between gold and the US dollar will remain intact, he will likely be *bearish* the greenback.

BULL AND BEAR SLANG

Now for the slang. *Bullish* and *bearish* aren't always used to portray markets. They can sometimes be used to describe expectations of the economy, the potential impact of news events or data, or an option or futures spread.

We generally all agree that the economy isn't a market, and it isn't *directly* tradable. However, it is possible to speculate on the health of the economy indirectly through the commodity and financial markets. Nonetheless, you might hear your broker mention being *bullish* on the economy. Although this isn't correct in the strict definition of the term, the phrase is commonly used. Accordingly, in a broad sense of the statement, this might insinuate that your broker is bullish the stock market and bearish bonds. This assumption is based on the common premise that investors favor stocks during good economic times and avoid bonds.

As you should recall, we discussed futures spreads in Chapter 1, "A Crash Course in Commodities." *Bull* and *bear* are often attached to futures spreads as a way to identify the intended direction of the market. Ironically, for futures spreads, *bull* doesn't necessarily mean that the futures market must go up for the position to be profitable; instead, a spread trader simply needs the spread to move favorably. Nonetheless, futures spreads are labeled *bull* or *bear* according to the trader's market sentiment.

Option spreads, also covered in Chapter 1, are similarly labeled in terms of the desired direction of the futures price. For example, a *bull call spread* involves the purchase of a close-to-the-money call option and the sale of an out-of-the-money option. Those familiar with options can easily see that this is a trade that stands to makes money if the market goes higher. However, those who haven't learned the basics of options trading could easily identify the intention of the spread simply by picking up on the fact that it is labeled a *bull*. Likewise, if your broker mentions a *bear put spread*, he is referring to an option strategy in which it is possible to profit if the market drops. With that said, I don't recommend that you participate in any trades that you don't understand. Simply being privy to the fact that *bear* is equivalent to the market going down should not be enough to entice you to participate in a recommended bear put spread; there's much more to it than that. However, knowing this is step one, and being aware of the clues surrounding you, might help lessen your learning curve.

SPREAD

The term *spread* is used loosely within the futures industry, and unless you are familiar with all the different uses of the word, you might be leaving yourself vulnerable to expensive miscommunications, or at least embarrassing misunderstandings. Here are a few of the broadest contexts in which you will hear the term used.

BID/ASK SPREAD

As covered in Chapter 1, the *spread* between the bid and the ask represents the difference in the highest price that a buyer is willing to pay (or the price you can sell it for) and the lowest price the seller is willing to accept (or the price you can buy it for). In essence, at any given time and in any market, there will always be a price at which you can buy an asset for and a price that the asset can be sold for. The "spread" between the two prices is known as the *bid/ask spread*. Prior to electronic trading, the beneficiary of the spread is the floor broker who takes the other side of your trade. In the current environment, market makers in options still benefit from the bid/ask spread but liquid futures markets generally don't have market makers. The bid/ask spread isn't necessarily earned by anybody; it is simply absorbed into the market as traders buy and sell securities.

In conversation, traders and brokers typically refer to the *bid/ask spread* simply as "the spread." Thus, any time you converse about the price of a commodity option or futures contract and someone mentions the *spread*, she is referring to the bid/ask spread.

Unfortunately, as a retail trader, you will always be forced to pay the ask when buying and sell the bid when going short. In other words, if you simultaneously bought and sold a futures or options contract, you would immediately lose the difference between the *spread*. Accordingly, you might hear your broker say that you need to *pay the spread* or *pay the ask* to get into a trade. This can come up if a limit order goes unfilled and it seems as though you need to increase your limit price to, or closer to, the ask to get filled. Similarly, if you hit the bid, you are agreeing to sell the contract at the bid price.

OPTION SPREAD

You rarely hear a broker or trader refer to an *option spread* as such; it is typically shortened to *spread*. When referring to the bid and ask of an *option spread*, a spread of a spread, the price quote is normally identified as the bid/ask, whereas the *option spread* is still referred to by a single word: *spread*. In reference to a *spread* between call options, it is common to hear *call spread* and, for those with puts, *put spread*. With that said, brokers have been creative in labeling specific types of option spreads with shortened terms. For example, a *put butterfly* is known as a *put-fly*.

FUTURES SPREAD

Based on my experience, option spreads are more common than futures spreads among retail traders. Perhaps this is why option spreads have become the default strategy identified by the single word "spread." *Futures spreads* are normally referred to in conjunction with the contracts involved. For instance, a trader who is spreading July and December corn might refer to it as a Dec/July corn spread.

CONTRACT MONTH SLANG

Throughout the years, traders have been determined to eliminate confusion in communication and keep it short and sweet. It isn't uncommon for indications of contract months to be shortened or even nicknamed. In view of that, don't be thrown off if you hear "deck corn," short for December corn. Likewise, a less obvious example is Christmas or Labor Day corn, to identify expiration months in those of the corresponding holidays.

RED MONTHS

Of course, each of the 12 months occurs only once every year; therefore, it is necessary to distinguish futures contracts expiring in March (or any other month) of the current year from those that expire in March of the following year. If there is no reference to the year, it is assumed to be the closest to expiration. When a trader or broker refers to the following year, the term *red* identifies it as such. Thus, in January 2018, a trader looking to speculate on March 2019 futures would refer to the contract as *red* March.

FILL

A *fill* is simply a price at which an order was executed. You might often hear it referred to as a *fill price*. Explicitly, if a trader buys a T-bond 155 call option for 1 15/64, then 1 15/64 is said to be the fill price. It is a bit embarrassing to admit, but after several years of college finance classes and months of rigorous studying for the Series 3 proficiency exam that is necessary to become a licensed commodity broker, I hadn't yet been introduced to the term *fill*. I distinctly remember the word showing up as I was taking the exam, and I was overtaken with a feeling of panic. Although

> The term *fill* is used to identify the execution price.

I assumed the definition based on the context in which it was used, there was no way to know for sure whether my conclusions were correct.

SPLIT FILL

A *split fill* occurs when a trader places an order to buy or sell a futures contract or option in a quantity in excess of one contract and receives a fill reported at more than one price. In other words, if a trader places an order to buy 10 December T-note futures at the market, the fills on each, or some, might be reported at different prices. For instance, a trader might buy four at 126'20, five at 126'20.5, and one at 126'21, and would be said to have gotten a *split fill*.

PARTIAL FILL

A *partial fill* occurs when some, but not all, of the stated quantity of a limit order (an order to buy or sell an asset at a specific price) is filled. Going back to our note futures example, if the order were placed to buy 10 December T-note futures at 119'20, and that was the low print of the day, it is possible that only a handful of the 10 contracts would be filled. Remember, in the case of a limit order, the market has to "go through it to do it." A trader isn't owed a fill unless the price ticks below the limit price. Had the low of the day been 119'19.5 (one tick below the limit price), the trader could have challenged any lack of fill on the trade.

BLOWOUT

For many, commodity trading is their first experience with leverage and margin. Beginners often underestimate the amount of control that a margin department rightfully has over their trading account in the case of an undercapitalized account.

> "I'm not nearly as concerned about the return on my capital as I am the return of my capital." — Will Rogers

A margin clerk, and even a broker responsible for a given account, is authorized to do whatever is in her power to prevent a trading account from going negative (losing more than the funds on deposit). For an account that is liquidated in this manner by someone other than the account owner, it is said to have been *blown out*. Similarly, an account on a persistent margin call might be liquidated to satisfy the exchange margin. This is also considered a *blowout*.

BLOWUP

A *blowup* is similar to a *blowout*, with the primary difference being who pulls the plug on a trade or an account. Thus, if a trader determines that he is undercapitalized and in danger of losing more money than was deposited in the account, he can liquidate the positions at his own hand. This is referred to as a *blowup*.

In the late 2000s and early 2010s, you likely heard of the many hedge fund *blowups* resulting from commodity bubbles and their subsequent busts. These were funds that simply lost all or most of the money deposited in their fund and could no longer continue trading.

Keep in mind that, for all intents and purposes, *blowup* and *blowout* can be used interchangeably, but their most common interpretations are as previously noted.

KEYPUNCH ERROR

A keypunch error is just as it sounds. It occurs when a back office brokerage employee, trading pit clerk, or order desk clerk mistypes a fill price, account number, quantity, or symbol on a reported fill. Given the massive volume and human involvement in open outcry trading, *keypunch errors* happened frequently. Fortunately, technology and electronic trade execution have dramatically reduced keypunch errors. If you notice what you believe to be a keypunch error in your account, contact your broker immediately instead of trying to trade out of it or offset the position.

In today's trading environment, the most common keypunch error is one in which a trade desk clerk or broker mistypes a client account number and subsequently places a trade in an incorrect account. As an account holder, if you attempt to exit a trade that was inadvertently placed in your account because a broker or desk clerk miskeyed an account number, you are responsible for the order that you entered, even though it was done so as an attempt to eliminate a keypunch error. Unfortunately, I have witnessed the peril of such actions, and I urge you to keep proper trading records and know your positions to ensure that this does not happen to you.

If a trade desk clerk or broker makes a mistake in the placement of your order, such as executing the incorrect quantity or trading the wrong product symbol or month, the order taker has made a keypunch error and is obligated to correct the situation in a manner that makes the traders account "whole." This can sometimes be extremely costly for the individual making the error.

BUSTED, MOVED, OR CANCELED TRADE

A *busted trade* is most often the result of a keypunch error and is simply a position that is removed from a client account due to an error of some kind. When a trade is *busted* or moved from an account, the account from which it is moved stands as if it never happened. The erroneous trade, along with any commission and fees attached to the position, is completely removed from the trading account.

> If you notice a trade that you don't believe is yours or that is inaccurate in price, contact your broker immediately. Don't try to offset it!

To the surprise of many, it is possible for trades executed on behalf of one client to be inadvertently entered into the account of another client. With thousands of trades being executed on a daily basis, it isn't hard to imagine a clerk on the floor, a broker, or a desk order taker mistyping a digit of an account number. This is the most common need for a *busted trade*.

A *busted trade* can also occur when the original fill was reported at an erroneous price (*keypunch error*), making it necessary to remove the executed trade at the incorrect price (*busting the trade*) and replacing it with an accurate fill price. As open outcry trading slowly dies, so does the frequency of these types of mishaps.

If you notice that your statement shows a position that isn't yours, if you are missing a position that should be yours, or if you see what seems to be an inaccurate fill price, immediately contact your broker. Don't panic, and whatever you do, don't try to offset a trade that isn't yours or reestablish one that is missing. It is highly likely that the absent, mysterious, or incorrect trade was the result of an error, either human or computer, and can easily be corrected. Any client attempt to "correct" the situation could lead to substantial chaos and large monetary damage.

Remember, whether it is a winning or losing position, if you didn't place or authorize the order, it isn't yours—regardless of what might be showing in your account. Additionally, the person who did place the order and expected to see the position on her statement is likely looking for it.

Again, busted or moved trades are occurring less frequently due to electronically executed futures and options. During the heyday of open outcry trading pits, they were common.

FAT FINGER ERROR

A *fat finger error* is a byproduct of technology. This term describes a situation in which a trader accidentally places an order for a much larger quantity than intended. For instance, a trader attempting to execute 10 contracts might add a zero, making it a 100-lot order. In extreme cases, this could mean thousands or tens of thousands of contracts inadvertently entered. The retail trading platforms most of you will have access to include risk-management parameters that prevent an overly excessive order from being placed, but professional traders might not have this safety net. If a fat finger error is large enough, it can cause a dramatic and temporary fluctuation in market pricing.

Limits placed on trading platforms to prevent *fat finger errors* are known as *clip limits*. For instance, a particular trader's brokerage might have set his clip limit at 100 contracts. This does not mean the trader cannot have more than 100 open contracts at a time, but it does mean he cannot buy or sell any contract on a single order ticket in a quantity higher than 100.

NET LIQ

Futures and options brokers often use the term *net liq* to refer to the *net liquidation value* of an account. The net liquidation value is simply a snapshot of what the account would be worth if all open positions were closed at the prices displayed on an account statement or within the trading platform intraday. Note that assuming that the positions held in the account could be liquidated at the displayed prices on the nightly brokerage statement is unrealistic, it doesn't reflect the impact of the bid/ask spread or any price change not accounted for in the snapshot. It is important to realize that values displayed on account statements reflect the price at which all positions were assigned at the close of a given trading session. In a 24-hour marketplace, statement values often differ greatly from actual market values almost immediately after they are issued. Traders are generally best off viewing their account via a real-time trading platform to get a more accurate picture of where things stand, but even then there are some quirks to be aware of.

Some trading platforms offer intraday valuations based on the current bid for long contracts or ask for short contracts. Accordingly, traders utilizing a platform that values positions in this manner are provided with an extremely accurate *net liquidation value* figure.

On the contrary, those traders using a trading platform that values positions based on their last trade, as opposed to the bid/ask quote, will likely see moderately inaccurate calculations of their *net liq*. This is because the most recent quote might not necessarily accurately reflect market value due to the amount of time that sometimes passes between fills of a given option contract.

Nonetheless, despite its imperfections, the *net liq* is the number that you should pay the most attention to on your brokerage statement and any intraday views of your account status.

EQUITY

Equity is a word used in the world of finance in a ridiculous number of contexts. However, in futures trading, the term is most commonly used to describe the amount of cash held in a given account. Unlike the net liquidation value, which gives you a bottom-line figure, your account *equity* is the top-line figure. Plainly, it is the beginning cash balance in an account before accounting for any premium paid for long options, premium collected for short options, and profit or loss sustained on open futures positions (unrealized profits and losses). In my view, the account equity is an arbitrary and relatively meaningless figure.

Before we look at details, you should know that options trades result in immediate cash inflows (when selling) or outflows (when buying). Futures trading, on the other hand, doesn't result in an actual cash transaction until the trade is offset. With that said, any commission and fees charged result in a cash transaction immediately.

> On a futures account statement, account equity is the equivalent to cash, not a marked-to-market value of your account.

In essence, if a trader put $5,000 into a new trading account and spends $300 on a March call option in the E-mini S&P along with another $8 in transaction costs, his account equity would be $4,692 ($5,000 – $300 – $8) because $308 in cash was taken out of the account. The cash left in the account is the equity and is the cash available to use toward the margin of a futures position, toward marginable option spreads, or to purchase long options and option spreads. In other words, it is the tradable account balance.

If the same trader went short an April crude oil futures position and has an *unrealized* loss of $550 after paying $4 in transaction costs (exchange fees and commission) to enter the trade, his equity balance would be $4,688 ($4,692 – $4). The $550 unrealized loss in the futures position has not been accounted for because there has yet to be a cash inflow or outflow. Assuming that the same trader took the loss of exactly $550, the equity balance would be reduced to $4,134 ($4,688 - $550 - $4). The additional $4 represents the other half of the transaction cost;

remember, futures trades are charged commission and exchange fees on a half in and half out basis in contrast to options in which the full round-turn commission is charged upon entry.

On the contrary, when a trader sells an option, there is an immediate cash transaction. Thus, the premium collected is added to the account equity. Using the preceding example, if the trader sold a March S&P put for $900 and paid a transaction fee of $8, the account equity would be back to $5,026 ($4,134 + $900 − $8). As you can see, the account equity gives you little information on the actual progress of the account. This particular trader has sustained a drawdown in net liquidation value in the account by approximately $574 (crude oil loss plus all transaction fees, and potentially more if there was a change in the option values, yet his account equity is showing a higher balance than the original deposited amount). Given this realistic example, it is clear that traders should focus on their net liquidation values instead of their account equity.

CUSTOMER SEGREGATED FUNDS ACCOUNT

Customer Segregated Funds Accounts are accounts held at a bank in the name of the Futures Commission Merchant (FCM) that houses client funds. Simply put, when a commodity client deposits funds into his account, rules and regulations dictate that the money is held in an account separate from the brokerage firm's operational funds. This separate account is known as *customer segregated funds*. The clear separation between the firm's money and customer's money is intended to protect customers in case of a brokerage firm bankruptcy. However, this safeguard exists only if firms follow the rules set in place and regulators enforce them.

BEANS

This might seem obvious to many of you, but for others (including myself at one point), it isn't so obvious. As an accounting and finance major in college, I became accustomed to precise wording, and anything less than exact references added unnecessary confusion. I have since gotten accustomed to the lax language futures traders use, as you will, too. However, I felt it necessary to point this out and avoid some of you the embarrassment that I experienced.

If you hear a commodity trader refer to *beans*, he is speaking of *soybeans*, not coffee beans, pinto beans, and the like.

COMMODITY CURRENCY

Commodity currencies are said to be correlated with the price of commodities. The two most common commodity currencies are the Australian dollar and the Canadian dollar, but the New Zealand dollar often is also lumped into this category. The correlation stems from the idea that the economies backed by the named currencies are tied to commodity valuations. If you pull up a chart of the Canadian dollar and crude oil futures, you will see exactly why the Canadian currency is referred to as a *commodity currency*.

THE AUSSIE AND THE LOONIE

The Australian and Canadian dollars have something else in common: They both have nicknames. The Australian dollar is often referred to as the Aussie, and you might hear industry insiders speak of the Canadian dollar using the term *Loonie*.

POUND, POUND STERLING, STERLING, THE CABLE

The British pound is often shortened to *pound*, but you can also hear it referred to as the *pound sterling* or the *sterling*. Although they are interchangeable, most brokers and traders refer to the currency used in the United Kingdom as the *pound*. Traders also sometimes refer to the relationship between the pound and the dollar as the *cable*.

DEAD CAT BOUNCE

A *dead cat bounce* is a figure of speech industry insiders use to describe a scenario in which a substantial decline in a futures market is followed by a temporary bounce in prices. Use of the phrase *dead cat bounce* typically implies that the speaker is expecting the market to resume its downtrend. The speaker often assumes that the subsequent bounce in pricing is mostly the result of short covering in the midst of a technically oversold market. Remember, if short traders are taking profits, they are buying futures contracts to exit their position. This buying can be enough to artificially prop up prices in the near term.

BOTTOM FISHING

In general, *bottom fishing* is a method of catching fish that stay at the bottom of a body of water. In finance, *bottom fishing* is the art of speculating on a price recovery in a market that is trading at what is considered historically cheap prices.

For instance, as natural gas prices drifted toward $1.60 mmBtu in early 2016, several *bottom fishers* were likely hoping for an eventual rally, and they got it. By the end of the year, natural gas was trading near the $4.00 price!

Expectations of higher prices typically stem from the cyclical nature of the market in regard to supply and demand. Bottom fishers know that as commodity prices become excessively cheap, producers cut back, and consumers demand more. The subsequent decrease in supply will eventually have a positive impact on price.

CHASING THE MARKET

A trader who enters a market well after a trend is established is said to be *chasing the market*. This scenario happens when a market has risen or fallen dramatically and traders try to enter in the direction of the move without regard to their entry price. Unfortunately, those *chasing a market* tend to regret it later when they discover the hard way that the trend is your friend only until it ends.

I have witnessed too many inexperienced traders anticipate a market move but talk themselves into waiting for confirmation of a trend. In the right context, confirmation might be a wise move. However, if the trader's idea of confirmation means several weeks or months of favorable market movement, the odds favor the miserable experience of getting into a trade just as the trend is ending. As a trader, you never want to be fashionably late to the party.

LIMIT MOVES

The futures exchanges stipulate specified price limits on most listed contracts. The largest amount of change that the price of a commodity futures contract is allowed to move in a single trading session is known as the price limit. A *limit move* is one in which the market rallies or falls in the largest magnitude allowable on that particular trading day and is measured from the previous session close, not from the current session open.

When the daily price limit is reached, it is said to be *locked limit*. When this occurs, trading a futures contract in the direction of the limit move is not possible. Therefore, if the set price limit in corn is 45 cents and the futures market rallies 45 cents from the previous session's close, it would not be possible to buy a corn futures contract (even if you are short and trying to get out). However, if you have nerves of steel, you could sell the contract. If there are enough sellers at the limit price, the market will eventually move off its limit and resume trading again.

While a market is *locked limit*, large numbers of orders waiting to be filled often accumulate at the limit price. These orders will be filled only if the market retreats from the limit price or in the following trading session in which the new limit price becomes 45 cents higher than the previous session's limit close (assuming a 45-cent limit, of course).

LIMIT UP

This occurs when a market rallies to its daily limit and ceases executing buy orders.

LIMIT DOWN

This occurs when the market declines to its daily limit and ceases executing sell orders.

THE TAPE

The *tape*, also known as the *ticker tape*, is a term borrowed from stock traders that was originally used to describe the running record of scrolling paper depicting the trading activity in each individual stock. The advent of computer technology has replaced the ticker tape with electronic records of trading activity, but the reference stuck.

In commodities, *the tape* is often used to refer to the *time and sales* data, which records each trade price and the quantity of contracts traded at each price.

TRADING SOLUTION, ENVIRONMENT, AND FRONT-END

The commodity industry is known for unnecessarily complicating otherwise simple terms. An order-entry platform that can be used to execute and monitor trades is often referred to as a *trading solution, trading environment,* or a *front-end*. Simply put, this is either web-based (accessed via an internet browser such as Microsoft Internet Explorer) or a downloadable software package that can be run directly from a trader's desktop that provides market access to retail traders. It might also be an application on a smartphone enabling traders to monitor their positions and place orders directly from their smartphone or iPad.

PROPRIETARY TRADING

The word *proprietary* indicates that a party holds exclusive rights of ownership, control, or use over an item of property, whether physical or intellectual. In reference to finance and trading, the term describes the practice in which a firm hires employees to actively trade in the financial markets with the firm's money as opposed to its customers' money. The goal is for the employees of the firm to profit from the speculative transactions executed by its employees. Of course, it also accepts the risk of losing trades executed on its behalf by authorized employees. *Proprietary trading* strategies are characteristically developed in-house and are considered trade secrets and are not released to the public.

PROP DESK

A *prop desk* is a trading desk where proprietary trading takes place.

RUNNING STOPS

When a market makes a quick and sometimes dramatic move through well-known support and resistance areas, it is often the result of stop running. In essence, this is a scenario in which market prices reach levels that contain a substantial number of buy or sell stop orders, and prices move rapidly as stop orders are elected.

For example, if the S&P 500 futures are trading at 12,322 with obvious technical support at 2,320, a price drop below 2,320 could trigger sell stops placed by those long the market attempting to defend their positions against adverse price moves. If this is the case, there will be a temporary imbalance of sell orders executed, and market prices may drop quickly as the sell stops are filled. When all the sell stop orders placed at or near 2,320 are executed, it is not uncommon for the futures contract to reverse higher. After all, the selling pressure is somewhat artificial, in that it generally isn't due to new bears entering the market with fresh shorts. Instead, it is the result of bulls exiting positions via automatically triggered orders as sell stops are executed.

> Don't get frustrated with markets running stops; this will always be part of the trading landscape. Instead, be informed of the characteristics of the market you are trading and adjust accordingly.

Some speculators believe larger market participants actively seek stop orders by pushing the market prices to known areas of support and resistance in hopes of triggering stop orders and benefiting from the price moves.

However, traders who speculate in markets with ample liquidity shouldn't believe this to be the case. Conversely, if a handful of manipulative traders can temporarily move the markets on the sheer size of their trading capital, it should be viewed as a market characteristic that can't be controlled but can be compensated for through trading strategy and decisions.

SHORT SQUEEZE

A *short squeeze* is a rapid increase in market price that occurs when there are large imbalances in buy orders over sell orders. A short squeeze scenario most often occurs when short sellers scramble to offset their open positions by buying back their contracts. As short traders continue to cover positions, a snowball effect in the quantity of buyers often takes place, and the resulting price increase can be surprisingly dramatic.

Short squeezes often begin as profit taking by the bears but are later fueled because a large quantity of buy stop orders are being executed or the market has rallied enough to force those short traders without working stop loss orders out of the market due to a lack of capital, margin, or faith. Specifically, traders are squeezed out of their positions. As the term *squeeze* suggests, this is a painful process for those caught on the wrong side of it.

Of course, long traders can also be squeezed out of positions in a sharp downturn. This is known as a *long squeeze*.

BABYSITTING

Babysitting a trade is the act of staring at a computer screen, quotes on a mobile device, or a business news channel seeking second-by-second updates on an open speculative position. Although it is true that there is substantial risk in trading and all risk exposure should be responsibly monitored, obsession over market activity could do damage to the psychology involved in the trade.

Traders who are glued to their screens are more likely to give in to the pressures of fear and greed, or perhaps the opposite scenario of analysis paralysis. Too much information can sometimes lead to a deer-in-the-headlights reaction to adverse price moves, in which the trader marries an open position and refuses to exit before losses mount to devastating levels.

I believe that traders should diligently evaluate their position before entering the market; if this is done properly, they should be comfortable enough with the trade to avoid the pressures of living and dying by each market tick. Hopefully, doing so removes some of the emotion that can negatively dictate trading decisions.

SCALP

Scalping is a day-trading method in which trades are opened and closed in a very short time scale. A scalper typically leaves a position open for anywhere from a second or two to a few minutes. Naturally, the risk and reward per individual trade is relatively low due to the time in which the trader is exposed to price risk. However, wins and losses can quickly mount along with transaction costs because most scalpers are trading large numbers of futures contracts.

SLIPPAGE

Slippage is the term used to describe the difference between the estimated fill price and the actual price. For example, if a trader places a buy stop order in January feeder cattle at 115.50 and was reported a fill price of 115.70, the trader would have suffered a fill that is 20 points worse than what was anticipated.

> Slippage is an ordinary cost of business for traders. However, the amount of slippage suffered is highly dependent on the markets being traded. Just as in business, you want to keep your costs low; therefore, traders should choose markets accordingly based on their strategy.

Remember, a stop order is an order to execute the trade at the market price when the named price is reached (assuming the order can be filled within the exchange's stipulated acceptable price limit). Thus, in a fast-moving market, the price can quickly surpass the stop order price and create a scenario in which the fill is significantly unfavorable, but within the exchange's price limit band.

Naturally, it goes both ways; it is possible for slippage to have a positive effect on traders and their accounts. However, slippage typically works *against* the retail trader. Slippage can occur with every order type and varies greatly by the market traded. A highly liquid market such as the E-mini S&P exposes the trader to much less risk of slippage than an illiquid and highly volatile market such as lumber. It should be clear that short-term day traders, or scalpers, should not be trading illiquid markets because slippage and a lack of fill quality would render such strategies guaranteed losers.

Although you often hear traders refer to slippage following what they believe to be an unfavorable fill on a market order, that usage is technically inaccurate. A market order is one in which the trader agrees to pay the best possible price. Because he is not specifying a price, he shouldn't refer to a deviation of his expected price as slippage—but he will. Instead, it is simply an unfortunate fill and, quite probably, the result of wide bid/ask spreads or excessive market volatility.

Conversely, while using a limit order, only positive slippage is possible. When a trader places a limit order, she is requesting to be filled at her price or better; therefore, a worse fill is not a possibility. For instance, an order to buy July soybeans at $10.45 on a limit might be filled at the stated price or lower; a fill at a price above $10.45 isn't acceptable. Once again, you shouldn't expect to see positive slippage often.

WORKING ORDER

A *working order* is any order, other than a market order, that has been placed but not yet filled. A day order is working until it is either filled or canceled, or until it expires at the end of the trading session. It is possible for a GTC (Good Till Canceled) order to be working for several days, weeks, or months before being filled or canceled, or until it expires with the contract.

UNABLE

If the market price fails to reach a placed stop or limit order, the exchange is unable to fill an order; therefore, it is said to have gone *unable*. In other words, the order placed was not filled and is no longer working.

HANDLE

Many brokers and traders refer to a full point of price movement as a *handle*. The definition of a handle is different in each market but is typically identified as the largest manageable increment of price movement. Keep in mind that, as with any slang, there are various interpretations of the meaning and uses. Therefore, you might hear or read slight deviations of the examples that I discussed in this book. Nonetheless, you likely can decipher the user's meaning based on the context.

When it comes to the grains and energies, a *full handle* is a dollar in price. Thus, if corn rallies from $3.00 per bushel to $4.00 per bushel, it is said to have moved a full handle. S&P traders most often refer to every 100 points in price change as a handle. As a result, the difference between 2,200 and 2,300 is a handle. You can determine the remaining contracts from here; if not, you will find comfort in knowing that, when using slang, there is room for error.

OVERBOUGHT/OVERSOLD

Overbought and *oversold* are terms that describe a market that is believed to have moved too far, too fast. In the case of *overbought* market conditions, prices are deemed to have rallied sharply to what are believed to be unsustainable levels. Conversely, in an *oversold* market, prices are said to have dropped beyond realistic valuations. In either case, the market is often expected to digest the condition with a corrective, countertrend move, but that isn't always the case.

Overbought and oversold market conditions are normally identified by technical indicators such as computer-generated oscillators. Technical counter-trend traders might look to sell markets that are technically overbought and buy those that are oversold.

DEBIT BALANCE/ACCOUNT DEBIT

Contrary to what you may have learned in Accounting 101, a commodity account *debit* implies a negative balance. If a client is said to have gone *debit* or to have a *debit balance*, it simply means that the trader has lost more money than was on deposit in the trading account. Under the right circumstances, it might be possible for losses to exceed the original investment and result in a negative account balance of $1,000, $2,000, or much more. For instance, if a trader starts with $10,000 and fails to properly manage risk causing a loss of $11,000, the account would have a *debit balance* of $1,000.

Keep in mind that brokers and brokerage firms do all that they can to prevent this from occurring because it poses a risk to their clearing relationships and their bottom lines if a trader cannot bring the account whole. Again, account debits are initially covered with the broker's commission. Clearly, legal consequences for the trader will follow, but in the meantime, it can be a large inconvenience for brokerage firms.

ROUND TURNS

All transactions in commodity futures or options are referred to in terms of *round turns*, which is a simplified way of describing the practice of getting in *and* getting out of a trade. For instance, if a trader buys a futures contract and later sells one of the same commodity and month, he is said to have completed one round turn. If multiple lots are traded, the trader has completed the number of round turns according to the number of contracts. Therefore, if a trader buys 20 contracts of the December E-mini S&P and then sells back 20, he is said to have done 20 round turns. In such a case, you might also hear this referred as 40 half-turns or 40 trades. You might also hear the entry or exit side of the transaction referred to as 20 half-turns.

Commodity brokerage firms traditionally quote commission rates on a round-turn basis but many of the broker dealers (stock brokers getting into the commodity business) quote rates in half-turns, or per side. It is important to realize this before you begin shopping for a broker. If you are quoted $25 for a full-service brokerage account, be sure to confirm that this is a round-turn rate that covers the cost to enter *and* exit the trade. If not, you might be unknowingly agreeing to a per-side charge of $25, in which you will pay $25 to enter and $25 to offset a position. Firms that charge commission in this manner are said to be working on a per-side basis. Some firms try to mislead traders, or at least take advantage of the marketing illusion of lower rates, by advertising their half-turn rate. Be sure you are clear on what you're negotiating.

INDEX

A

aging margin calls, 184

algorithmic trading, 23–24, 75

application, iBroker, 82–83

arbitrage, 39–40, 61, 160

asset, underlying, 38, 40, 42, 44, 60, 132, 153–55, 159, 162–66, 172, 174, 210, 214

asset prices, 19, 210

Australian dollar, 176, 178, 224–25

B

balances, negative, 96, 213, 230

Barchart Trader, 74

BarchartTrader, 82, 84–85

BarchartTrader's mobile platform, 85

basis, per-side, 46–47, 76, 231

bean oil, 137–38

beans, 57, 137, 224

bear, 204, 217–18

bearish, 26, 197, 217

bear markets, 16, 161, 200, 217

or better order, 115–16, 130

bid, 45, 50–51, 53, 114, 116, 150, 218–19

bid/ask, 45–46, 48, 50–52, 59, 64, 80, 116–17, 123, 127, 150, 159, 218–19, 222

blowout, 220–21

blowup, 221

bodies, regulatory, 30, 89–90, 105, 198

bond futures, 30-year, 169

bond futures prices, 167

bonds, 20, 47, 89, 91, 163–67, 170, 174, 218

  long, 163, 166, 170

boom-and-bust cycles, 16

bottom fishing, 225

bounce, dead cat, 225

breakout traders, 117–18

Brent, 35, 73, 150–51

British pound, 176, 178–79, 225

British pound futures, 178

brokerage firms, 27, 29, 31, 65–66, 75–77, 80, 85–86, 93–94, 97–99, 108–9, 180, 182, 185–86, 215, 230–31

brokerage industry, 85, 103, 110

brokerage services, 77, 85, 94, 107

brokerage statement, 222–23

broker/dealers, 89, 91–92

broker-dealers, 46

brokers, deep discount, 98, 106, 109–10

bull, 156, 217–18, 227

bullish, 44, 197, 217–18

bull market, 17, 21, 140, 217

business plan, 27, 196, 199, 202

C

call option, 49, 51–52, 78, 82, 116, 138, 151–52, 168, 183, 202–3, 213, 219

Canadian dollar, 176, 178, 224–25

Canceled Trade, 221

cancel/replace, 125

capital preservation, 193–94

Carley Garner, 4–6

cash market price risk, 57–58

cash market speculators, 55

cash market transaction, 38, 57

cash price, 38, 57

cattle

  feeder, 139, 141, 229

  live, 139–41

CBOE (Chicago Board of Options Exchange's), 200

CBOT (Chicago Board of Trade), 33–35, 68, 132–33, 145, 155, 162, 165–68

CBOT division, 33–34, 135

CFTC (Commodity Futures Trading Commission), 30–31, 70, 73, 89–91, 105, 176, 198

charting, 74–75

charts, 64, 68, 70–71, 74–76, 82, 131, 224

Chicago Board of Options Exchange's (CBOE), 200

Chicago Board of Trade. See CBOT

Chicago Mercantile Exchange. See CME

CityTrader, 82–83, 85

client funds, 27–29, 31, 90

client money, 27, 29, 89–90

CME (Chicago Mercantile Exchange), 33–35, 68, 70–73, 88, 126–27, 132–33, 139, 142, 145, 148, 154–57, 161–63, 171, 176, 192

CME exchanges, 71, 74

CME Group, 6, 33–35, 37, 54, 63, 67, 71–73, 132, 135, 139, 148, 150, 154–55, 162, 174

CME Group exchanges, 71–73, 154

cocoa, 35, 73, 142

coffee, 35, 73, 142–43

COMEX (Commodity Exchange), 34–35, 132–33, 149, 151

COMEX division, 35, 148–50

commission, 27, 30, 32, 45–47, 88, 90–91, 93–97, 102–3, 108, 110–13, 142, 144, 158–59, 223

  round-turn, 46, 95, 224

commissions and fees, 46, 116, 135, 137, 139–40, 144–45, 155, 159, 168, 178, 213, 221, 223

commitments of traders, 82

commodities, underlying, 37, 40–42, 60, 64, 133, 135, 143, 146, 149, 210

commodity brokerage firms, 26, 28, 99, 231

commodity brokers, 25, 30–31, 66, 71, 73, 76, 85, 96, 104, 106

commodity currencies, 178, 224

Commodity Exchange. See COMEX

commodity futures contracts, 26, 35, 54, 59, 226

Commodity Futures Trading Commission. See CFTC

commodity market volatility, 17, 21, 24

commodity prices, 21, 23, 33, 47, 55, 178, 210, 225

commodity trading, book Higher Probability, 17, 78, 148, 150, 183, 200, 202, 204, 206

Commodity Trading Advisors. See CTAs

commodity trading platforms, 77, 83–84

contango, 38–39, 57

Contract Expiration, 40

contract month, 44, 48, 125

contracts

  mini futures, 155–56

  standardized futures, 37, 165

contract size, 10, 133, 135–37, 139, 143, 145, 148–51, 155, 162, 170–71, 176, 178

contract specifications, 167, 178

contract symbols, 64, 102, 131

contract values, 132–33, 158, 167, 174

copper, 116, 146, 149–50

copper futures, 11, 148–49

corn, 33, 37, 41, 45, 52, 55, 62, 64, 122, 133–35, 137, 149, 153, 163, 208–11

cotton, 35, 73, 142, 145

coupon payments, 163–65

CQG Q-Trader, 82–83

crop, 33–34, 36, 55, 57–59, 68, 134

crude oil, 22, 24–26, 34–35, 48, 52, 55, 73, 78, 80, 92, 120, 128, 150–51, 191–92, 214

crude oil futures, 46, 78, 151

CTAs (Commodity Trading Advisors), 20, 70, 152, 198

currencies, 18, 146, 166, 172, 176–78, 224–25

Customer Segregated Funds Account, 29, 224

D

data, real-time, 63, 87

data fees, professional, 73

day order, 126, 130, 229

day trade, 66, 181, 210, 212

day trade futures, 78

day traders, 80, 99, 107, 119, 156, 180, 182, 206, 213

day trading margin, 65–66, 98, 181

debit balance, 230

DeCarley Trading, 29–31, 75, 77, 85, 196

default risk, 37, 163

delivery, 37–38, 40–42, 44, 49, 133, 163, 165, 187

delivery date, 37–38

delivery notice, 40–41

delivery process, 41–42, 209

discount bonds, 164, 171, 174

discount brokerage, 81, 94

Discount Brokerage, deep, 47, 94

discount securities, 163–64

DOM, 83

E

electronic trading, 35, 52, 61, 63–67, 71, 172, 218

electronic trading platforms, 51, 61, 65, 118

E-Micro Gold, 146–48

E-mini, 53, 128, 147–48, 150–52, 155–59, 161, 187

E-mini Dow, 119, 154–55

E-Mini Dow Jones Industrial Average, 155

E-mini futures contract, 128, 150, 210

E-mini NASDAQ, 156

E-MINI NASDAQ, 156, 183

E-mini silver, 149

E-MINI S&P, 53–54, 64, 67, 92, 115–16, 123, 128, 154–56, 159–60, 181–82, 187, 209–10, 212, 223, 229

energies, 16, 24, 34, 47, 61, 150–51, 230

energy markets, 16, 26, 55

equity markets, 17, 21, 23–24, 64, 152–53, 209

ETFs (exchange traded funds), 20, 209–11, 213–14

Euro, 92, 176–78

Eurodollar futures, 172

Eurodollar Futures, 172–73

Eurodollars, 59, 147, 162–63, 166, 171–73

exam, proficiency, 104, 106, 220

exchange, traded, 34

Exchange Data Fees, 63, 70–71, 92, 142

exchange fees, 46, 171, 223–24

exchange floor, 62, 65–66, 95, 158

exchange margin, 80, 181, 220

exchange margin requirements, 80

exchange's price limit band, 229

exchange traded funds. See ETFs

expiration, 40–42, 44, 53–54, 78, 80, 154, 164, 166, 168, 171, 173–75, 219

F

FCM (Futures Commission Merchant), 29–30, 60, 72, 81, 88–93, 224

fees, 46, 71–73, 76, 80, 82, 86, 135, 137, 139–40, 142, 144–45, 185, 211–13, 221, 223

  clearing, 47, 93

  desk, 86, 94, 109

Fill or Kill (FOK), 122–23

FINRA (Financial Industry Regulatory Authority), 104

firms

  deep discount brokerage, 86, 184

  futures brokerage, 27

  stock brokerage, 211–12

flash crash, 23–24, 94, 128

floor traders, 29, 64, 68–69

FOK orders, 122–23

forward contracts, 36–37

  exchange-traded, 37

free-to-use trading platforms, 71, 75–76, 79, 87

free trading platforms, 74–75

full-service broker, 85–86, 88, 94, 102, 108–9, 112–13, 118, 129–30, 207

fundamentals, 20–21, 23, 163

funds, segregated, 28, 31, 224

futures

  coffee, 143–44

  currency, 34, 167, 171, 176

  financial, 154–55, 166

  fund, 163–64, 171, 174

  meat, 139–40

  sugar, 144

  yen, 176

futures and options markets, 20, 67, 83–84, 105, 108, 154, 209, 214–15, 217

futures brokers, 27, 46, 84, 97, 104, 210, 212–13

Futures Commission Merchant. See FCM

futures contracts, 21, 36–37, 39–40, 42–43, 58, 62, 77, 115, 130, 134, 157, 210, 213

futures exchange, 34, 48, 64, 72, 89, 162, 213

futures expiration, 41

futures markets, 20–22, 33, 36, 38–39, 52, 55–60, 78, 114, 128, 132, 154, 162–63, 209–12

futures position, 57–58, 60, 67, 193, 200, 202, 207, 223

futures price, 38–39, 46, 53, 57–58, 71, 78–79, 135, 138, 143, 158, 176–77, 204, 218

Futures Spreads, 47

futures strangle, 120

futures trading, 35, 37, 42, 61, 65, 103, 108, 169, 200, 204, 208–11, 214–15, 223

futures trading pits, 62

futures trading platforms, 66

futures trading systems, 196–97

G

gold, 16–19, 24, 34, 52–53, 64–65, 119, 146–48, 150, 190, 210–11, 217

gold futures, 146, 150

  e-micro, 148

gold prices, 17, 146–48, 210, 217

Good Till Canceled. See GTC

grain futures, 134–35

grains, 16, 24–25, 33–34, 47, 57, 134–35, 137, 148–49, 153, 230

greeks, 78–79, 84

GTC (Good Till Canceled), 125, 130, 229

GTC orders, 125–26

H

hedge, 48, 55–58, 78, 112, 128, 146, 154, 162, 185, 202–3, 206–7 long, 58–59

short, 58–59

hedge price risk, 55–56

hedgers, 23, 39, 55–56, 58–60, 137, 159

commercial, 171–72

hedging, 55–57, 59, 129, 148

Higher Probability Commodity Trading, 49–50, 59, 79, 129, 193

I

iBroker, 85

IBs, 89–91, 93, 101

ICE (Intercontinental Exchange), 35, 73, 127, 142, 145–46, 148–51, 154, 161

ICE Price data fees, 73

Immediate or Cancel. See IOC

Index value, 154–55

indicators, 32, 83, 187, 200–201

initial margin, 180–81

Intercontinental Exchange. See ICE

interest rate futures, 162

interest rate risk, 164–65

interest rates, 27, 162, 164, 166, 168, 172–74

Introducing Broker, 27, 88–90

IOC (Immediate or Cancel), 123

IRA, 214–15

K

keypunch error, 221–22

L

lean hog futures, 141

lean hogs, 139–41

leverage, 58–60, 66, 98, 150, 153, 155, 158–59, 180, 186, 209–12, 215, 220

leveraged markets, 24, 107, 155

LIBOR (London Interbank Offered Rate), 162, 172–73

limit order, 48, 53, 82, 114–17, 119–23, 125–26, 128, 130–31, 133, 141, 149, 202, 219–20, 229–30

limit price, 116, 126–27, 219–20, 226

liquidate, 17, 53, 98–99, 112, 117, 155, 182–83, 186, 221

liquidity, 21, 23, 34–35, 45, 52–53, 56, 59, 145, 148–50, 153–55, 157, 159, 161–62, 211, 214

liquid markets, 45, 51, 67, 229

live cattle futures, 139–40

live trading platform, 71, 87

London Interbank Offered Rate (LIBOR), 162, 172–73

lumber, 11, 58–59, 142, 145, 229

M

margin, 26, 36–37, 43, 78–81, 89–90, 97–98, 102–3, 155–56, 158–59, 180–86, 210–12, 220, 223, 228

  maintenance, 181–82

  required, 66, 79, 81, 184, 204

margin accounts, 180, 211–12

margin calls, 16, 25, 60, 98–99, 103, 112, 124, 180–86

margin deficiency, 182, 185, 192

margin deficit, 124, 182, 184–85

margin requirements, 24, 26–27, 70, 78–79, 89, 92, 98, 180, 183, 186, 210

  initial, 181, 183–84

market access, 16–17, 64, 70, 75, 77, 86, 98, 227

market analysis, 68, 85, 93

market characteristics, 102, 105, 150, 162

market conditions, 128, 158, 168, 184, 187, 197–99, 206

  normal, 38, 126, 160

market depth, 63

market liquidity, 45, 56, 65, 161

market makers, 29, 45, 48, 52–53, 64, 66–67, 81–82, 116, 123, 150, 213, 218

Market on Close (MOC), 124

Market on Open. See MOO

market order, 53, 63, 114–15, 117, 120, 122, 124–29, 141, 206, 229

market reversal, 192, 203

markets

  electronic, 64, 67, 123–24

  forex, 176

  grain, 128, 134

market sentiment, 49, 68, 188

matching, electronic trade, 34–35, 63–65, 127

meats, 16, 139, 141–43, 202, 208

MEME (Multiple Entry, Multiple Exit), 10, 126

metal futures, 148

metals, precious, 19, 146

MF Global, 25, 28–29, 31, 91, 157

mini Dow, 118–19, 155

minimum tick, 134–35, 137–38, 143, 145, 149, 158–59, 171, 176

mobile platform, 72, 74, 85

mobile trading platforms, 84

MOC (Market on Close), 10, 124

MOC orders, 124

modified order, 125

MOO (Market on Open), 10, 123–24

MOO orders, 123–24

Multiple Entry, Multiple Exit. See MEME

multiplier, 133, 135–39, 141–43, 145–46, 148–51, 158, 161, 167–68, 176–78

N

NASDAQ futures, 153, 156–57, 183

National Futures Association. See NFA

natural gas, 21, 26, 34, 52, 120, 151–52, 211, 225

natural gas futures, 151–52

net liq, 222–23

net liquidation value, 65, 210, 222–24

New York Board of Trade (NYBOT), 35

New York futures exchange, 34

New York Mercantile Exchange. See NYMEX

NFA (National Futures Association), 31, 46–47, 73, 89–91, 104–5, 176, 198

notice day, first, 7, 40–42, 44

NYMEX (New York Mercantile Exchange), 34–35, 68, 95, 132–33

O

OCO (One Cancels the Other), 118, 120, 130

OCO orders, 76, 118, 120–21

offset, 37, 42–46, 50, 56–58, 80, 95, 98, 112, 135, 167, 181, 183, 221–23, 228, 231

oil, heating, 48, 151

oil futures, crude, 22, 24, 35, 80, 117, 144, 151, 224

One Cancels the Other. See OCO

One Sends the Other. See OSO

online trading, 64, 92–93, 101–4, 106, 111

online trading platforms, 68, 86, 102, 122, 129, 131

open interest, 115, 156–57, 166, 172

open outcry, 35, 61–64, 124, 154, 172, 213

open outcry pits, 29, 61, 64, 66, 68, 127, 157, 159, 172

open positions, 29, 41, 43–44, 75, 94, 114, 117, 137, 173, 180–81, 193, 222, 228

option analytics, 78, 83–84

option prices, 78, 127

option sellers, 49–50, 54, 77, 80, 131, 158, 203–4

options markets, 5, 20, 45, 52–53, 67, 79, 83–84, 105, 108, 114–16, 149, 154, 209, 214–15, 217

options orders, 53, 82–83, 131

options traders, short, 77, 97, 99, 151

options trading, 45–46, 50, 53, 63, 76–77, 81, 92, 94, 98, 107, 114, 116, 123, 137, 139

orange juice, 73, 130, 142–44

orange juice futures, 131, 143

order desk, 8, 63, 85–86

order entry, 67, 71, 75, 78–79, 82–83, 85, 131

  point-and-click, 83

order entry server, 72, 83

order flow, 52, 64, 68

order rejections, 80–81

orders

  bracket, 76, 120

  cancel/replace, 125

  contingency, 76, 120–21, 130

  placing, 75, 92, 102, 111, 131

  rejected, 81, 92

  working, 52, 105, 116, 120, 229

order tickets, 46, 48

order types, 53, 114, 119–20, 122, 124–25, 130–32, 148, 161, 204, 229

OSO (One Sends the Other), 10, 121–22

P

PFGBEST, 27–31, 91

pits, 35, 62–68, 127, 154, 157

pit trading, 53, 61–62, 64–65, 68

placing stop orders, 126, 206

platform risk parameters, 79, 81

platforms, 51, 64, 66, 70–86, 92, 94, 97–98, 101–2, 104, 107, 118–22, 124–27, 129, 131, 182

  desktop, 84–85

  free, 75–76, 82, 84, 87

  order-entry, 126, 227

  upgraded, 74, 76, 86

platinum, 146, 148

point values, 133, 135, 139, 148, 155, 159, 162, 167, 170–72, 174, 177

precious metals futures, 34, 146

premium trading platforms, 74, 76

price

  best possible, 114, 122–23, 128, 229

  closing, 183

  last traded, 52

  stop/limit, 119

  stop order, 141, 229

  target, 126, 195

price change, 57, 133, 137–38, 141, 148–49, 152, 173, 222, 230

price chart, 82–83

price data, 67, 70, 72–75

  live, 35, 70

price hedge, 56–57, 60

price ladders, 63, 82, 85, 131

price limit, 226, 229

price movement, 17, 42, 45, 118, 134, 137–38, 143, 145, 148, 150–51, 158, 200, 230

price prediction, 59, 108, 199

price protections, 57, 127, 206

price risk, 36–37, 42–43, 45, 55–59, 137, 150, 228

producers, 22, 33, 36, 39, 55–56, 59, 143, 225

professional traders, 70–74, 82, 222

profit

  realized, 138, 141, 155, 173, 178

  taking, 190–91, 225

profit target, 115–16, 120, 178, 203

Q

QST, 18, 20, 22, 25–26, 43–44, 82–83, 118, 121, 136, 138, 140–41, 144, 147, 177, 179

QST Mobile, 85

quote, real-time, 70, 75–76

quote board, 123, 134–35, 138, 167, 170

R

risk

  credit, 180, 182

  limited, 50, 97, 202, 212

  unlimited, 50, 97, 119, 131, 141, 203

risk and reward, 50, 96, 155, 179, 182, 200–202, 228

risk capital, 49, 201, 215

risk-free profit, 39–40

risk management, 35, 96, 122, 127, 193, 199, 202–3, 205–7

risk-management, 122

risk-management techniques, 199, 206–7

risk managers, 66, 70, 73, 80, 91, 94

risk parameters, 51, 79, 81

risk tolerance, 165, 173, 195, 197, 200–201, 203, 207

round turn, 46, 76–77, 94, 231

Russell, 153–54, 156–57, 161

S

scalpers, 116, 228–29

securities, fixed-income, 163–65

segregated funds account, 30

selling options, 91–92, 112

service, customer, 100

Short squeezes, 228

silver, 19–20, 34, 52–53, 146, 149–50, 211

slippage, 81, 117, 119, 127, 141, 149–50, 157, 192, 206–7, 229

soybean meal futures, 11, 137–38

soybean oil futures, 11, 138

soybeans, 33, 46, 48, 51–52, 57, 127, 134–35, 137, 149, 153, 163, 210–11, 214, 224

speculators, 17, 22–24, 39, 41, 43, 55–56, 58–60, 65, 67–68, 145, 148–49, 153, 171–74, 199, 213–15

S&P futures, 157–58

stock index futures, 34, 54, 98, 153, 156–57, 160

stock market, 20, 23–24, 200, 217–18

stop, 18, 117–22, 125–30, 141–42, 170, 202, 206–7, 227

  trailing, 118–19, 202

stop/limit, 119, 127

stop/limit order, 119–20, 126–27, 204

stop loss, 117, 120, 122, 127, 130, 192, 206

stop loss orders, 117–22, 126–29, 178, 193, 206

stop loss price, 127–28

stop orders, 64, 111, 114, 117–22, 125–28, 130, 133, 141, 149, 159, 192, 206–7, 227–29

  working, 117–18, 192

stop order slippage, 117, 119

stop price, 117, 126–28, 141–42, 145, 170

strategy, 48–49, 51, 77, 80, 88, 97, 99, 126, 129, 148, 150, 183, 195–97, 200–210, 229

strike prices, 49–50, 52–53, 79–80, 127, 130, 137, 139, 169, 202, 204 sugar, 35, 73, 142–45, 213

supply, 21–22, 33, 39, 47, 225

symbol, 62, 64, 148, 221

system trading, 196–97

T

T-bond, 163, 166–67, 169–70, 219

T-Bond Futures, 166–68

tick value, 142, 170, 173, 176–78

T-note futures contract, 181

trade

  busted, 221–22

  clear, 31, 85, 90

  last, 52, 67, 223

    place, 52, 81, 83–84, 97, 102, 129, 131

trade desk, 81, 100, 109, 130

trade desk clerk, 130, 221

trade execution, electronic, 65, 91–92, 221

trade futures, 17, 65, 78, 210, 214–15

TradeNavigator, 82–83

trade online, 62, 75, 102, 107, 113–14, 126, 131

trade options, 52, 77, 79, 116, 124

traders

  algo, 24

grain, 33, 48

  non-professional, 71–72, 74

  position, 74, 97, 119, 136, 201

A Trader's First book on Commodities, 5

trading floor, 35, 61–62, 64, 68–69, 159

trading pits, 29, 45, 61–64, 66, 68, 115, 157

trading plans, 194–96, 199, 202, 205

trading platforms, 51, 62–63, 65–68, 73–75, 77–84, 86, 90–92, 99–100, 102–3, 107, 110–11, 120–25, 142, 222–23

trading session, 65, 80, 98–99, 123–24, 127, 181, 184–85, 209, 229

trading systems, 23, 29, 187, 196–99

trailing stop order, 118–19

transaction fees, 46, 67, 75, 77, 224

Treasury bonds, 19–20, 47, 164–65, 168

Treasury futures, 53, 163, 166, 168, 171

V

volatility, 21–24, 45, 53, 55, 65, 67, 137, 144, 155–56, 158–59, 161–62, 171, 201, 204, 207

W

wheat, 24–25, 33, 55, 62, 134–35, 137, 149, 153, 211

WTI, 150–51

CPSIA information can be obtained
at www.ICGtesting.com
Printed in the USA
BVHW021210210223
658923BV00017B/633